D1475853

540

RETRAINING THE WORK FORCE

RETRAINING
THE WORK FORCE

*An Analysis
of Current Experience*

IDA R. HOOS

UNIVERSITY OF CALIFORNIA PRESS
Berkeley and Los Angeles 1967

University of California Press
Berkeley and Los Angeles, California

Cambridge University Press
London, England

Charity, it is written, suffereth long and is kind; so also is my husband, Sidney Hoos, to whom this book and all my endeavors, intellectual, culinary, and uxorial, are lovingly dedicated.

Preface

This book had its experiential if not its existential beginning in the 1930's when, as director of vocational services in a social agency, I was convinced of the one-way causality between lack of jobs and unemployment. Now, thirty years later, I am wiser. Lack of jobs might have been the primary cause of unemployment in the Great Depression. But when prosperity returned and people still remained jobless, I became less certain that availability of work was the one deciding factor. Mere numbers of open jobs or unattached workers could not explain unemployment statistics or rates. People were still without jobs even though help was wanted in factory, office, and laboratory. If the assumption was valid that jobs were going unfilled because of a shortage of competent applicants or that people were remaining unemployed because they had no marketable skills, then it seemed reasonable, logical, and necessary to examine retraining as the means by which a better matching could be achieved, in which the supply of manpower could be adjusted to the skill demands of a technological civilization.

Empirical research into retraining as a way to attaining this socially and economically valuable goal was made possible by a grant from the Ford Foundation. Coverage in breadth was facilitated by the active interest of many people in high places in federal and state government, private corporations, labor unions, and social agencies. Perception in depth was achieved through the cooperative spirit and patience of the men and women whose personal experiences contributed the human dimension to the dynamics of retraining. I wish it were possible to thank by name each person whose help I so gratefully acknowledge here, but to do so would in some instances betray confidences and reveal identities carefully guarded. If the perspective gained from this critical analysis serves as a useful guide to policy decisions regarding retraining programs and thus improves their effectiveness, then perhaps a small part of my debt to all those who participated will be repaid.

vii

Living in the household with a book a-borning is something one would not wish on one's worst enemy, let alone one's dearest loved ones. My husband and family have provided support, encouragement, and understanding to an extent for which my gratitude is unbounded.

I.R.H.

Berkeley, California

Contents

Introduction

As technology advances and the structure of work life changes, the need for an empirical assessment of current retraining measures and practices becomes ever more apparent. Experts may disagree about the general causes and cures of unemployment; a high level of economic activity has somewhat quieted the controversy about aggregate demand as against structural imbalance. But persistent prosperity unemployment underscores the vital necessity of vigorous retraining measures for providing workers with marketable skills. Business, government, and labor, charged by the President of the United States with estimating the impacts of automation on employment, have debated the issue of displacement without reaching definitive conclusions.[1] On one point, however, there is unanimity: worker retraining is urgently required. And along with the recommendation that industry retrain its employees, the Commission favors federal programs for at least 750,000 persons per year. There is, in short, almost universal acceptance of retraining as a prime factor in achieving optimal manpower adjustment and utilization.

The research reported in this book was undertaken with a view to acquiring factual information about the kind of retraining programs available to the work force, their sponsorship, the reasons for their establishment, the way they were conducted, their extent and limitations, their procedures and problems, their prospects for continuation, and their results in terms of upgrading, job security, and employment opportunity. Identified as the chief agents for job-skill development were adult vocational schools, the Civil Service, private companies, labor unions, and the federal government. Accordingly, case studies under each of these headings were carried out with the interest of ascertaining the extent of commitment on the part of the various sponsors to keeping American workers employable. Not to be regarded

---

[1] National Commission on Technology, Automation and Economic Progress, *Technology and the American Economy*, Vol. I (Washington, Feb., 1966).

as a bias but rather as a hypothesis were the interrelated assumptions that large sectors of the population were not being served through the traditional channels and that federally sponsored endeavors needed improvement and strengthening.

Such an assessment of ongoing programs serves several useful social purposes. It provides a clearer picture of the realities of retraining, or the conditions under which private corporations, labor unions, and government agencies are likely to assume responsibility for providing such programs. It places in sharper focus the portions of the labor force likely to be included in or bypassed by such endeavors. It highlights the factors impeding or contributing to successful operation of programs. The comprehensive data, acquired through case studies of retraining under varying types of sponsorship, contain the guidelines for developing realistic and effective courses of action in both the private and public sectors, within and outside traditional educational institutions, and reaching hitherto neglected segments of the population.

During the present period of relative prosperity, when the national unemployment rate stands at its lowest point in nine years, under 4 percent, and is expected to drop still farther, a certain tendency toward complacency can be discerned. Neglected is the disquietingly high rate that persisted even during years when the economy was regarded as healthy. Slighted is the fact that even as the country's employment totals reach new heights there exist deep and desperate concentrations of jobless persons—notably members of minority groups, young men and women, workers in obsolescent occupations, and inhabitants of permanently depressed regions. Overlooked is the possibility that the present low rate of unemployment is ephemeral, a reflection of war time conditions, and that many problems are merely masked but not solved. What are the social and economic realities facing each of these problem groups, how well have endeavors going on now served them, and how are their prospects for successful labor force participation being affected?

NEGRO WORKERS

Job opportunities for educated Negroes, both in private industry and government service, have improved considerably in recent years. In fact, there seems to be a shortage of qualified Negro applicants for openings. At the same time, however, the unemployment rate among Negroes remains high—exactly how high no one really knows. Authorities agree that present definitions and measures of unemployment, as well as statistics gathering methods, fail to include the true hard core. Not counted because they are not actively searching for work are untold numbers who have given up the quest or who see no use in starting one.

Unemployment has been identified as a key factor in racial violence in many sections of the United States. The exact 1966 rate in Greenville, Mississippi, and Harlem may not be known; it is a matter of record, however, that in 1963, a prosperous year, 29.2 percent of all Negro men in the labor force were unemployed during the year.[2] It is further established that the rate of joblessness in Negro slums remains disproportionately high. In the Watts Area of Los Angeles, one of California's sixteen "tension areas," the estimate was placed at 30 percent or higher.[3] In Oakland, California, for example, another of the state's potential trouble spots, the Negroes' unemployment rate is moving counter to the national trend, more than 20 percent being the current estimate. Competent observers generally concede that the overall rate of joblessness among Negroes can be arrived at by doubling that of the white population, and that a refinement of terminology and improvement of data collection would reveal a more serious discrepancy.[4] Moreover, the Negroes' exact employment situation may be further obscured by their status with respect to military service. Since Negroes are less likely than white boys to qualify for deferment because of vital jobs or studies, they are being drafted at a higher rate proportional to their numbers in the population, and their reenlistment record indicates a similar relationship.[5] Their return to civilian life will no doubt affect the employment ratios. Labor force projections suggest the demographic pattern of the near future: Negroes at present account for about 10 percent of the population of working age, but indications are that they will comprise close to 18 percent of the manpower increase just ahead. It is estimated that in the next five years, nearly 1.5 million nonwhite[6] persons will be added to a work force that has not demonstrated a reassuring absorptive capability for the current number.

What kinds of retraining programs must be designed to serve the needs of those portions of the Negro population which, despite some improvement in opportunities, appear caught in the self-perpetuating deprivations of slum living, inadequate education, and overwhelming

[2] U.S. Department of Labor, Office of Policy Planning and Research, *The Negro Family* (March, 1965), p. 21.

[3] Edmund G. Brown, *Economic Report of the Governor*, Sacramento, California, 1966, p. xiii.

[4] U.S. Department of Labor, Bureau of Labor Statistics, *The Negro in the West* (1966), p. 5.

[5] Eric Pace, "Negroes' Draft Ratio Exceeds Whites," *New York Times* (Jan. 3, 1966).

[6] Negroes represent over 90 percent of the nationwide population listed by the U.S. Bureau of the Census as nonwhite.

competition for jobs? Their demand for equal right to work comes at the very time when the occupations which they traditionally entered are disappearing.[7] It can best be met by adequate provisions for skill development through remedial instruction and training. A full understanding of the special problems of poverty-engulfed minorities and the steps that must be taken to involve their members effectively in programs of vocational readjustment is a basic ingredient in community action design and in national manpower policy. This research study of retraining, in order to broaden the horizons of our comprehension, investigates the degree of Negro participation not only in programs sponsored by adult education, the Civil Service, labor, and industry but also a number of special programs such as job preparation efforts of county welfare agencies, the Neighborhood House in North Richmond, California, and the Job Corps.

YOUTHFUL ENTRANTS

The original research design of this study called for analysis of retraining programs, with the express exclusion of those intended for new entrants into the work force. Early in the investigation, however, it became apparent that arbitrary demarcations between the concepts of training and retraining had only semantic reality and that artificial boundaries between youth and adulthood violated the real life continuum. Moreover, because programs developed to prepare young people for the world of work form an intrinsic and significant part of current federal manpower policy, failure to evaluate their performance and potential would constitute a gap in as comprehensive a spectrum as the one presented here.

Clearly deserving exhaustive research and critical appraisal are matters pertaining to the role and efficiency of the public education system in vocational preparation. Such considerations cannot be ignored, for it is recognized that the quality and character of the school experience determines and conditions an individual's subsequent need for retraining, his receptivity to it, and his response. The very importance and complexity of the issues involved in building suitable curricula reflecting and inculcating the values of a democratic society, consonant with the technology of the times, and sensitive to a vast array of talents and aspirations preclude coverage of public education here. Formal apprenticeship programs have likewise been omitted because of their limited and contested impact. Serving relatively small

---

[7] Charles C. Killingsworth, "Structural Unemployment in the United States," *Seminar on Manpower Policy and Program,* U. S. Department of Labor (Dec., 1964), p. 8.

numbers of young people, this means of skill development is even regarded by some authorities as an anachronism.

For purposes of this empirical investigation, a unique program for young Negro men (one called the Job Upgraders because "this was the only direction they could move in; they could go no lower") was singled out for intensive study. The findings show that the multidimensional and complicated problems of social and vocational maladjustment do not yield readily to ameliorative measures, and the cry of "Freedom now" has fired the embers of youthful rebellion and impatience into a flame of protest against both low-level entry jobs and the process of skill acquisition. The techniques of progressive development as embodied in this pioneer program, which now receives federal support through Manpower Development and Training Act funds, appear to have real merit, especially when a supervised work experience is built into the training process. Case studies of Job Upgraders provide an extreme example of the interrelated problems of youth from low socioeconomic classes. Analysis of the program as a whole indicates that its contributions are real and necessary, quite irrespective of the state of the economy, and it provides guidelines for the United States' cradle-to-grave war on poverty.

The more generalized approach of the Job Corps, another federally financed youth training program, serves as an interesting contrast. This endeavor, under the Office of Economic Opportunity, cost the nation $190 million from June, 1964 to June, 1965, and has about 18,000 enrollees in its 88 urban and conservation centers. A new manifestation of government-industry cooperation, the Job Corps has so far involved such major corporations as Litton Industries, Westinghouse, Ford Motor Company, and Federal Electric, an affiliate of International Telephone and Telegraph. Some twenty-five companies are at present bidding for retraining contracts. For purposes of this study of retraining the Job Corps center at Camp Parks, California, operated by Litton Industries, has been analyzed.

The one year's experience is too recent to supply definitive answers to basic questions such as whether this program is reaching and remedying the vocational deficiencies of the young people most in need and to what extent the business community is as willing to hire Job Corps enrollees as to train them. But all available empirical data have been analyzed, and responsible staff members and officials have been consulted so that meaningful conclusions can be distilled from this large-scale effort.

With demographers predicting a labor force explosion as the high birth rates of the post Second World War period are translated into job seekers, adequate and appropriate skill preparation for all entrants is a matter of public interest and concern. One million young men and women reached the age of 18 last year, one-third more than the year before. Many members of this vast army of youthful entrants have adult responsibilities, for early marriage and parenthood have become the norm in American society today. Their vocational adjustment is an integral part of the economic and social scene and requires sound long-range planning based on substantive research.

OBSOLESCENT WORKERS

Skill obsolescence is the main occupational hazard of the technological era whose threshold we are just approaching. Blue-collar, and professional workers are vulnerable as computers demonstrate their ubiquitous capability in field and factory, under seas and in outer space. The full dimensions of the changes ahead defy quantification; there are, however, a few hints. The new Dictionary of Occupational Titles, compiled by the U. S. Employment Service, lists the 23,000 job categories in the United States. Out of these, 6,000 were nonexistent ten years ago. Authorities foresee a fundamental alteration in the pattern of the work life, with as many as three vocational changes involved. This estimate may prove to be conservative; aerospace industries regard six months as the maximum skill life in many phases of their operations.

What have been the channels traditionally used in American society for keeping the work force up to date? Can we look to private industry, labor unions, and vocational schools to carry forward the retraining prescribed by experts as the sine qua non in intelligent manpower planning and preparation? In order to obtain a factual base for an evaluation of the training accomplishments of vocational schools, the Civil Service, private companies, and labor unions, case studies of each were included in the research design of this book. Of particular interest were such matters as the extent of commitment of the sponsors to vulnerable workers, the response and involvement of such persons, and the results in terms of job security, upgrading, and updating. The dynamics of the training process came under close scrutiny, for there was much to be learned from the selection procedures, teaching techniques, and worker morale and motivation.

The results of the investigation underscore the inadequacy of public education policy, point up such promising procedures as those established by the U. S. Civil Service for skill salvage and redeployment of personnel, and indicate the contributions as well as the limitations of the activities of private companies and of labor unions. The realistic view of retraining thus achieved forms the basis on which not only to judge the present need for the federally initiated and supported programs but to formulate long-range policy.

DEPRESSED AREAS

Although national attention has been directed most dramatically to the region of the Appalachian Mountains, there are many other areas immersed in or facing potential decline. Sluggish economic development, with a concomitant high rate of joblessness, causes a drain on community resources; industrial facilities deteriorate as services falter and taxes rise; commercial enterprises fade; substandard wage scales become the norm; the school system suffers; and there is an emigration of ambitious young people from such areas. These conditions stunt the work lives of many Americans besides mountaineers and miners. The pattern is just as familiar in once-prosperous textile-manufacturing towns of New England and in the lumbering centers of the Northwest. Programs for ameliorating the misery of residents of high poverty areas include, among others, vocational rehabilitation through training and job development. The Area Redevelopment Act passed by Congress in 1961 included provisions for such steps. During recent months this legislation has undergone some changes; its training functions have been largely merged with those of the Manpower Development and Training Act. Consequently, in the research design of this study, case materials from local MDTA programs were drawn upon to yield data on depression-bred disadvantage. It may be noted that in Oakland, California, which has been designated a depressed area, the discrete categories of vocational handicap are commingled into one of gigantic proportions. Here are minorities: Negroes, Mexican-Americans, and American Indians. Here, the out-of-school, out-of-work youthful population is reaching explosive proportions. Here, too, are the victims of technological change: carpet makers whose needle-trade skill is useless in handling synthetic fabrics; cannery workers displaced by machines; warehousemen rendered surplus by modern equipment. As evidence of the depth and persistence of Oakland's unemployment problems, this city was selected by the federal government as the pilot for a massive, many-fronted public works program. The U. S. Economic Development Administration in mid-1966 allocated $23,289,000 for a multifaceted plan to serve as a model for helping other chronically depressed cities.

This comprehensive analysis of retraining as conducted under all types of sponsorship in the United States underscores the sporadic character that has dominated such endeavors. The findings strengthen the case for continuous dedication to the complicated problems of labor force adjustment. The conclusions indicate that while a permanent, viable federal manpower policy is urgently needed, this by no means precludes articulation and expansion of union and industry commitment to retraining the nation's workers.

LOCATION AND FOCUS OF THE STUDY

Although the study on which this book is based draws upon retraining developments in the country at large, focus is directed to the greater San Francisco Bay area. Hence, while the aspects of retraining discussed and the findings set forth apply in a specific sense to the situation in a particular region, broader inferences can be drawn. This is especially true because of the socioeconomic structure of the area.

The San Francisco Bay area was selected as the focal point of the study because of its multidimensional aspects relevant to factors involved in retraining. The population reflects a distribution of age categories pertinent to people in search of jobs. Included are middle-aged job seekers, but also teen-agers and the elderly. The ethnic composition of the population comprises Negroes, Mexican-Americans, Chinese, Japanese, and North American Indians, as well as Caucasians. The income pattern ranges from the highly opulent to the truly needy. The San Francisco Bay area's proportion of jobless in the work force exceeds the national average, thus indicating a substantial need for interest in training and retraining. Further, the status of developments in retraining, because of the area's jobless rate, underlies as a distinct advantage the study's focus on the San Francisco Bay area.

The area includes a mixture of industry, commerce, and trade. San Francisco itself is an important commercial center with a vast concentration of financial activity. The east side of the Bay and its southern fringe include manufacturing and some heavy industry. Thus, the area as a whole includes a composite of various types of job possibilities, a range from office work to heavy industry which includes commerce, manufacturing, and a substantial amount of civil service activity at various governmental levels. The types of potential retraining programs are as varied as the economic texture.

It is not suggested that any area of the United States can be accepted as a truly representative sample of the country at large. The San Francisco Bay area is a variegated entity from the viewpoint of economic activity and population characteristics, and it incorporates significant features common to other geographical regions of the nation and thus provides an appropriate laboratory. Observation and analysis of retraining in this area can, therefore, serve as a reliable basis for indications of the status of and prospects for retraining.

The retraining resources investigated in this study include five major divisions: (1) adult education, (2) the U. S. Civil Service, (3) private industry, (4) labor unions, and (5) the public sector, in which local social welfare and federal programs figure. Although the projects selected for intensive research were for the most part located in the San Francisco Bay area, it should be noted that the implications of the findings far exceed the geographical boundaries and are applicable to the country as a whole.

Of special interest were the concept, scope, composition, and execution of the retraining programs; why they were initiated and how they were operated in terms of trainee selection, teaching techniques, and financing; and whether they were effective as a means to job security, updating, or upgrading. Analysis of case materials brought into focus the individual trainees, their age, education, previous work record, and ethnic origin. These personal characteristics were often crucial in determining motivation for enrolling or continuing in programs. They certainly had strong bearing on the benefits derived from them and, to an important extent, influenced the outcome from the standpoint of the participants.

Each program was approached as an entity, and all its dimensions were explored. This was done through participant observation, consultation with responsible officials and teachers, interviews with the trainees, perusal of all pertinent records, and personal, telephone, and mail follow-up on dropouts and graduates. In the case histories, fictitious names have been used. Some of the courses were chosen because they were typical, illustrative of retraining practices under particular auspices. Others were selected because they were unique, a demonstration of promising techniques.

Welding, licensed vocational nursing, and electronics assembly were selected from the catalogue of public vocational education for special study. The welding program was chosen because predominant among its enrollees were the hard-to-place—unskilled Negroes and Mexican-Americans and untrained youths. The practical nurse class merited investigation because training in this field is being offered under all kinds of sponsorship, public and private, throughout the country. The program promised to yield valuable insights into successful operation, for its graduates had achieved first place with highest grades ever attained in the California State Licensing Board Examinations. The electronics assembly class was of special interest because it pointed up the urgent importance of realistic labor market information if retraining is to accomplish its desired objective: employment.

The two case studies of government retraining present data on skill salvage and personnel redeployment at both the blue- and the white-collar levels. The former deals with instrument repair mechanics at a Naval Air base, and serves as a blueprint for on-the-job upgrading;

the latter, the Internal Revenue Service activity, serves as a model for effecting smooth transition to automated data processing. The study of private industry yielded case materials from several major firms, such as Kaiser Aerospace and American Can, as well as a small company whose retraining endeavors exemplify a unique cooperative effort involving the employer, workers, and the local school system. The data on trade union retraining programs move somewhat beyond the immediate San Francisco Bay area. This is because some unions, such as the International Brotherhood of Electrical Workers, have set up special national training funds. What is of interest in a comparative analytical study such as this is to ascertain how these funds are utilized at the local level and whether membership in a union offers job security in the face of technological change and protection against skill obsolescence.

Case materials on programs designed for vocational preparation of long-deprived minority groups include the Job Upgraders at Neighborhood House (North Richmond, California), special courses conducted by county welfare offices, and the Job Corps. The final chapters of the book provide research findings on a number of courses financed under the Manpower Development and Training Act. Among those of an institutional nature—that is, using school facilities already in existence—were courses for clerical workers, retail sales clerks, chemists' assistants, and licensed vocational nurses. Noninstitutional, or on-the-job, training projects included one for operating engineers and others for journeyman printing pressmen and linotype operators.

The empirical investigation of retraining as conducted under every major type of sponsorship in the United States today provides a foundation on which to assess and design public policy and private strategy. Such a basis of factual material becomes increasingly important as technological advances alter occupational patterns and as successful labor force participation remains central in our society. This research, comprising past experience and encompassing the multidimensional human aspects of the problems involved, can serve as the foundation on which industry, labor, and government can build retraining programs consonant with economc need and social reality.

[1

Adult Education as a Means to Skill Development

INTRODUCTION

Education on the adult level cannot be considered meaningfully as an entity apart from the total educational process in the United States, nor separate from the vocational curriculum within that system. Skill shortages in our economy have caused observers to note that while young people in the schools of the industrialized countries of Western Europe receive job preparation which is consonant with labor market demands,[1] the American educational system has practically no vocational orientation. Whatever such training is available at the high school level is virtually limited to large cities and to only a small segment of the student body.[2] Few of the young people to be found in the vocational classes are there by choice; most of them drift in through failure to perform successfully in academic programs. While one may consider that, whether liberal or vocational, all education enhances employability, the general curriculum contains little of direct vocational value. The fact that at least two-thirds of the students now in school will enter the labor market with neither a college degree nor vocational training indicates a serious gap in our educational system and underscores the present need for adult courses which will ensure a successful work experience. The following brief account of the history, development, and present status of vocational guidance and training in the school system will provide the frame of

---

[1] "Technical Progress and the Employment and Training of the Young," *International Labor Review*, Vol. LXXXIII, No. 5 (May, 1961), pp. 483–507.

[2] U.S. Department of Health, Education, and Welfare, Office of Education, *Education for a Changing World of Work* (Washington, 1963), p. 108.

reference for the research findings on adult education. The definition of vocational education used in this study is the one proposed by the President's Panel of Consultants on Vocational Education. The term refers to "all formal instruction for both youth and adults, at the high school, post high school, and out-of-school levels, which prepares individuals for initial entrance into and advancement within an occupation or group of related occupations." [3]

HISTORY AND DEVELOPMENT OF VOCATIONAL INSTRUCTION IN THE UNITED STATES

Until the early years of this century, the nation's need for trained manpower was met largely by the immigration of European journeymen. By 1914, however, recognizing that trial-and-error entry into the labor market with skills acquired informally on the job was costly and wasteful, President Woodrow Wilson appointed a commission to inquire into the need for federal support for vocational education.[4] Under the Smith–Hughes Act of 1917, a sum of $7.2 million annually was appropriated in perpetuity to the states according to their respective rural, urban, and total population, for expenditure on an equal matching basis for vocational education in agriculture, home economics, and trade and industry in the secondary schools. A prerequisite for eligibility for funds was that the individual state submit an approved plan for expenditures and appoint a state board to administer the program.

During the subsequent thirty years, Congress authorized three additional statutes in support of vocational education, differing from the Smith–Hughes Act mainly in that they specified terminal dates. These short-term subsidies having served to highlight the need for substantial and continuing aid to such programs, the government in 1946 approved the George–Barden Act, which provided an additional $29 million annually and inclusion of part-time and evening courses for adults in distributive occupations. As originally introduced, the bill would have covered training in office occupations, but this proposal was dropped at the insistence of lobbies representing private secretarial schools.[5] Federal legislation to aid practical nurse training and occupations related to the fishery trades and industries was enacted in 1956. In response to the nation's need for highly skilled technicians in work associated with defense, Congress passed in 1958 the National Defense

---

[3] *Ibid.*

[4] Louis Levine, "Manpower, Our Most Critical Resource," Address before the Regional Manpower Conference (Little Rock, Ark., March 18, 1960), p. 12, mimeo.

[5] Sar A. Levitan, *Vocational Education and Federal Policy*, W. E. Upjohn Institute for Employment Research (Kalamazoo, Mich., May, 1963), p. 3.

Education Act, Title VIII of which authorized an annual appropriation of $15 million. Each area vocational education program was (1) to consist of one or more below-college grade courses conducted under public supervision and control on an organized, systematic basis; (2) to be designed so as to fit individuals for useful employment as highly skilled technicians or skilled workers in recognized occupations requiring scientific or technical knowledge; and (3) to be made available to residents of the state or area of the state designated and approved by the State Board of Control for Vocational Education. It was stipulated that the trainees must either have completed junior high school or, irrespective of their school credits, have attained the age of 16 and could profit by the instruction.

The National Vocational Education Act of 1963 amended the 1958 National Defense Education Act, the 1964 form of which was amended in the First Session of the 89th Congress to be extended for a three-year period. This legislation was intended to increase the scope and effectiveness of federal and state vocational education. Some of its major provisions were as follows. (1) It removed categorical limitations and thus qualified all occupations for support. (2) It encouraged student vocational counseling services. (3) It authorized programs for unemployed, partially employed, and handicapped persons not served previously. (4) It provided in-service education for vocational teachers. (5) It permitted experimental programs and encouraged development of instruction materials. (6) It made permanent the practical nurse training program as a vocational field. These objectives are worthy; their implementation is, however, a slow process. With funds moving through established bureaucratic channels, disbursements reflect familiar patterns, with little evidence of innovations in allocation and use.

Certain portions of the Economic Opportunity Act of 1964 pertain directly to vocational training. Part-time jobs in situations where no regular paid employee is displaced are found for young people from sixteen to twenty-one as an incentive to continue or resume their education. Funds are allocated to community action programs which offer remedial reading, literacy instruction, and vocational rehabilitation. The creation of an Office of Economic Opportunity to carry forward the mandate of the Act has occasioned considerable resentment on the part of many professional and governmental agencies. Accusations of encroachment, duplication, and confusion have obscured basic issues and prevented proper evaluation. Under the sobriquet, "The War on Poverty," these efforts have drawn political fire from opponents of the present administration in Washington— criticisms quite unrelated to the merits of either the philosophy, the executing, or the results of these efforts. Lacking objective measures for

the success of the myriad programs initiated or supported by the legislation, we are forced to think in future social terms; many of the
beneficiaries are still in free nursery schools, day care centers, and
enrichment programs. The specifically vocational activities, which are
germane to this research on retraining, are for the most part closely
tied in with other hard-core-oriented endeavors, to be addressed later
in this book.

The Area Redevelopment Act of 1961 and the Manpower Development and Training Act of 1962 are often included in discussions of
federal measures to assist vocational education, but their primary
emphasis has been on persons out of school and out of work. Because
the resultant programs merit special attention as means primarily to
retrain individuals and groups with certain designated characteristics
related to age, status in family, and occupation, it is more appropriate
that their operation and impacts be reported in later chapters of this
book. Later chapters are devoted to retraining endeavors stemming
from this legislation.

Present Status of Vocational Guidance and Education in the United States

According to the fact-finding survey conducted by the President's
Panel of Consultants on Vocational Education,[6] there are wide variations among the states as to the effective use of these federal funds.
Enrollments in the vocational curriculum represent about 13 percent
of those aged fifteen to nineteen years and 2 percent of the out-of-
school youth and adults between the ages of twenty and sixty-four. In
large cities, an enrollment of 115,575 students has constituted a mere
18 percent of the total student body in grades 10 through 12. In the
Panel's evaluation, "in comparison with present and projected needs
of the labor force, the enrollments of in-school youth and out-of-school
youth and adults are very small." [7] Not only do many schools lack this
type of program entirely, but offerings of occupation are limited.
Moreover, the curriculum is considered insufficiently sensitive to trends
and supply-and-demand factors in the labor market.

Nowhere has the need for up-to-date vocational education been
voiced quite so eloquently as in the context of the Review Panel of
the President's Cabinet Committee on Juvenile Delinquency and
Youth Crime.[8] Having recognized that these complicated social prob-

---

[6] U.S. Department of Health, Education, and Welfare, *Changing World*, p. 108.
[7] *Ibid.*, p. 109.
[8] Herbert F. Striner, "Training in the Perspective of Technological Change,"
Seminar on Manpower Policy and Program, U.S. Department of Labor, Manpower
Administration, Office of Manpower, Automation and Training (Jan., 1966), p. 4.

lems require something more than the traditional handling by courts and corrections agencies, the Panel tried to develop a comprehensive prevention program. With vocational training high on their priority list, they examined school curricula throughout the country. They encountered a decided lack of awareness on the part of community officials of changes taking place in the structure of their own local job market areas. With no understanding of the impacts of advancing technology and little sensitivity to the shifts in industries, services, and business establishments, the school superintendents, heads of local employment services, and others interviewed displayed little interest in the adequacy of job training facilities available to the young people. Moreover, it was apparent that they not only were complacent about their educational system but also failed to grasp the possible relationship between manpower development activities and juvenile delinquency.

Failure to coordinate vocational education with the realities of the world of work has come about at least in part because schools have far too few vocational counselors, usually inadequately trained; effective use of labor market data is not made;[9] the amount of solid, verified information on the current situation and on the outlook for the future are markedly deficient. It has been found that training programs are frequently organized for jobs which no longer exist.[10]

With fewer than half of the states using their vocational education federal grant for vocational guidance and less than 1 percent of the total amount devoted to this purpose,[11] it becomes apparent that this vital area has been much neglected. Among the consequences of failure to provide sufficient guidance services is the rising incidence of early school leaving.

An authoritative study shows that only one individual out of every three in a sample of 22,000 dropouts had received counseling of any kind.[12] If these youngsters had been given help in finding themselves early in relation to school and the world of work, they might have benefited from compulsory education. Instead, they fled from it with memories so unpleasant as to be carried over into adulthood, there to block successful participation in classroom-based retraining programs. It is almost axiomatic that guidance services should begin early

---

[9] Harold T. Smith, *Education and Training for the World of Work*, The W. E. Upjohn Institute for Employment Research (Kalamazoo, Mich., July, 1963), p. 42.

[10] Joseph Froomkin, "Jobs, Skills, and Realities," *Columbia University Forum*, Vol. VII, No. 2 (Spring, 1964), pp. 30–33.

[11] U.S. Department of Health, Education, and Welfare, *Changing World*, p. 49.

[12] Seymour Wolfbein, "The Transition from School to Work: A Study of the School Leaver," *Readings in Unemployment*, Prepared for the Special Committee on Unemployment Problems, U.S. Senate, 86th Congress, 1st Session Washington: U.S. Government Printing Office (1960), pp. 712–714. (Condensed from the original.)

in the school career, continue for all students through high school, and be available to both out-of-school youths and adults.

Although it is clearly evident that vocational education has not maintained a position of prestige in the eyes of the general public, identification of which factors are cause and which are consequence presents some difficulty. Whether we fail to ascribe value to the job-oriented curricula because of their poor quality, or whether their weakness is due to a lack of respect and support from the public is hard to say. Certainly there is a reciprocal relationship, and its basis may be largely historical. The very immigrants who made a good life for themselves in this country by dint of hard work recognized that education would provide the magic key to opportunity for their children. The sons of pushcart peddlers could become doctors; the sons of hod carriers could become lawyers; the stepping-stone for betterment was seen to be free education. Inherent in these aspirations was a hierarchical value system vis-à-vis occupations, with the white collar a symbol of status and manual work considered generally inferior even though the latter sometimes provided better earnings.[13] This rank order is reflected in the school system, with the academic high school attracting the bright students and the trade school being the place where the less talented find themselves.

In the comprehensive secondary schools, this process of selection takes form in the "tracking system." Pupils rarely elect the industrial arts track; they are in it by default. Thus, it has earned the reputation —as it has indeed become—a dumping ground or custodial service for the unmotivated and the less capable. By and large, the teaching staff mirrors the unfavorable image; with second-class citizens as their students, the faculty enjoys little prestige. Instruction in English and mathematics, required in all tracks, is of a notably poor quality in the vocational curriculum.

With the sharp dichotomy between education on the one hand and vocational training on the other, students who will not go to college but who cannot avoid assignment to the industrial arts emerge from their years of compulsory school devoid of occupational direction and preparation. It is estimated that two out of every three children now in American schools will enter the labor market with neither a college education nor vocational training.[14] For these sixteen million, due to enter the labor force in this decade, jobs are likely to be a matter of luck and a process of trial and error. This situation has come about because of the built-in assumption in our educational philosophy that

---

[13] Alex Inkeles and Peter Rossi, "National Comparisons of Occupational Prestige," *American Journal of Sociology*, Vol. LXI, No. 4 (Jan., 1956), pp. 329–339.

[14] Levitan, *Vocational Education*, p. 1.

all students want to be doctors, lawyers, and engineers. Only after a period in limbo, of idleness and sporadic work experiences, will some of them recognize the value of specific training and take positive steps to remedy the deficiencies. In some states, high school graduates may turn to junior or community colleges, many of which have a variety of vocational curricula. California has 76 such schools, and New York and Texas have 33, out of a national total of 452. Aggregate enrollments country-wide exceed 900,000, with California accounting for 442,818. The California figure includes 253,769 adults registered for classes; pupils listed in September, 1965 for grades 13 and 14 full- and part-time were reported at 289,456. For young men and women, classes beyond secondary school may serve as a reclamation project. For their elders, adults who may have entered the labor force without skills at a time when jobs were plentiful, evening trade classes could provide a means of self-improvement and insurance against obsolescence.

California has already made full use of federal funds for vocational education by matching these appropriations on a dollar-for-dollar basis.[15] But even this record leaves much to be accomplished. Statistics show that more than 4 million persons now twenty-five years of age and older in the state have not graduated from high school. Of these, 1.3 million lack even an eighth grade education, the past decade having shown an increase of 16 percent.[16]

THE USE OF PRIVATE VOCATIONAL SCHOOLS

To a very limited extent, vocational institutions financed by endowment or for private profit fill gaps left by our system of public schools. As was indicated earlier in this chapter, there have been instances of actual prevention of certain vocational courses by lobbies of entrepreneurs bent on preserving their own bailiwick. To be sure, not all commercially sponsored educational endeavors are self-seeking. Some on the contrary maintain high standards and, indeed, serve as a model for and impetus to public institutions.

It must be pointed out, however, that these high norms are not universally characteristic of private endeavors. In fact, because in too many cases public vocational education has failed to meet the needs of the out-of-school youth and adults, there have sprung up large numbers of commercial organizations which attract persons who have been

[15] Wesley P. Smith, "Vocational Education in California," in Harold T. Smith, *World of Work*, pp. 95–107.

[16] Wesley P. Smith, Testimony before the Assembly Interim Committee on Industrial Relations (Sacramento, Calif., Dec. 2, 1963), p. 5.

casting about for direction. A combination of zeal to acquire a salable
package of training and naïveté stemming from lack of knowledge
about specific entry requirements and opportunity in given fields
makes this group highly vulnerable to the glib advertising and pressure exerted by purveyors of these courses. Enterprises of this sort are
likely to ride the wave of technological change. At present, electronics
and automation schools abound, waving a banner of permanent employment, glowing opportunities, and a fabulous future. Far from un-
profitable, these institutions reap an abundant harvest by trapping
the hapless into exorbitantly expensive programs with contracts bind-
ing to the last penny.

A factor which frequently beguiles and misleads the vocation-hungry
enrollee is that of official authorization. The California Superintendent of Public Instruction has the responsibility for approving
courses, both public and private, according to certain specified regulations.[17] The list of criteria to be met includes items bearing on
finances, administration, ethical practices, course of instruction, physical facilities, and instructional staff. But such imprecise requirements
as that "the school operate(s) on a basis of sound administrative principles" or that "the school at all times adhere(s) to ethical practices"
undermine effective quality control. Consequently, the calibre of the
courses and their value as acceptable preparation for particular occupations may be open to question. The fact that the catalogue of
approved courses[18] serves as a Bible to employment and school counselors and to the general public underscores the need for more intensive and careful evaluation procedures. Many less scrupulous institutions flaunt their "official approval" as an advertisement and endorsement of their capability. The case study of an enrollee in one such
school underscores the urgency of more rigorously articulated and
enforced criteria.

Case Study of a Student in a Private Program

Mrs. Martin, a 45-year-old widow, was attracted to a newspaper
advertisement put forth by a school which accepted students irrespective of age for training as doctors' assistants. It stated, "We are authorized by the Superintendent of Public Instruction to confer the
Merit Certificate of Completion upon our graduates," and that fact

---

[17] State of California Education Code Title 5, Administrative Regulations, Register
64, Subchapter 21. "Private Schools," Article 2 (Register 64, No. 13, 6-20-64), p. 410.
[18] California State Department of Education, *Courses Offered by California Private
Schools*, Authorized or Approved Under Division 21—California Education Code
(Sacramento, Calif., July, 1965).

carried sufficient assurance of the school's respectability to warrant Mrs. Martin's confidence. Somewhat troubled, however, by the pressure exerted by the school to get her to enroll after her preliminary interview, she sought the only professional guidance she knew of, the State Employment Service. There an interviewer consulted the above-mentioned catalogue and found the school approved for "Health Services." As a consequence, Mrs. Martin paid the $75 registration fee and signed the contract calling for six additional monthly payments of $75 each. In total seven months' training, comprising three evenings per week, amounted to $525, and she was committed to complete the course and pay for it in full.

Upon attending the first week of classes, Mrs. Martin discovered that the teacher was a young woman so poorly equipped that even in the rudiments of first aid, her instructions ran counter to what Mrs. Martin had learned in a Red Cross course for homemakers. What was being taught was not only incorrect but downright dangerous. Instead of techniques in blood and urinalysis, as the registrar had promised, the class hours were devoted exclusively to thermometer reading, pulse taking, and patient positioning. Mrs. Martin soon learned that the school was legally barred from teaching urinalysis and blood counts because it had no arrangements with any laboratories licensed by the State Department of Public Health.

Thoroughly disillusioned by her experience, Mrs. Martin tried to withdraw from the school. She was reconciled to forfeiting the $75 registration fee but determined not to compound the price of her gullibility by continuing the course and the payments. The school was adamant; a contract had been signed and the student was held liable for payment of the full $525. Only after some discussion was a slight concession made. Mrs. Martin could drop out if she promised to complete the training at some later date or if she stated in writing that, due to circumstances beyond her control, she was forced to leave but was fully satisfied with the course. The first proposal was patently unacceptable; the alternative represented an abrogation of her ethical principles. The testimonial implicit in a statement of this kind was so repugnant that Mrs. Martin sought the aid of an attorney to extricate her from this trap. When he notified the owners of the school of his intention to pursue the case in court, they relinquished their claim on Mrs. Martin. Evidently, the quiet release of one recalcitrant student was preferable to jeopardy of their entire lucrative operation. Not only were bad publicity and a court record to be avoided, but there was also the strong likelihood that the case would provide the Public Health authorities with evidence sufficiently damaging to put the school out of business.

That untold hundreds of schools of this kind flourish in America and that lawyers are kept busy liberating the unwary from entanglement with them indicates a serious gap in our vocational services. Guidance and training must be made available to all sectors of the population with choice of occupation and course of instruction dependent not on glossy advertisements but on carefully compiled and analyzed data on the realities of the employment situation.

THE ROLE OF PUBLIC FINANCED
ADULT EDUCATION

Apprenticeship, one of the oldest training techniques, combines classroom instruction with on-the-job training according to regulations both private companies and unions are parties to. Entrance requirements set up by labor-management agreement vary widely among industries. The elite trades, such as plumbing, electrician, and others of the construction family, supplement conventional examinations in reading and mathematics with aptitude tests and other screening devices to select from among the applicants, who outnumber the openings often in the magnitude of ten to one. The courses set up by the schools can admit only accredited apprentices and journeymen and cannot serve as preparation for entry into these trades for any others. Because of these limitations we do not include California's 4,500[19] such classes in this research, nor do we attempt an analysis of apprenticeship within the framework of the present retraining study. Such an orientation would be more appropriate in the context of an inquiry into means of initial entry into the labor force, perhaps in a study directed to the special problems of youth, and problems arising from union restrictions.

Classes for adults maintained in connection with day or evening high schools or junior colleges are conducted in 80 percent of the state of California's school districts. Locally administered and controlled and tuition-free, the classes may at any one time in the school year have an enrollment of nearly 500,000 adults.[20] Covering a large range of subjects and pitched at various levels, the curriculum defies generalization. Some courses are remedial, others serve as an extension of previously-acquired knowledge or skill. Anything from folk-dancing to philosophy is available. In its combination of liberal, recreational, and vocational activities, "adult education covers virtually all areas

---

[19] Wesley P. Smith, "Development of Vocational, Technical, and Related Classroom Programs to Meet the Changing Skill Requirements," California Labor Federation, AFL-CIO, Conference on Unemployment, Retraining, and Skill Development, Los Angeles, California, November 17–19, 1961, p. 3, mimeo.

[20] Wesley P. Smith, "Vocational Education in California," p. 101.

of human existence where more knowledge and skill are needed to assume the adult social roles in the complexity to today's social world." [21]

As was pointed out earlier, it is difficult to identify among the courses outside the apprentice and journeyman area a cohesive curriculum that can properly be viewed as a source of retraining. In general the catalogue of adult evening schools lists discrete offerings set up in response to public request; assured enrollment of 15 persons can effectuate a class almost irrespective of subject content or applicability to labor market conditions. From the array of courses conducted in local public trade schools, three have been selected for special analysis. The first, a course in electronics assembly, exemplifies the situation in which retraining was initiated for a group of older women displaced from their factory jobs when their employer moved to another part of the country. The effort merits consideration because it indicates clearly the need for vocational guidance for adults and for closer liaison between school and the public employment service, especially for a better utilization of labor market information.

The second course, selected for study because most of the students were the hard-to-place, that is, unskilled and of minority status, points up the fact that even when motivation to learn is present, students' ambitions may be defeated unless some kind of financial subsidy can be arranged. As seen in the case materials on the welding program, the Indian men, who were receiving aid from the U.S. Bureau of Indian Affairs, were able to achieve independence by completing the training program and finding employment. Many of the other students had to dilute their school efforts by night jobs or had to drop out for lack of money on which to live and support families.

There are several reasons for having included the training for licensed vocational nurses. To begin with, this type of course has found favor throughout the country and exists to a greater or lesser degree in every state. A second important desideratum is that licensed vocational nursing is an occupation for which Manpower Development and Training Act funds have been allocated all over the United States. In answer to such questions as whether the federally financed courses duplicate local efforts and how the two types of programs differ with respect to selection procedures, instruction, persons served, and placement results, a locally financed course is studied in this chapter; the research findings on a comparable course under the MDTA are set forth in a later section.

---

[21] Jack London and Robert Wenkert, "Some Reflections on Defining Adult Education," unpublished report, Survey Research Center, University of California (Berkeley, Calif., March, 1963), p. 4, mimeo.

ELECTRONICS ASSEMBLY CLASS

Through an item in a local newspaper, the employees of the Marchant Division of Smith-Corona Company learned that within a year their firm was moving to Orangeburg, South Carolina. It was reported that some 1,800 workers, many of them women who had been with the company for ten or more years, would lose their jobs. Anxious to remain employable, a group of them, encouraged by a plant foreman, asked the public school to organize an evening class in electronics assembly. Most of the 39 persons (38 women and 1 man) who enrolled in the course during the following year were relatively unskilled production workers. Their hourly wage range, from $2.35 to $2.75, was somewhat higher than the prevailing average at this skill level, largely because of increments through seniority. After the class had begun, the State Employment Service administered aptitude tests which had been postponed in the interest of making optimal use of time left before the students lost their jobs. Surprisingly low were the scores in muscular coordination and small tool manipulation, both of which were closely work related. The causes for this phenomenon might have been: (1) inappropriateness or inadequacy of the test battery; (2) slowing of pace due to advancing years; or (3) a sort of "trained incapacity," in which experience on a given operation improved performance of the special task to the detriment of general dexterity. No systematic study of the employment outlook in this occupation was made by any of the responsible agencies involved. A representative of the Department of Employment indicated, however, that the electronics industry in the area had declined sharply in recent years, with a decrease in demand for assemblers.

The majority of the students was in the over-45 age bracket. Figures provided by the women themselves were found to understate the facts by several years, a discrepancy which appeared when the data were compared with official records. Although it is suspected that many of them also misrepresented and exaggerated their years of education, the extent could not be ascertained because of a lack of available evidence. The forms which they filled out and their written replies to the questionnaires gave basis to the assumption that a certain amount of wishful thinking with respect to age and education had gone into the reporting. Further inquiry revealed that desperation and not vanity prompted these falsifications. Two-thirds of the group were self-supporting—single, widowed, or divorced. Some of the married women were the primary wage earners in their households, their husbands disabled or jobless. In several instances where a husband was listed as working, Marchant was his employer too.

The students' replies to the question, "Why are you taking this course?" were a catalogue of anxiety and hope. A widow who gave her age as fifty-five and her school years completed as ten wrote, "I am self-supporting and Marchant Division of Smith-Corona is moving to South Carolina leaving me unemployed and I must prepare for another job." She had done machine assembly work since 1941, a total of 22 years. A college graduate of fifty-six who had started working for Marchant in 1942 stated, "I am self-supporting, so need to find employment until I reach retirement age. I thought 'electronic assembly' an active field." The answer of a forty-six-year-old divorcée reflected the typical pattern: "very interesting and to plan for the future and upgrading myself. Electronics will be here to stay."

The attraction of electronics as a green pasture for jobs and the necessity of taking steps to assure continued employment served as sufficient motivation to carry many of these women through two semesters of evening classes; some enrolled in the summer session as well. Although an interval of six months or a year is usually allowed before the results of a training program are assessed through follow-up, a somewhat shorter period seemed preferable in this instance because (1) the rather shallow skill base might disappear over a prolonged period, and (2) the actual shutdown of the plant would occasion movement into lower rental areas and the doubling up of families, both of which would complicate the tracking of persons. Investigation into the employment status of all former students was, therefore, undertaken four months after the plant closed. Eight graduates were found to be working as electronics assemblers; nine were in some other kind of job; the rest were either unemployed or failed to respond. The high correlation found in other research between non-respondence and unemployment suggests that these graduates had little success to report.

The post-layoff experience of all Marchant's production workers was surveyed six months after the shutdown.[22] It was found that only 19 percent of the women of forty-five and over had found any jobs, although this age group accounted for 81 percent of the female factory force displaced. A general decline in wage expectations had taken place, with a drop from 15 to 25 percent. Apparently, the women who had taken the course had fared no better than the rest. Two years later, the prospects for employment in electronic assembly were reported to have decreased. With more advanced calculators in production, 7,000 moving parts had been reduced to fewer than 100, and

---

[22] U.S. Department of Labor, U.S. Employment Service, *Marchant Moves South*, Automation Program Report No. 8 (May, 1965).

these were put together automatically with printed circuits instead of human hands.

Some Illustrative Cases

Mrs. Mary Coburn, a fifty-five-year-old widow with two grown-up children, had worked at the Marchant Division of Smith-Corona for almost 21 years. In another ten years she would receive a monthly pension of $39.43 but was in such serious need of immediate employment that she returned the questionnaire in person to the University office of the sociologist conducting the research in hope of receiving some kind of guidance. Mrs. Coburn had completed tenth grade and had once taken what she called a "Seven Day Aventist course in home nursing care of the ill," prior to her machine assembly job at Marchant. This had consisted of "putting together various sections of the Calculating Machines." She had done some commercial laundry work and had put in six months at the "sycleton" (the University of California Cyclotron). Before that, she had served as a practical nurse for "virious peoples"; this involved "house to house caring for convalescent and new mothers and babies." The records show that she failed the State Employment Service tests and that her grade for the first semester, which she did not complete, was C. During the personal interview, she explained that she had dropped out because she was not learning enough in the electronics course. She was emphatic, however, about her sincere desire for retraining and realistic in her awareness of the unlikelihood of finding another job paying the $2.77 hourly wage that she had achieved. She was actually willing to accept the kind of impersonal domestic work that one might expect to find in a college dormitory or dining commons. There being no vacancies on the campus, an appointment was arranged for Mrs. Coburn to see the State Employment Service interviewer in charge of selection for an MDTA-sponsored course in licensed vocational nursing. If Mrs. Coburn could meet the educational and physical requirements, she would be eligible for subsidy during the period. If she lacked the qualifications for this program, efforts were to be made by the Employment Service to direct her to other possibilities.

Mrs. Coburn was accompanied on her visit to the University of California by a friend, Mrs. Laura Stone, whose only employment had been with Marchant where she had worked on the assembly line for 17 years. Considering that she completed only seventh grade, Mrs. Stone expressed herself quite well, better orally than in writing. She was smartly dressed and used hair coloring and make-up to achieve an appearance that made the purported fifty-three, which she put down as her age, fairly plausible. Mrs. Stone stated that her husband's occupation was steamfitter, but that he did not work regularly. She had failed the State Employment Service test battery and received a grade of D in her first semester of electronics assembly. She did not continue because "I dident feel like I was learning anything." Like Mrs. Coburn, she knew that the job market provided sparse opportunity for earning her accustomed $2.77 per hour and was willing to accept less or enroll in a training course "if it is something I could do." Impressed with Mrs. Stone's apparent flair for clothes, the University sociologist, to whom she had turned for advice, strongly recommended that she capitalize on her sewing ability and apply for saleswork in a store specializing in fabrics or in the yard goods section of a department store. For help in obtaining this kind of job, an appointment was made for her with the local State Employment Office.

Inez Hale, a fifty-six-year-old divorcée with two grown-up children, wrote that besides being a graduate of the University of California she had completed one year of graduate work for a general secondary teaching credential. She had entered the employ of the Marchant Division of Smith-Corona Company in 1942, and, at the time of their closing down, was in the final inspection department, where correct operation of the completed machines was the prime responsibility. Her wage rate was $2.39 per hour. Although she had failed the State Employment Service tests, she achieved a grade of C for the first semester and finished all the class work in the second. Mrs. Hale ignored the request for follow-up information and there is no record of her having found employment either as a machine inspector or in electronics assembly, which she had chosen because it was an "active and expanding" field.

The sole male in the program deserves honorable mention. Mr. Brian Yancey, forty-eight-year-old father of three, had graduated from high school in 1935 and begun his work life as a bus driver in Pontiac, Michigan with a salary of $300 per month. Seven years later, he and his family moved to the Bay Area, where he found a job in commercial furniture delivery. Here, he earned a monthly salary of $324. After one year, he was hired by Marchant, where he worked up to the position of final inspector at $550 per month. At the age of forty-five, Mr. Yancey started attending evening courses in machine shop, mechanics, electronics, and electronics technology at the various local community colleges. He passed the State Employment Service tests, completed the electronics assembly class with a B and continued with the more advanced course while studying theory at another junior college. Within weeks after the plant shutdown, Mr. Yancey was working in electronics at a local laboratory and soon was upgraded to an engineering aide classification.

Judged on the basis of the number of graduates employed in jobs related to the training, these classes can claim little success. It is depressing to calculate the number of hours fruitlessly spent by a group of women desperate to maintain their earning power. The waste of time, energy, and emotional strength exemplified in this experience is not of course limited to this particular program, which was selected for analysis not to serve as a scapegoat but rather to point up the problem germane to the retraining process.

Viewing the records of this course, one feels impelled to raise some basic questions about the role and responsibilities of the schools in providing trade education on the adult level. For example, should preparatory classes be offered in occupations for which there is small local demand? Is it justifiable, under a democratic system advocating equal opportunity for all comers, to exclude some persons and include others? If so, what should be selection criteria and who is to determine them? In the electronics assembly class, it may be recalled, the relationship between score on State Employment tests and subsequent performance was nebulous; the predictive value of the former was not confirmed. Assuming a greater degree of refinement of the screening procedure and closer liaison between the Employment Service and the schools, would the result be an exclusion of persons who are motivated to improve their skills? Can any test be so definitive as to provide a foolproof basis for changing an applicant's career aspirations? It is known from experience that the test-wise can often make a satisfactory showing quite irrespective of vocational competence and that test results are often inadequate and even misleading in assessing capability.

The compelling question arises as to allocation of the responsibility for vocational guidance in adult education. When a group of women such as those who were displaced by Marchant's shutdown is cast out of what they must have considered their lifelong occupation, where can they turn for direction? At the age of fifty a person thrown upon her own resources cannot afford the trial-and-error, hit-or-miss course of action. But what alternatives can be found in the present adult education system? A completely open admissions policy, which may be favored by local school authorities because it provides financial underpinning through the operation of state reimbursement for student attendance, may only perpetuate the misguided or unguided flounderings of the unqualified and the incompetent. Courses that are set up with due regard for local labor market conditions and adhere to qualification criteria appear to provide a much more effective vehicle for realistic skill development. The program in welding serves as an illustration.

WELDING PROGRAM

Since welding as such is not considered a trade but rather a technique, this occupation is not included among those covered by apprenticeship agreements. This allows for a freedom of entry that makes welding attractive to men who cannot, for a number of reasons, compete successfully for the relatively few openings handled through formal apprenticeship channels.

The job of the welder is to join metals by applying intense heat and sometimes pressure to melt the edges and thus form a permanent bond. Within the occupation there are wide skill variations, ranging from single manual and arc welding to more complicated operations which require knowledge of blueprint reading, welding symbols, properties of metals, work planning, and electricity, as well as the use of new processes and equipment. While the better-trained workers are to be found in steel mills, metal-stamping establishments, and machinery factories, there is a market for the less skilled in boiler shops, motor vehicle and equipment plants, automobile body and other metalworking repair shops. There is a generally favorable long-run outlook for employment in this occupation.[23]

The program singled out for special study is geared to the lower level entry and conducted by a public school; it is open to male youth and adults who have completed the tenth grade or its equivalent. The one-year instructional plan calls for five hours per day of manipulative training and one hour daily of related course work. In the welding curriculum, there is considerable emphasis on metallurgy, with study of the characteristics of the various metals to be used. Mechanical drawing and blueprint reading are included. Another portion of time is devoted to arithmetic—whole numbers, fractions, decimals, percentages, weights and measures, power and roots, and simple geometry. Although a certain amount of schooling is required, it has been found that much of this material is unfamiliar to the students. In some instances they lack knowledge of even elementary fractions and decimals.

The sources of referral are mainly the State Employment Office and the U.S. Bureau of Indian Affairs; but some students hear of the course from friends or former enrollees and apply on their own initiative. The State Employment Office selects the men it will refer by

---

[23] U.S. Department of Labor, Bureau of Labor Statistics, *Occupational Outlook Handbook*, Bulletin 1255 (Washington, D.C., 1959).

means of a battery of tests which emphasize finger dexterity and spatial relations. The Bureau of Indian Affairs selects its applicants, usually ranging in age from eighteen to thirty-six, through aptitude tests administered in the home district by State Employment Offices. On the basis of the results, each individual is helped to select three occupations in order of preference and to designate the geographical area of his choice. Upon his arrival there, the Field Office of the Bureau of Indian Affairs again assesses his aptitude and tries to guide him into a suitable training program. It may be noted that welding is a particularly popular occupational choice, probably because the men are likely to be familiar with it. Screening of those persons who apply without formal referral is handled by the instructor, who interviews each and then tries him out on the various operations. It is the teacher's opinion that performance is the best test and more reliable than any other.

There is a registration fee of three dollars per semester. Since each student is required to wear a special kind of heavy shoes or boots, these along with protective leather aprons and jackets must be acquired at a cost of $30 to $40. The school furnishes hoods and goggles. Students attending the day course pay four dollars per week for the materials used. For heliarc welding there is a flat fee of one dollar per hour.

Characteristics of the Trainees

The ethnic composition of the class was as follows: ten Indians, five white, three Negro, one Filipino, and one Mexican. Their ages ranged from nineteen to fifty-three, with a median age of twenty-five and an average of thirty. Although the average number of years of schooling was claimed by the trainees to be eleven, there is the possibility that this may have been somewhat exaggerated. Irrespective of the tenth grade requirement, two of the students had gone through only the eighth grade, one the ninth, and four the tenth. Two of the eleven who had graduated from high school had also attended junior college.

Research into jobs held prior to the welding course indicates that four men had done some work as general laborers, three had been farm hands, three had been janitors, two had been commercial fishermen, two had retired from the Armed Forces, one had been a stock boy, and one had done odd jobs. Four members of the class were currently employed—three as welders and one as a carpenter. This means that all but four of the twenty students were unemployed at the time of enrollment. The period of joblessness ranged from two months to three years. Three of the working students were already doing welding but needed more training; the fourth employed member, who was spray-painting cars, regarded welding as a valuable sideline. Fourteen of the men were married, one was widowed, and five were single. The ten Indians were receiving full subsidy from the Bureau of Indian Affairs: one man was on pension after service as a cook with the U.S. Navy, six men were self-supporting, two were receiving Unemployment Compensation, one was on welfare, and one was being supported by his parents.

In order to ascertain the pertinent facts about previous enrollees, an investigation of those who had completed the course the previous year was conducted. It was found that of the 41 former students, 19 were Caucasian, 11 Negro, eight Indian, one Chinese, and two of unknown ethnic origin. One year after graduation, 23 were employed as welders—13 Caucasian, four Indian, four Negro, one Chinese, and one unknown. Employed, but not as welders, were four Caucasian and two Negro men.

Although the sample studied was small, the research brought into focus many problems that have been almost overshadowed by the understandable national concern for the gross needs of the heavy concentrations of the unemployed. Almost forgotten have been Indians, Mexican-Americans, and other minorities requiring special vocational help; virtually overlooked have been the underemployed for whom work has not provided a living wage. The current emphasis on the negative characteristics of school dropouts has obscured the fact that motivation and aspiration are often just as strong drives for them as for their graduating friends. The enrollees in the welding class represented a heterogeneous gathering of unskilled workers who had identified a clear vocational objective and were, with the exception of the subsidized Indians, pursuing it quite independently.

Many of the welders persevered in the program in the face of pressing financial difficulties. Some of them had to withdraw when their Unemployment Compensation was exhausted; others managed to continue by dint of part-time jobs. Among the group, so many of whom had to make considerable personal sacrifice in order to complete the course, there was an undercurrent of bitterness. "The way to get a good training," one said, "is to throw a rock through the windshield of a police car. Then, you'll get sent to San Quentin. They've got a real good training setup there, and you get free room and board besides."

No such financial deprivation beset the vocational efforts of the Indians. Under full subsidy from the Bureau of Indian Affairs, they usually stayed through the year unless the adjustment to urban life or the demands of the occupation were too difficult. Their low rate of dropout may have been due to some extent to the close liaison maintained with social workers and employment counselors from the Bureau.

Several more months of training would probably have led to employment for these men, so early withdrawal seemed a sad waste. On their way to acquiring skill in an occupation for which there is a fair demand, already positively oriented toward work—difficult, dirty-hands work at that—these men had to return to the ranks of the undifferentiated, unemployed general laborers. The cavalier assumption, encouraged perhaps by the huge expenditure of public funds on retraining, that no serious student need suffer from lack of support, is totally erroneous. Social legislation that has been designed for the greatest good of the greatest number does not cover all contingencies. It is urgent even in a metropolitan setting where public manpower programs are being implemented, but the problem of persons for whom there is no coverage is compounded in large sections of the country where little has been attempted or accomplished with respect to vocational rehabilitation through skill development.

Some Illustrative Cases

Mr. Young Horse is a typical example of the currently-enrolled student. He was born in Red Lake, Minnesota in 1934 and completed the tenth grade of an industrial program in a 1934 Bureau of Indian Affairs school in Wannaska, Minnesota. He is married and the father of three children, aged five, four, and two. His work history consisted of (1) three months on a landscaping job at $1.50 per hour, and (2) self-employment in commercial fishing, a seasonal activity that yielded about $50 weekly. Mr. Young Horse heard of the welding training through the Relocation Program of the Bureau of Indian Affairs and is receiving financial aid from that agency. He gave as the reason for taking the course, "to be experienced and for a better paying job."

Among those who have completed the training, the case of Mr. Graham Hopkins is a good example. A graduate of the industrial course in high school, twenty-five years old, married and claiming seven dependents, he had worked at gardening at $2.50 per hour when such jobs were available. This was his means of support during the training, which cost between $90 and $100. His reply to the question, "How did you hear about the welding course at the Berkeley Trade and Technical College?" was, "I called them and asked." Mr. Hopkins is employed as a welder, earning $3.10 per hour.

Another graduate, Mr. Wilbur Bates, a Negro aged fifty, indicated that he had completed tenth grade and had done some welding in the Army. This course, which he had sought out himself and paid for out of savings, led to a welding job at which he receives an hourly wage of $3.10.

PUBLIC SCHOOL PROGRAM FOR LICENSED VOCATIONAL NURSING

As was pointed out earlier in this chapter, a program for licensed vocational nursing was selected for special study because (1) it represents a cohesive training curriculum; (2) it is commonly found in adult schools throughout the country; and (3) it has more recently become part of the core of projects financed under the Manpower Development and Training Act. Analysis of findings on the course given by the Berkeley, California, adult education department will serve as a basis for substantive comparison with the one offered under the MDTA examined in a later chapter.

Nature of Work

Licensed vocational nurses, also known as licensed practical nurses, usually perform such duties as observing and recording symptoms and reactions of selected patients. They give prescribed treatment and medication, take patients' temperature, pulse, and blood pressure, and help with personal hygiene tasks. Vocational nurses frequently provide most of the nursing care given to newborn babies, mothers, and chronically ill persons. In doctors' offices they assist in many routine medical and often some clerical services. Their duties in industrial establishments may vary from first aid and emergency care on the premises to home visiting for health reasons.[24] Employment opportunities exist in hospitals, nursing homes, private health agencies, doctors' offices, industrial plants, and in the homes of the individual patients. The Nurses' Registry reports that the younger vocational nurses tend to prefer positions in doctors' offices, while bedside nursing is the preference of the older graduates.

Since the Second World War, when a critical shortage of professional nurses occurred, there has been a redistribution of nursing duties among personnel with different degrees of preparation and training. Although the number of registered (professional) nurses has increased steadily, this growth has not been sufficient to meet the needs of an expanding population alert to the importance of medical care. The employment outlook for nurses at all levels of proficiency is judged by the U.S. Department of Labor to remain very promising.

---

[24] Ibid.

With respect to vocational nurses' salaries, the San Francisco Bay area observes a scale somewhat higher than that prevailing in other parts of the country.[25] The monthly rate negotiated by the Hospital and Institutional Workers' Union begins at $393 per month for hospital duty; in private homes an eight-hour shift calls for a fee of $20.

In California, where the 1953 State Legislature passed the vocational Nursing Practice Act of 1951, there are about 40 courses going on in junior colleges and adult education programs. In accordance with the Act, the State Board of Vocational Nurse Examiners set up regulations as to academic qualifications of applicants, curriculum, and eligibility for licensure criteria. This board prepares and administers the statewide examination at completion of the training, 400 being the minimum passing score and 800 the maximum attainable grade.

In Berkeley, California, where training in this occupation has been carried on for the past 15 years, the program was of 12 months' duration, seven hours per day, five days per week. After an initial three weeks' period spent in class work on hospital premises, the students devoted five hours daily to work in the wards and two in class. The teacher, a registered nurse, received her salary from the Berkeley Public School. Predominantly, training was carried on at a local general hospital where the requirements in medical, surgical, and obstetrical nursing, as well as such specialties as physical therapy, could be fulfilled. California regulations limit vocational nursing to women because of the obstetrical requirement, a restriction which prevails in many other states.

Applicants had to have completed the tenth grade or show competence at that level. There appeared to be no special premium put on schooling of a higher order. In fact, the records of students graduating from the four classes reviewed showed little correlation between years of schooling and scores on aptitude and subsequent State Board examinations.

The lack of meaningful relationship between schooling and aptitude (as ascertained by the Otis Beta Test) is attributed to the fact that many of the enrollees were products of schools in states where the calibre of education is generally poor. It should be borne in mind that a considerable number of students were Negro, and the quality of their education may have been inferior. With the rather heavy emphasis in most intelligence tests on verbal and arithmetic skills, usually acquired in school, the lack of correlation between scores achieved and school grade completed probably indicates that the graduates of some high schools were less adequately prepared for

---

[25] U.S. Department of Labor, Women's Bureau, *1962 Handbook on Women Workers* (Washington, D.C., 1963), p. 82.

the tests than applicants who had completed tenth grade in regions where higher standards prevail. While there is still some question as to what intelligence tests actually measure, there is no gainsaying their usefulness in screening out persons whose linguistic skills are not sufficient to cope with the requirements of the training and the subsequent job.

The absence of statistically significant relationships of years of school and I.Q. score to subsequent rating on the State Board Examination should be noted, for it implies that these factors, relied on so heavily now in the selection of trainees, are not necessarily predictive of successful achievement on the State Boards. To be sure, the sample studied was not large nor one that was selected at random. But recognizing these limitations, there is still no objective basis for rejection as null of the hypothesis that the examination results relate to years in school and I.Q. score. It is conceivable that the State Boards relate closely to the actual subject matter taught in the course, and that ability to absorb this training was the decisive factor irrespective of years of school attended and score on the Otis Beta, which may not be a workable measure of intelligence for this purpose. Or it is possible that a more meaningful index would have been score on the Practical Nursing Test (to be described later), an instrument used only a short time and not administered to the classes included in this study.

In many cases, students whose background included college and even post-college education performed poorly. They were found to have emotional and personality problems that had probably hampered their attempts at a career in other occupations and could be detrimental here as well. The use of this course as therapy for persons undergoing psychiatric treatment was strictly discouraged.

Applicants were given the Otis (Beta Form) Test. In recent years a cutoff point of 90 was considered desirable, although classes prior to that of September, 1960, did range from a low of 78. Most of the scores clustered about the 90 mark. But the I.Q. rating is not a firm desideratum, for the test score on the Psychological Services Bureau Test for Practical Nursing Aptitude, the personal interview and other factors often bear more weight in the final selection. It was only recently that this test was used as a screening device. The scoring of this three-hour test was paid for by the student. There are five sections. The first part, assessing general mental ability is pitched at a considerably higher plane than the Otis Beta. In the second part spelling is tested. The next tests information in the area of natural sciences by having the applicant identify the correct answer among several choices. Part four tests judgment in practical nursing situations by requiring the prospective student to select the most appropriate course of behavior under certain circumstances from five possibilities. The final section of the test, called "The Personal Adjustment Index," contains statements that concern one's feelings about oneself in relation to the social environment; the respondent is asked to indicate agreement or disagreement with such statements as, "Most people get a raw deal out of life."

In addition to the battery of tests, each applicant had to write an essay on "Why I want to become a Vocational Nurse." This varied from a paragraph to several pages of a personal chronicle, depending on the personality and the degree of articulateness of the individual. Two themes predominated: (1) desire to help others, and (2) a longstanding interest in nursing, often evidenced by preliminary steps toward training, possibly frustrated by lack of funds or opportunity early in the career. Another motive, expressed especially by women over 35, was the wish to become or remain self-supporting.

The women who had been selected had to pass a physical examination, which they paid for. Because of the nature of the work, they had to be strong and healthy. Although height and weight requirements were not specifically defined, extremes were considered a deterrent to effective performance. Obesity, for example, frequently barred applicants from entry.

The students ranged in age from seventeen to fifty. The median age for those who completed the four most recent classes was thirty, the average was thirty-two. Except in instances of noteworthy maturity, girls in their teens were not encouraged to go into this occupation. While many recent high school graduates in quest of a career applied for admission, the teachers found that only a small proportion of them were seriously motivated enough to persevere. At the upper end of the age scale, the picture was somewhat different. This training program seemed to be especially appropriate for women between thirty-five and fifty who were seeking reentry into the labor force or who, for one or another reason, wanted a change of occupation. Although some hospitals placed 55 as the top age limit for hiring, others, finding qualified personnel in short supply, followed a somewhat more flexible policy.

Interesting to note, among the applicants for training were secretaries threatened with job loss because of advancing years, clerical workers faced with displacement by automation, domestic and factory workers in quest of upgrading, housewives seeking reentry into the labor force, and women with the entrepreneurial intent of opening their own nursing homes.

The teacher reported that as many as 300 applicants were screened in order to organize a class of 15 to 20. It was her judgment that numerous applicants are attracted because this relatively short and inexpensive training qualifies the graduate for participation in a dignified subprofession that, with its uniform and visible relationship to doctors and nurses, enjoys a sort of reflected status. Careful screening at the outset was considered a sine qua non in achieving a stable group with a minimum of dropping out and failure. Despite the care exercised, however, the rate of attrition over the past few years stood at between 25 percent and 30 percent. Such reasons as family illness and personal injury could not have been anticipated or prevented, no matter how selective the screening nor how strong the motivation of the students.

The students paid no tuition fee. Their total expenses amounted to about $150 and included the six dollar registration fee for two semesters of classes, the scoring of the special aptitude test, the fee for the physical checkup, the cost of books, uniforms, and pin, and ten dollars for the State Board application. It was found that almost half of the enrollees depended on husbands for support during the training; one-fifth had been financed by parents; one-tenth were welfare clients; and another tenth drew on their own savings.

The racial distribution among those who completed training during the period under study was as follows: 18 white, 32 Negro. Scrutiny of all available data indicates that race was not a factor within the frame of reference of years of schooling, I.Q., attrition rate, or performance on State Board Examination. Similarly, a spot check on subsequent employment indicated that job opportunities were available equally to all graduates and at a standardized salary. It is interesting to observe that, by and large, becoming a licensed vocational nurse represented more of an upgrading for the Negro than the white licensees. Although no precise hierarchy of the former occupations of trainees has been attempted, the records indicate that those lower on the job scale, namely, domestic, waitress, and laundry worker had been held by Negro women. Also, the group who had had no previous work experience was predominantly Negro.

To report that there was an attempt to keep a balance between Negro and white students is in no way to ascribe discrimination or bias to any of the persons responsible for this program. In fact, by following this practice the authorities demonstrated a deep sensitivity to and understanding of the delicate matter of race. They saw that white enrollees dropped out after the first meeting if the class was overwhelmingly Negro. By the same token, a strongly negative reaction was observed on the part of prospective Negro students who, upon visiting the class prior to making formal application, discovered that the student body was predominantly Negro. Evidently, from their own point of view, it was not desirable to be identified with an all-Negro group, nor with an occupation that ran the risk of becoming identified with exclusively Negro workers. Thus, some kind of balance was maintained so that a high calibre of students from all racial sectors of the community would be attracted and served. This policy was regarded by school authorities as a benefit to the occupation as well as to all who entered it.

Experience with the Practical Nursing Aptitude Test

Because the Psychological Service Bureau Test for practical nursing aptitude was used as a screening device for only one class, it seemed advisable to separate this group for purposes of analysis. From about 200 persons interviewed, 28 were given the three-hour test, and 15 were enrolled in the class for September, 1962. Three dropped out before the course ended a year later. This class placed first on the State list, thus giving Berkeley the distinction of leading all California programs in licensed vocational nursing. The entire graduating group, with the exception of the one who elected to study to become a registered nurse, found immediate employment.

It would be premature on the basis of one small sample to draw conclusions about the definitive value of the new test in identifying traits that lead to successful entry into the field of vocational nursing. If the Berkeley graduates maintained their high rating on the State list,[26] there might have been justification for research into the relationship between scores on the various parts of the special aptitude test and subsequent performance, not only on the licensing examinations but in actual employment. There is little in the ratings to justify a priori assumptions; some students who rated "low average" on sections of the Practical Nursing Aptitude Test placed well on the State Board Examination. The teacher's view was that performance during the training was the key consideration and that as yet no screening device has proved that it can predict this vital ingredient. Moreover, it was her opinion that this top-ranking class was comparable in every respect to its immediate predecessor—three-hour selection tests notwithstanding. The differences, which could have accounted for their superior showing, were twofold. (1) The most recent class had all of its hospital training at one of the best

---

[26] Subsequent followup showed that in October, 1964, the Berkeley graduates placed second, with a score of 577.11, and in March, 1965, they attained an all-time high for the state—first place with a score of 707.67 out of a possible 800. As of July 1, 1965, the Berkeley Public School District discontinued the program because of an internal administrative adjustment and the simultaneous withdrawal of participation of the hospital. The latter decision was occasioned by involvement with a two-year registered nurse program under the aegis of the junior college district. The teaching facilities of the other local hospitals were reported to be strained beyond capacity.

teaching institutions in the area, in contrast to some lesser assignments in the previous class. (2) The teacher herself had had the
opportunity to work closely with each individual student, to the point
where she could anticipate shortcomings and needs. By actually
teaching each enrollee according to her own strengths and weaknesses,
the teacher custom-designed the training.

Some typical case histories

Mrs. Helen Johnson, a Caucasian divorcée of thirty-seven, with
working sons aged eighteen and twenty-one and a dependent twelve-
year-old daughter, was allowed to enter the class on probation in 1959,
since her test score indicated an I.Q. of only 87. She was a high
school graduate and eager to acquire this training, because of a
lifetime interest in nursing and the need to be self-supporting. She
completed the course in September, 1960, passed the State Board with
a score of 515, and was immediately hired by a local general hospital.
After about two years, Mrs. Johnson realized that her daughter required more of her time and that the seventy-year-old grandparents
could supply little more than custodial care to a teen-ager. Consequently, she left the hospital and has been steadily employed on
private cases ever since.

Mrs. Janice Coulter, a Negro, entered Class 29 when she was
forty-seven. She is married and has no dependent children. A graduate
of high school in Mississippi, she attended Xavier College in Louisiana
for one year and took a typing course at a local junior college. Her
work experience included employment at the Berkeley Post Office
and a forelady's job at Treasure Island (U. S. Naval Base). She had
been a president of a Parent-Teachers Association and Worthy
Matron of the Eastern Star. Her I.Q. score on the Otis was 102.

Mrs. Coulter wrote in her essay that she had had a considerable
amount of schooling but felt the need for some kind of degree or
certificate of completion; then she had read about this course in a
local newspaper. She indicated that the reasons for wishing to take
the training were: (1) to help mankind and (2) to earn extra money
so as to aid her grandsons with their education. During the training
period, her husband was her source of support.

Several comments by the teacher during the early months bear
mention: "She is extremely loquacious, at times argumentative and
petulant to the point of rudeness. Has a tendency to use poor grammar. At times her classroom behavior is deplorable. Other times, she
is the most attentive student in the class." The supervisor at the
Children's Hospital, where part of the clinical training was done,

noted that Mrs. Coulter displayed "a somewhat defensive attitude." The record stated that this student "carried a chip on her shoulder," and the teacher devoted many sessions to talking things through. The final notations testify to substantial improvement in the situation: "good worker, gives excellent nursing care to patients, uses good judgment."

A very interesting letter from Mrs. Coulter appears in the files: "I know that I have caused my teacher to be disturbed about my attitude, I have appreciate her constructive criticism, and learning to think before I speak. I plan to take public speaking two nights a week after graduation. Thanks. Hope I will be a good L.V.N. to make school and teachers proud of this program." Mrs. Coulter passed the State Board Examination with a score of 442 and is now employed at the Children's Hospital of the East Bay.

Mrs. Grace Lawrence, a Caucasian student in Class 30, was a thirty-nine-year-old high-school graduate who had worked as a shipping and receiving clerk and at a production bench job. She is married and has three children, one aged fifteen, one seventeen, and one who is married. She scored 106 on the Otis. Although she depended on her husband for support during the year's training, it was known that he is a serious alcoholic, very unstable, and a poor provider.

Her essay stated that she had always wanted to be a nurse but that she had had to find employment early in order to help her family. "I want to be able to support myself if necessary," she wrote. "I have worked quite a lot in factories, but it is difficult for a woman past 40 to obtain factory work." Mrs. Lawrence received the grade of 624 on the State Examination and would have been placed immediately except that she required surgery. Upon recuperating, she was placed.

Mrs. Madeline La Croix, a white student who indicated that her age was "48+" and whose birth date was "3-15-13," had completed the tenth grade. She was married, with no children. Her work experience included registration clerk at a hospital and some sales. Her Otis score was 109. The essay she wrote was two pages long. It described her childhood in an orphanage, her lifelong dream of becoming a nurse, and the vicarious satisfaction she had derived from serving in a clerical capacity in a hospital. "To me, a nursing profession would be one of dedication, for I think it is a 'place' where one can do for others, entirely forgetful of 'self' or 'ego.' In this troubled world a word of wisdom or a smile or a clasp of a warm hand sometimes gives the depressed, sick, and weary the desire to live again." Mrs. La Croix' husband was her source of support during the training. After passing the State Board Examination with a score of 568, she joined the staff of a Berkeley hospital.

CONCLUSION

If the proximate goal of vocational guidance and education at the secondary school level is to provide students with adequate skills for jobholding, these services must be expanded and improved. Even in such states as California, which enjoys a better record than many others, the amount and quality of counseling nowhere nearly meet the needs of the growing enrollments. Occupying a position of low regard in the public's estimation, the industrial arts curriculum in our schools often functions as the repository for misfits and failures. The active manpower policy sought in America depends to a great extent on effective guidance and training in occupational skills for the young people in our schools. Through the strengthening and reorientation of vocational programs, the number leaving school early may be reduced and entry into the labor force eased.

While strong economic advance is vital, it alone cannot achieve substantial reduction in the unemployment rate. Remedial education and retraining are prime factors in successful adjustment of workers' skills to job demand. It is largely because of lacks in the vocational educational system that retraining for adults has had to assume an inordinately heavy burden of responsibility. Case materials in this chapter indicate some of the strengths and weaknesses of programs and policies now in existence. The research findings indicate that even in school districts which have a tradition and commitment to this kind of activity the problems are far from solved. Programs such as those for vocational nurses achieve their purpose; they are in tune with the occupational supply-and-demand realities and provide a vehicle by which the untrained and jobless can become usefully employed. Similarly, the course for welders attained its goal. But there, it will be remembered, some of the promising students were forced to withdraw for lack of funds. Despite their potential ability to derive benefit from the training, they had to fall back into the already glutted ranks of unemployed and compete for jobs with the totally unskilled. This is all the more regrettable when one recognizes the amount of effort being expended all over the country in motivating workers to take advantage of training opportunities. The students in the welding program demonstrated a strong drive; they simply could not support themselves and their families while learning the trade.

That effective operation of the adult education system must be accomplished by development of competent guidance services to the out-of-school sector of the population as well as to young people became apparent in the case of the electronics assemblers. Random input, in the sense of unqualified applicants, points up the pressing need for appropriate selection criteria. Failure to make intelligent use of labor market information was a vital factor in the unsatisfactory placement results of this and any other programs instituted merely at workers' requests and not on substantive data about occupational facts and employment trends. That there has not been better prognosis of future technological changes is no excuse for neglect to utilize the available materials. To continue offering programs inconsistent with economic reality, as is evidenced by the repetition of the electronics assembly course, compounds the waste of resources. Whether and to what extent these far from isolated instances of gaps and short-comings in the vocational education system are being overcome by the policies, provisions, and procedures of the Manpower Development and Training Act will be the subject of analysis in later chapters.

[2

Technological Change
in the Government Enterprise:
Retraining in the Federal Service

INTRODUCTION

Employment in the public sector of the economy represents so significant a portion of the total labor force that examination of the ways in which the government prepares its workers for technological changes is especially germane to this retraining study. As can be readily seen, the government plays a dual role; it both affects and is affected by technical innovations. By its heavy investment in research and development in various institutions throughout the country, it provides impetus to innovation. This may be inspired by military or scientific need, but the feedback is unmistakable. When changes resulting from scientific research become operational within the civil service framework, the government is faced with the necessity of arranging for orderly adjustment to them. Thus, the federal role is one of action in stimulating research and development, and of reaction in coping with the changes that result.

Government agencies and installations must cope with a volume of work that keeps mounting, and at the same time provide prompt service. Then they must take advantage of technological innovations and adopt them. But concomitant with such changes, or inherent in the process of technical change, is worker displacement. This prospect is not welcomed by any conscientious administrator but it is evidently unavoidable. Government operations, except for various types of services, are not faced with competition as are private

41

business firms. New concepts in weaponry bring drastic changes; labor-saving devices are introduced in all shops and every office; there appear directives to perform at maximum efficiency or face shutdown—all of these affect the work force engaged in defense activities. The pressure is not so severe in other government operations, but every bureau and each program is at least answerable through Congress to the taxpayer for economical and efficient operation. So, everywhere the government is put in the anomalous position of having to destroy jobs to get more work done.

How it adjusts its workers to these shifts is the focus of the research reported in this chapter. The case studies are typical of the programs designed to get optimal use of manpower. They show that retraining is the vital center of these programs; it is the vehicle for getting to their destination. And they show the government's commitment to education, remedial and adjunctive, at all occupational levels.

THE GOVERNMENT AS EMPLOYER

Government employment has increased steadily during the past fifteen years. In 1947, 5.5 million persons were on state, local, and federal payrolls; in 1965, over 10 million. This rate of increase substantially exceeded that for all nonfarm salary and wage employment during the period. The greatest expansion took place at the state and local levels, with such employment accounting for more than one out of every two jobs added to the nation's economy since 1957. It is anticipated that this trend will continue, but somewhat more moderately, with state and local public employment expected to increase by about 25 percent from 1965 to 1970.[1] The following chart (Fig. I) shows how the government has utilized this work force and compares its growth rate with that of industry at large.[2]

As the country's largest employer, the government has had to cope with a full measure of adjustments to change wrought by technological innovation. To handle the increasing task of record-keeping, the federal government utilizes about 2,000 computers, not counting those used in unique military and certain classified activities.[3] Since the first computer installation, for scientific purposes in 1949, and

---

[1] U.S. Department of Labor, *Manpower Report of the President* (1966), pp. 40 and 41.

[2] U.S. Department of Labor, *Employment Trends and Manpower Requirements in Government,* Manpower Report No. 9 (July, 1963).

[3] U.S. Congress, Subcommittee of the Committee on Government Operations, House of Representatives, 89th Congress, 1st Session, on H. R. 4845, *Automatic Data Processing Equipment,* Testimony of Hon. Joseph Campbell, Controller General of the United States (March 30, 31, and April 7, 1965), p. 5.

the second, for administrative and business management functions in 1950, government agencies have experienced at first hand the enormous readjustments in terms of system and staff that accompany changeover to automatic data processing. While due emphasis has been given to the technical planning connected with the installation of computers, extraordinary attention has been paid to the re-

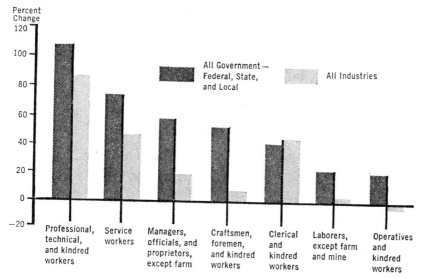

Fig. 1. Percent change in government employment, 1948–1962, compared with change in all industries, by major occupational group. (Source: U. S. Department of Labor, Bureau of Statistics and U. S. Department of Commerce.)

deployment of personnel. The Government Employees Training Act of 1958 and its subsequent extensions called for programs "designed to lead to improved public service, dollar savings, the building and retention of a permanent cadre of skilled and efficient government employees, well abreast of scientific, professional, technical, and management developments both in and out of Government." [4]

Executive Order 10800 implementing the Act, delineated specific measures, some of which placed certain responsibilities on the head of each department. He was to:

(a) review periodically the immediate and long-range needs of the department for employee training and in so doing take special care to identify those instances in which training will increase the economy and efficiency of de-

[4] President's letter of referral of "The Government Employees Training Act, 1958" (P. L. 85–507), p. VI.

partmental operations; b) formulate plans of action to meet such training needs; (c) establish and maintain, to the maximum extent feasible, needed training programs; (d) establish adequate administrative controls to insure that training improves the performance of employees, and contributes to the economy, efficiency, and effective operation of the department and to the attainment of its program goals; (e) stimulate and encourage employee self-development and self-training; (f) utilize the training facilities and services of other departments to the extent practicable, provide training facilities and services to other departments when practical and without interference with the department's mission, and cooperate in the development of interdepartmental employee training activities.[5]

In practice, departments train employees for new positions, update existing skills so that workers may qualify for jobs involving the preparation of data for processing, and provide courses for the development of new capabilities which will qualify affected employees for available categories. In maintaining a policy of job security, federal departments have tried to convert to electronic data processing with minimal displacement, thus salvaging, developing, and utilizing the potentialities of its work force through retraining.

The magnitude of the task involved in the changeover can best be appreciated by examination of the pattern of personnel adjustments during fiscal year 1961 through fiscal year 1963.[6] Ten agencies whose aggregate employment was about 1,325,000 persons reported a total of 1,628 actions involving employees whose positions were eliminated. Three-quarters of the workers affected were in clerical jobs. It may be noted that continued reduction of office personnel has been forecast for the fiscal 1964 through fiscal year 1968 period. Predominant among the positive adjustment steps taken was reassignment, which accounted for 77 percent of the workers. Responsible government officials, charged with minimizing automation's future impacts, anticipated that retraining and redeployment may become more difficult as advancing technology usurps more functions and leaves fewer unfilled lower-level slots. While remaining job opportunities become scarcer, the gap between present and required skills may spread. Moreover, greater sophistication with electronic data-processing equipment will undoubtedly reduce the lead time between planning and converting operations and thus preclude reliance on attrition to siphon off surplus workers.[7]

---

[5] Executive Order 10800, "Implementing the Government Employees Training Act," Section 2, Federal Personnel Manual Supplement 990–1 (Jan. 15, 1959).

[6] U.S. Senate, 89th Congress, 1st Session, Committee on Government Operations, Report to the President on *The Management of Automatic Data Processing in the Federal Government* (March 4, 1965), p. 94.

[7] Hoos, *Automation in the Office*, p. 120.

RETRAINING IN GOVERNMENT AGENCIES

Retraining of civil service workers is a matter of vital importance to the maintenance of efficiency of operation of government bureaus. Always in competition with private industry for capable workers, and usually at a disadvantage as to salary, the government perforce must offer other attractions. Relative stability of employment is one of these, but unless coupled with well-defined training opportunities for advancement, job security could lead to bureaucratic stagnation. To counteract this and to encourage self-development, federal personnel policy has placed significant emphasis on continuing education. How this is reflected in the operation of the various agencies differs markedly.[8] The contrast between the federal and other levels of government is even more apparent. As federal programs impinge more and more on state and local jurisdictions, with the extensive proliferation of grants-in-aid, loans, shared revenue, and direct action projects, personnel practices by state and local administrations become relevant, especially since it is at these levels that the largest work force growth has occurred. Implementation of new programs, no matter how carefully conceived in Washington, founders in the district or regional office when qualified personnel are lacking. And yet recent studies indicate that, with the exception of California, Michigan, and New York, state governments have taken practically no steps toward developing progressive manpower policies,[9] and municipalities have been even less active.[10]

There are continuous arrangements in the federal service for the training and retraining that contribute to upgrading and career development. In addition there are ad hoc programs for purposes such as the redeployment of workers made surplus by organizational changes, or the development of in-house capability to man new posts brought about by such changes. These may range from manual to managerial categories and may be designed for a single individual or for hundreds. Government usage of computers, which has been limited except in military and classified installations to fairly routine chores, is now being extended to more complex tasks. It can therefore be assumed that the need for retraining will increase. Develop-

---

[8] U.S. Senate Committee on Government Operations, Subcommittee on Intergovernmental Relations, *The Federal System as Seen by Federal Aid Officials* (Dec. 15, 1965), p. 197.

[9] Earl Planty and George Kanawaty, *Training Activities in the State Governments*, Personnel Report No. 622, Public Personnel Association (Chicago, Ill.), p. 16 (no date).

[10] Municipal Manpower Commission, *Governmental Manpower for Tomorrow's Cities* (New York: McGraw-Hill, 1962).

ment of support skills for the costly equipment, creation of innovative ability to devise programs to utilize fully the electronic systems, and salvage operations for the benefit of the displaced can be foreseen as permanent features of government personnel policy—federal, state, and local.

In the federal service, the Civil Service Commission plays an active role in these matters. It not only sets up agreements covering certain individuals or groups, but also, through the granting of special authorities, it permits variations from normal procedures and requirements. These may include temporary appointments and promotions as well as waivers of qualifications for a given time. As indicated above, the purpose for the retraining may be quite general, as in career development, or specific, as in the case of employees faced with displacement. The procedure for redeployment is regularized and follows the practices incorporated in reductions-in-force procedures. Such numerical reductions are not a simple matter of dropping the excess employees. Persons so "bumped" are entitled to certain privileges, based on their "retention points." In this way, the worker with veterans' preference and high seniority can displace someone with fewer such items. But even if he stays employed, such a worker must often accept downgrading and possible assignment to a blind-alley post. The total process has a domino effect downward, in which the persons laid off are the last hired, least experienced, and least capable of competing for other jobs. For example, when electronic data processing was introduced at a military supply base, the clerical workers who finally were laid off were those whose routine duties required little more than knowledge of the alphabet. The same, a common occurrence in the civil service, was the result when an automated, computer-controlled conveyor belt system for moving supplies went into operation at a naval base. Some of the 90 warehousemen whose jobs were taken over exercised their reduction-in-force prerogatives and were downgraded to the classification of laborers and stevedores. The unskilled workers they bumped lost their jobs without fully realizing that they were the victims of automation. Exceedingly limited educationally and vocationally, they faced real hardship in finding other jobs.

Government officials have recognized that advanced technology has made it possible to carry heavier work loads with a smaller complement of workers. They have also noted that, in some instances, new systems demanding higher skills or knowledge may have an escalator effect, in the sense of promotions that move present employees into better classifications. Inventory control, for example, now tied into a standardized worldwide requisition system, involves a higher order of precision and accuracy than ever before. Persons who are assigned to handle the exceptions that the computer rejects must have much more competence than the workers who dealt with the conventional procedures. Many of the support personnel for the electronic installations occupy classifications farther up the occupational ladder than those displaced.

In the effort to develop and maintain humane policies, the Civil Service Commission arranges seminars and institutes through which all levels of personnel, from supervisors to top administrators, can become more alert to the impacts of change on individuals, jobs, and organizational structure. Sessions are devoted to discussion of the complex problems involved. Invariably, there emerges the consensus that constant training and retraining are a sine qua non in retaining workers and using their services effectively. It has become apparent that in many cases of redeployment of personnel such basic skills as elementary arithmetic and written communication, not necessary when first the employees were hired, are now essential for effective performance on the job. At the Naval Supply Center in Oakland, California, with a civilian contingent of some 4,500, the training department has conducted a base-wide inventory of training needs. More than 600 respondents recognized their own deficiency in English grammar and reading, oral and written expression, and basic mathematics. The strong desire for improvement was evidenced by the response to the Center-sponsored courses in these subjects; they were over-subscribed within several days of their announcement.

After high-level consideration of the Navy Department's responsibility for helping its employees adjust to the changes confronting them, a decision was reached in July, 1964, that when automation or other factors change the system and impose new requirements, the agency has a responsibility to supply training opportunity, even to the extent of remedial education. To this end the training officer of the Center has recommended a liberal use of release time with the understanding that any drop in production can probably be offset by the long-run increase in the employee's efficiency on the job. Operating under the same philosophy, the Civil Service Commission stands ready to set up training agreements intended to provide a way to rapid upgrading. For qualified workers the training is telescoped and organized realistically in terms of production in the areas used for the practical instruction. As will be shown in the case study of the Alameda Naval Air Station instrument technicians, the shops were allowed specified "handicaps" in output as the students progressed through them. Research data on this program and on those carried out at McClellan Air Force Base in Sacramento, California, indicate that the success of such endeavors depends on early identification of obsolescent skills on the one hand and anticipation of future requirements on the other, coupled with thoughtful screening procedures and carefully constructed courses of training.

ALAMEDA NAVAL AIR STATION: INSTRUMENTATION MECHANICS' TRAINING PROGRAM

The instrument mechanics' program was begun in October, 1960, when the Overhaul and Repair Division of the Avionics Branch expanded its instrument shop. Needed were men with a high degree of skill and versatility, since the units to be worked on are growing increasingly complex; electronics and instrumentation are now becoming more closely linked than ever before. In view of the dearth of persons qualified in this special trade, vital to the overhaul and repair of the components in modern aircraft, the Alameda Naval Air Station developed a program in which men with a mechanical background in aircraft could be retrained in instrument work. It was assumed that all apprenticeable trades associated with aircraft overhaul have in common many aviation technical requirements. By the addition of specialized training, some degree of interchangeability with aircraft-instrument-mechanic could be achieved.

The ultimate program was the result of joint effort on the part of the U.S. Naval Air Station Avionics Branch, the Industrial Relations Department at that base, and the Civil Service Commission. Attention was given to such matters as length of period of training and selection devices. The contractual agreement set up with the Civil Service Commission included specific details on scheduling, rotation, theory to be required, and means of grading. The objectives of this program, as stated in the Training Agreement, were "to broaden the work experience and trade knowledge of certain artisan employees and to improve the Naval Air Station's ability to meet changing production workload requirements." Designed to train selected personnel for lateral movement, the program was not specifically intended to be promotional, although acquisition of new skills subsequently qualified the men for promotions otherwise not accessible to them. The basic goal of the program was to provide a certain group of journeymen with trade knowledge and skills appropriate to the new materials and equipment, thus increasing the effectiveness of employees, improving the efficiency of overhaul and repair activities of the shops involved, and supplying management with a more flexible work force. Eligible for this retraining were employees who had completed an apprenticeship in one of the aircraft trades or who had attained full journeyman status with two years of related experience. Excluded were journeymen in the family of processing occupations, as for example, painting.

It is estimated that about 1,800 men were technically qualified for

the program, but in response to a notice disseminating information
on the proposed training, only 65 applied and 53 emerged as likely
possibilities. Three tests were given: (1) Abstract reasoning, (2) Co-
ordinative symbol (visual perception combined with mechanical ability and manual dexterity), and (3) Mathematics. Cutoff points were
set for the tests, and those persons at the cross section of each were
selected. This narrowed the group down to 35, from which 12 trainees
were chosen according to certain specified criteria: (1) vouchers from
supervisors as to character and attitude on the job, (2) official standing
on the register, and (3) personal interview. The latter was considered
valuable, for it provided an opportunity to judge men on their ability
to express themselves, describe their work, and demonstrate their
prowess in handling a hypothetical problem involving the use of
reference materials. Its primary utility was related to actual physical
appearance and to certain personality traits not likely to be identified
in the other screening methods.

Since instrumentation is a "clean" job, it is imperative that trainees
be meticulous in their personal habits. "Clean" refers to the environmental control regulating temperature, humidity, and cleanliness in
the work area, the contamination point having been determined by
micron count. In the "ultra clean" room, where many of the trainees
are assigned, even more rigid standards are maintained. Also, because
instrument repair involves concentrated effort with men working together closely, certain personality factors are important. Individuals
who display strongly aggressive characteristics do not function well in
this occupation. The interview served to bring this tendency more
clearly in focus than did the other selection media.

The total training time of 3,744 hours (minimum) was designed to
cover two years, and it consisted of two phases: (1) The shop phase was
carried on within the instrument shop and used on-the-job rotation
consonant with planned work assignments. Instruction, for individuals
or small groups, was conducted by a competent shop instructor,
journeyman, or supervisor. (2) Related study consisted of group instruction under teachers qualified in trade-related subjects. Lectures,
directed reading, and lesson assignments comprised this aspect of the
program. Each trainee's performance in the two phases was evaluated
monthly, the understanding being that unsatisfactory performance
would mean disqualification and a return to the trade rate previously
occupied.

The trainees ranged in age from thirty to fifty, with a median of
thirty-nine. All but one (who dropped out after one year) were married. The ethnic composition of the group was as follows: three Orientals, one Greek, one Portuguese, one Negro, and six Anglo-Saxon. All
but one trainee, who was born in the Philippines, were native Ameri-

cans. Ten of the men had completed at least high school, the exceptions being one who had finished only tenth grade and another who had left high school after the eleventh grade but studied two years at a watchmaking institute. Nine of the high school graduates had attended junior colleges or had taken specialized courses—radio, electronics, and watchmaking the most frequently chosen. The majority of the men had been in the employ of the Alameda Naval Air Station for more than five years. The actual range was from 4 to 21, with a mean of 9 and a median of 7.5 years. Some of the men had started as common laborers or helpers; four had served an apprenticeship on the base; five had received training in aircraft mechanics as part of their military service.

Nine of the trainees had taken advantage of after-working-hours courses offered on the base and at the local high school. These covered a wide variety of subjects, with mathematics, electronics, and English predominating. Even though the official program included 150 hours of basic instrument theory taught on government time in classes on the base, about half of the men were enrolled in Army Air Force correspondence courses in electronics during the training. Prior to the inception of the program, eight of the trainees had received a total of twenty-eight awards and commendations for suggestions contributing to efficiency and safety on the job.

There was only one dropout from the program. Mr. Wong, 43, stayed in the group for about a year. Three months after the beginning of the training, there was a notation on his record that he had been cautioned to "spend more time at his work area to utilize his working time for training." In May, 1961, six months later, the supervisor's comment was that he "had good ability and produces good work, however . . . he could use time more wisely. Too much time spent away from bench." The September, 1961, report was: "Employee performed his work satisfactorily. He gave the impression of marking time rather than of enthusiastic drive to learn a new trade." From then until December, 1961, when he was transferred at his own request, Mr. Wong's performance with respect to quantity and quality dropped steadily. Reluctant at first to admit that he did not feel suited to the close work in the instrument shop, he stayed away from his bench; his record showed more and more absenteeism. Finally, it was learned through interviews that he was complaining of sleepless nights, jittery nerves, and general tension. His voluntary return to the electric shop, where the work is not as confining, is reported to have solved these difficulties. The comment on his record dated September 26, 1962, states: "Doing fine as journeyman electrician. Happy, satisfactory employee."

The twenty-four month program graduated eleven instrument

mechanics in November, 1962. Two blanket wage increases, which they had received during that period, brought their rate from the original $3.03 per hour (bench-level grade 11) to $3.18, then to $3.32. In applying for the training the men knew that, officially, it would lead only to lateral transfer. But they recognized the value of achieving dual journeyman status, at the threshold of a new and rapidly developing sphere of technology. With constantly increasing miniaturization of components, instrument repair work is becoming more and more critical. The next level for these men is that of the glamour occupations dealing with exotic systems. As of April 15, 1963, two of the graduates had been promoted into the instrument-mechanic-electrical field where they were receiving a higher wage. By December, 1963, three had been selected for assignment to the electronics aspects of the work, a direct avenue to a higher level.

Following the formal training, some of the men attended after-hours classes in advanced mathematics and electronics. According to a mid-1966 report, four of the men have remained in the trade area for which this training prepared them. At this level, base pay is $3.68 per hour. Four others have moved to one level above this, at $3.87 per hour. Two men have reached two grades higher, at an hourly rate of $4.07. One of the graduates of the program has moved into a salaried classification and is an industrial engineering technician, which has an annual range of $7,479 to $9,765. Supervisors rate these men as the most competent in their respective shops.

The exact dollars-and-cents cost of the program cannot be computed. No wages were involved, since production was maintained in all the shops through which the trainees passed. But overall expense must be assessed from the viewpoint of efficiency. There is an estimate of a cut of approximately 15 percent in production, for journeymen on the bench carried out most of the on-the-job teaching. Thus a substantial burden was put on the production group. This factor warrants special emphasis because it often acts as a serious deterrent to cooperation from supervisors, especially in cases where the "handicap" is not recognized and adjusted for.

The importance of the supervisory echelon in private industry as well as in government becomes increasingly great as changes occur in work content, organizational structure, and processes and procedures. Their willingness to cooperate in training, in adjusting schedules, and in revising production goals is often the prime determinant of the effectiveness of a program. As will be further exemplified in the McClellan Air Force Base study and as will be seen in the Internal Revenue Service research findings, operating personnel often evince great reluctance to release workers for retraining, even though this may facilitate redeployment in the face of vanishing jobs. Anxious to maintain output until the end, many department heads relinquish the least qualified of their work force. This practice has the perverse effect of giving the poorest equipped individuals first chance at the ongoing occupations and delaying if not denying the more capable the opportunity to acquire the skills necessary for continued employment.

The role played by middle management in implementing or blocking organization goals is central, but it has not been fully appreciated. But there is strong evidence both in government agencies and in private industry that supervisory participation can be a key factor in the success of a mission. For example, in some government agencies there have been established rating procedures that allow for selection of persons lower on the roster but with greater potential than some of their seniors. This system provides a means for identification and retraining of really promising people almost regardless of their place on the register. But it is not in wide use. This is attributed to inertia or sometimes sheer laziness on the part of middle management, a factor equally prevalent in government and in private industry, and just as likely to stymie the best-laid plans.

At the Alameda Naval Air Station, for example, the heads of the various shops were on the whole favorably disposed toward the program and accepted the 15 percent cut in production allowance as fair compensation for time devoted to trainees. At McClellan Air Force Base, where actual changeover was in progress, the desire of some foremen to cope with present work load took precedence over the need to face ultimate, ineluctable change. In industry, such preoccupation with day-to-day production was found to be a major handicap in the successful operation of formal on-the-job training programs.

Because of the production-cost factor, subsequent programs at the Alameda Naval Air Station provided training on certain specialized instruments in one trade area only, as compared with the four previously covered. Instead of following the full instrumentation concept, a one-year, somewhat more limited project was conceived for the concentrated preparation of men from the intermediate classification, that is, lower than journeyman. Recognizing the danger of overspecialization, however, the Station officials had the trainee move systematically through various shops under careful supervision, so that he could develop well-rounded skills. Thus each of the men would be in a better position vis-à-vis promotion, and would also be sufficiently versatile to cope with some of the technological changes that are bound to occur in this rapidly developing field. If ever the need should arise for a massive reassignment of journeymen due to skill obsolescence in a particular work area, officials at the base would use the original instrument technicians' program as a model.

McCLELLAN AIR FORCE BASE, SACRAMENTO, CALIFORNIA

Retraining is defined at this base as "the situation where one civil service group is moved to another occupation through a deliberately planned program." Changes in technology and consequent changes in the industrial structure are affecting the content of jobs so radically that workers in both the blue- and the gray-collar areas would be faced with skill obsolescence and dismissal but for such programs. Not only the mechanic who could overhaul and repair reciprocating engines, but the workers doing the "clipboard tasks" in the area felt the impact when jet propulsion of aircraft was adopted. The chronicle of events by Civilian Personnel Division was revealing. "We suppose we've been talking about the impact of technological change for years. Practically everybody has. We watched the Air Force grow from fabric- to metal-covered planes and from piston to jet engines. One by one we wrestled with the problems of training people to repair and maintain increasingly complicated equipment. . . . The only real problem came from the . . . acceleration of technology. The equipment was growing in complication faster than the man at the bench was able to keep up with it." [11]

At first the philosophy underlying the retraining effort was largely humanitarian. "We looked at the succession of RIF's (reductions in force) that had been our lot since 1956 and the fact that old timers with 10 or 20 years of service were going involuntarily out the gate. . . . We wanted to find a niche for those old timers." A closer, educated look on the part of the same personnel officials clarified their primary objective as the one that would ensure "that we have people on board who are ready to support the new system or the new weapon as soon as it is ready to perform." The officials realized that it was for the ultimate well-being of the organization as well as employment security of individuals that there be a concerted salvage of skills.

Basic to the planning was the ascertainment of just what combination of aptitude and knowledge was common to various categories of aircraft work. It was discovered that certain ingredients were sometimes common to some blue-collar as well as white-collar classifications. In face of a ten-year-old trend to decrease manual work at the base and a marked acceptance attitude on the part of industrial workers toward a change to "gray-" if not white-collar occupations, it is not surprising that there had already been considerable drift

---

[11] McClellan Air Force Base, Hq. Sacramento Air Material Area, *Report by Civilian Personnel Division,* mimeo.

without formal retraining programs. Mechanics with an eye to career development had enrolled through the years in various classes and upgraded themselves, with strong encouragement from top executives. Many of the engineering and equipment technicians had made their own way up this ladder. Such "accidental migration," as it is called at McClellan, is an everyday phenomenon and the ideal antidote for the "clay pigeon" [12] reaction to technological change.

With the changeover to jet engines came the necessity for much more than this laissez-faire policy. Retraining and reassignment of some 250 reciprocating-engine mechanics became imperative in the face of a mass obsolescence of skill. The personnel office set about this task by appointing a committee, which delineated the objectives, examined all available program documents, and made some perspicacious calculations about the future. They decided to concentrate on technical advances in the trades and crafts on their own station, with secondary emphasis on changes in management and method. Kept in focus were the hardware already invented and devices still on the drawing boards.

It became evident that three basic questions underlay the formation of thorough, detailed, and long-range training plans. (1) What kind of work force would be needed in one, five, and ten years? (2) In what respects would this work force differ from that employed at present? (3) What were the steps necessary to get from the current work force to the one attuned to requirements when needs occurred in the future?

The following excerpt from the McClellan Civilian Personnel Division report is a revealing demonstration of the candid approach taken by the committee.

The answer to the first question is complicated, and if we continue to update the base-line, the question will probably never be completely answered. We find that we can make specific answers only when we know the specific hardware that we will work on. But there is one redeeming feature. We find that we can generalize quite effectively and go from the general to the specific quite rapidly when necessary. The best example of this is in the field of electronics. We may not know with any certainty what specific electronic equipment we will maintain and repair in years to come. It may be LORAN, TACAN, Missile Flight Control, Satellites, Read Out, or Space Communications. Actually, we don't care, as long as we know that the electronic requirement itself is going to exist, for the basic knowledge of fundamentals of electronics applies just about as much to one piece of hardware as another. And we do know that the hardware of the space age cannot function without electronics. Therefore, our problem is to build electronic capability to meet this requirement. The specific instruction can follow.

We find that we can use this method generally to determine the kind of

---

[12] Hoos, *Automation in the Office*, p. 60.

work force we need for the future. Then, when the requirement becomes specific, we are already 50 to 90 percent of the way toward our objective.

In answer to the second question, as to how the anticipated work force would differ from the present one, it was felt that for the most part there would be a change only of emphasis within the trades. No truly new occupations seemed likely, but merely a logical extension of skills already acquired. It was recognized, however, that an extra measure of precision and reliability would be called for.

The formula that applied to the third question, relating to achievement of the goal, was three-fold: selective hiring, training, and retraining, with upgrading as the prevalent theme. As the skill requirements are perceived to shift, the personnel, group by group, will be prepared to meet the change by training that "fills the gap between what they already know and what they need to know in the new assignment and on the new equipment."

A simultaneous surplus of aircraft mechanics on the one hand and shortage of systems electricians on the other inspired the first program (January, 1960) in which men were deliberately moved from one career field to another. The 2,080 hours of training, a combination of classroom, on-the-job, and work experience, covered just over 16 months. By July, 1961, with the supply of superfluous aircraft mechanics exhausted but the demand for electricians still unsurfeited, the base for selection of trainees was broadened to all maintenance shops where there might be extra workers. The comment in the report[13] was: "It isn't really Space Age training, but it does upgrade people—and from surplus to shortage categories."

Under other training agreements with the Civil Service Commission, 62 men who were auto mechanics in oversupply were prepared in three separate groups for power ground-equipment repair and maintenance, where the needs for persons skilled in working with the increasingly complex units that support modern fighters are growing. A fourth group of surplus engine mechanics later took this 1,040 hour course, which, like any others requiring from three to eighteen months, now comes under a general Civil Service Retraining Agreement. This allows the base much more flexibility than did the previous system of one-by-one approval of programs.

As the labor market could not supply men for radio repair and industrial electronics, courses ranging from 2,080 to 2,120 hours and including classes, on-the-job instruction, and work experience were set up to convert journeymen from other trades. In this way, some of the best of the long-time employees were supplied with a new trade when the need for their old one became evanescent.

---

[13] McClellan Air Force Base, *Civilian Personnel Report.*

To supply the persistent demand for qualified staff in the electronics department, the Personnel Placement, Classification, and Maintenance Management offices conducted an inquiry into job components and thus established a substantive basis for what had previously been a matter of intuition, namely, that much of the work of electronic technicians was actually mechanical. So substantial an amount of similarity in task content was discovered through comparative analysis that only a short period of training (520 hours) sufficed to prepare 27 mechanics from the engine repair department to handle the mechanical jobs in electronics. In addition, 50 surplus engine mechanics completed a 2,080-hour training in free gyroscope mechanisms and electromechanical instrument repair. It was considered that their subsequent performance on the new jobs was probably superior to what might have been expected from applicants from the open market.

About 250 men have been enrolled in such programs as were described above. At one time, there were as many as twenty projects under way simultaneously; at present, due to consolidation of those which were related, there are eight. All of these have been under the aegis of the maintenance division. The projects have concentrated on trade and craft skills, and they certainly reflect a strong element of skill salvage. But a pioneer step has also been taken in the direction of developing technical sophistication in middle managers, so that they will be able to cope adequately with changing technology. This program, for specialists in the management of equipment and supplies, is under the direction of Material Management at McClellan Air Force Base.

The Civilian Personnel Division report[14] gives the underlying motive for the program:

Our aircraft workloads are phasing down. Our space material management workloads are going up. With the assignment of SPADATS, SAINT, and FSG 18 (Space Group) in addition to SAMOS/MIDAS, it becomes clear that the electronic knowledge possessed by the maintenance types in DMM (Directorate of Material Management) is not sufficient in quality or quantity. We have two choices. Get electronic types and teach them logistic management or take our present logistic management people on the maintenance side who would in time be surplus and give them a new technical background. We choose the latter.

The advantages of this policy of retraining and retaining are readily apparent. The employees have learned to live with the organization; they have developed facility in coping with the higher echelons and with the system generally. Moreover, their experience with the materials and the nomenclature almost always shows up as relevant. For

---

[14] McClellan Air Force Base, *Civilian Personnel Report*, p. 8.

the equipment specialist who once took a device apart, technological change often is mere logical technical advance. Such orderly retraining procedures have also demonstrated their efficacy as an antidote against the poor morale, job insecurity, and worker resistance often generated by innovations.

As trainees, the men received 1,040 hours of classroom instruction and laboratory work in electronics, four hours a day for one year. The other one-half day was spent on their old jobs. In mathematics, they went from basic concepts to analog and digital computers, with such related subjects as infrared and optics also included in the curriculum. Emphasis in this program was on establishing the firm foundation needed in the logistic management area. Eligible were employees serving in graded positions in areas of operation which were on the decline. About 20 journeymen were included in the first group to be selected.

It may be noted that here, as at the Alameda Naval Air Station, only lateral transfer was at first in store for graduates, but the element of job preservation by updating of existent skills and attainment of new ones was of paramount importance. Workers who for some reason did not qualify for retraining or who did not persevere when the opportunity was provided were downgraded to the unskilled laborer classification, a status very vulnerable to reductions in force. It was observed that some older workers, especially at supervisory levels, opted early retirement in preference to such downgrading. But the successful participation of "middle-aged" trainees is noteworthy. At the Alameda Naval Air Station, the age range was from thirty to fifty, with a median of thirty-nine. The age distribution at McClellan was very similar.

In the battery of tests used for screening of applicants at McClellan, intelligence is weighted heavily since in each of the programs there is a premium placed on ability to learn and to apply information. The verbal and mathematics sections are deemed particularly important. For the most part, the continuing jobs require more than average performance in these respects. The failures and dropouts were due not so much to deficiency in aptitude as to personality problems. Even if these were temporarily undetected, they were likely to emerge early in the course of training. In fact, it has been the experience at this base that of all the workers fired, the reason in 99 percent of the cases is difficult personality, regardless of the official excuse or the guise taken by the problem behavior of the individual.

Accepting seriously its tradition of training and of planned obsolescence, McClellan Air Force Base regards in-service, on-the-job training as an intrinsic part of its organizational functions. Journeymen and graduate apprentices in the trades, as well as supervisors, are accustomed to working with learners; the Civilian Personnel Division has training-oriented people in all the shops. Under "Operation Bootstrap," the Air Force provides a variety of courses at the junior college level. These are intended primarily for enlisted men but are open to civilians as well. Recently, under "Operation Deep Look," several thousand staff technicians were scrutinized through interviews, supervisors' evaluations, and specially constructed tests, with the objective of ascertaining the men's capability and improving it where necessary.

The annual report for the year ending June, 1965, showed that 12,947 man-courses were completed during that time, with a total investment of 223,702 man-hours of training. The emphasis was on the technical level, where officials recognized that rapid developments in the state of the art call for prompt skill adjustments. Of the 314 man-courses included in the off-base training contract, 67 were categorized as of a factory type and 208 of a specialized or scientific character.

Emphasis on retraining as a means to redeployment of the work force in the federal Civil Service is not limited to the defense agencies nor to the production areas. The case materials just presented are typical and not isolated examples of the personnel policy of the government. It should be noted that while careful planning led to enhanced utilization of existing skills and helped accomplish fairly smooth transition, the evidence does not suggest that retraining solved all the problems created by automation and technological change. Some of the workers affected by altered requirements were not willing to accept retraining, others could not learn the new skills, and still others refused reassignment to new posts or locations. Whether there was a net increase or decrease in job openings at any one base could not be ascertained meaningfully because of such variables as changes in concepts of weaponry, contract-letting to private manufacturers for entire or partial units, shifts of operations to bases in other parts of the country, and so on. Even though responsible government officials agreed that the new equipment and processes appeared to call for a higher order of competence, there seems to be no basis for the assumption that the skilled worker is, therefore, immune to technological displacement. The most that can be said is that for the present he is certainly not as vulnerable as his not-so-well-trained fellows. To a marked extent, the same situation prevails among clerical workers in the federal Civil Service. With procedures and machines for handling data undergoing tremendous change, many government agencies are experiencing vast personnel alterations.

The following case study of the Internal Revenue Service illustrates the role of retraining in the shift to automated data processing.

RETRAINING FOR AUTOMATIC DATA PROCESSING IN THE FEDERAL ESTABLISHMENT

The Atlanta Experience

The experience of the Internal Revenue Service in taking its first major step toward a nationwide conversion to automation serves as a striking prototype of the government's approach to redeployment of manpower resources. In the Atlanta region, covering seven Southern states, new hardware and attendant procedures brought about changes not only in numbers and types of jobs but also in their location. Similar adjustments are foreseen as inevitable in the step-by-step changeover that will encompass the Internal Revenue Service on a national scale and will concentrate the processing of business tax returns, individual tax returns, and the miscellaneous returns and information reports in seven centers, located from Boston, Massachusetts, to Ogden, Utah.

Specifically, with returns-processing and accounting work first to be automated and centralized, some 12,000 permanent employees in 62 district offices have been directly affected and about 10,000 more indirectly involved. Half of the permanent jobs in the districts will disappear, while as many as 10,000 persons will have to be selected and trained for positions in the new service centers.[15] In view of these substantial changes, the Internal Revenue Service has been faced with the urgent necessity of setting up policies and procedures that will accomplish the reorganization with a minimum of disruption, upheaval, and displacement, as well as an optimal utilization of present staff. The magnitude of this task can be appreciated best when viewed in the frame of reference of other studies of office automation, where the road to labor force adjustment has frequently been a sequence of frantic decisions, random reassignment and ad hoc measures.[16]

In most recorded instances of the introduction of electronic data-processing, first emphasis—often exclusive emphasis—has been placed on technical feasibility: the kind of hardware and its purchase or rental price; the functions amenable to programming and the order of their integration into the new system; the procedural and corporate restructuring that will hasten the break-even point and optimize opera-

---

[15] A. J. Schaffer (Director, Personnel Division, Internal Revenue Service), "Personnel Management for Conversion to Automation," Thirteenth Federal Personnel Management Conference (San Francisco, Calif., Oct. 29, 1965), p. 3, mimeo.

[16] Hoos, *Automation in the Office.*

tion. All these matters receive expert attention. The usual policy as regards personnel displacement is, however euphemistically expressed, one of economy, with little attention to the human problems that may be involved.

In the Internal Revenue Service, by contrast, the amount of planning devoted to the manpower aspects of the enormous changeover has been described as "extraordinary." [17] The basic personnel policy for conversion contained the least possible hardship to employees and the greatest utilization of present workers in new assignments. Articulated were the implications of this switch to automation for the entire organization. First to be noted were the possible effects on efficiency and morale in continuing functions. "If unwise policies are followed, or if you fail to communicate the wisdom of your policies to your employees, there will be widespread loss of morale, increased instability and turnover, loss of interest and efficiency, not only in affected areas, but even in functions which would be unscathed by the changeover." [18] Also taken into account was the unfavorable public image which might be created if the agency were guilty of callous treatment of its staff. The Internal Revenue Service was far from unmindful of the adverse impression that reckless handling of employee-citizens might have on the controlling legislative bodies.

To permit regional offices the opportunity to achieve orderly transition, several years' lead time was given for the retraining and reassignment of affected employees. Identified as particularly vulnerable were clerical workers who posted, checked, and maintained records, as well as supervisors at the lower levels in the districts. About 1,000 of the more than 4,000 employees in the seven local offices included in the Atlanta area were thus directly threatened, for at least 50 percent of these jobs were slated for ultimate elimination. Increased and expanded by the enlarged enforcement facilities made available through the automatic data-processing centers will be the public information and assistance services, as well as the volume of correspondence.

The 261 new jobs directly associated with the computer operation covered eight occupations:[19] programmers and management or systems analysts accounted for two-thirds; managers and administrators, one-fifth; the rest were console and equipment operators, schedulers, and tape librarians. Adhering to the policy of recruiting from within, the

---

[17] Richard Riche and James Alliston, "Impact of Office Automation in the Internal Revenue Service," U.S. Department of Labor, Bureau of Labor Statistics, Bulletin No. 1364 (July, 1963).

[18] A. J. Schaffer, pp. 1–2.

[19] Cardpunching has been intentionally excluded from consideration here, because of the evanescent nature of the occupation. Optical scanning, electronic transmission, and other rapidly improving methods of input are effectively bypassing this step in data preparation.

Internal Revenue Service filled 80 percent of these ADP jobs with former employees. But it must be noted that relatively few of the latter came from the ranks of the vulnerable district office personnel. Not only skill deficiency, but the myriad of circumstances usually encountered in reassignment of personnel presented obstacles. Fear of financial loss on sale of a house, likelihood of the necessity of spouse to resign from job, possibility of higher living cost in a new community, reluctance to sever home ties, and health and age problems were some of the deterrents to mobility. For female workers, after-hours retraining interfered with family commitments, relocation would have forfeited the prime wage earner's employment, or the real possibility of shift work loomed as an insurmountable threat to the normal way of life.

At the point halfway through the conversion, a total of 315 employees from the affected units had been reassigned to other jobs. About 64 percent of these were within commuting distance of their homes. The Audit Division and the Delinquent Accounts and Returns Branch, where enforcement measures are taken, received most of the transferees, half of the group having attained such technical and semi-technical status as interviewers, reviewers, and audit technicians. Over one-third qualified for clerical, stenographic, and typing jobs; the rest went into semiprofessional and administrative positions. Thirty-six percent of the original group of 315 relocated in other units of the Internal Revenue Service or other federal agencies, the majority having accepted appointment to technical jobs as tax examiners and accounting positions in the Atlanta Service Center.[20]

That these readjustments were achieved smoothly is attributable in large part to the retraining programs made available to employees in vanishing jobs and the training offered those selected for automatic data-processing jobs. Since the Internal Revenue Service has for many years conducted courses in administering new tax laws, it was not unprepared for the responsibility of setting up appropriate curricula. In the Atlanta region, local officials by mid-1960 had begun to encourage vulnerable employees to enroll in voluntary study programs in accounting and income tax law. When it was recognized that classroom instruction was the best means by which to supply the necessary preparation, courses were set up in all seven district offices. Although all employees were eligible for participation, special attention was paid to those whose jobs were directly affected by the restructuring. Such persons were counseled to enroll in classes most closely geared to ongoing, expanding, or newly developing occupations within the organization.

---

[20] Riche and Alliston, "Impact of Office Automation," p. 32.

Table 1 gives a summary of the contents and extent of courses offered.

TABLE 1

CONTENTS AND LENGTH OF RETRAINING COURSES[a]

Name of course	Contents of course	Length[b]
Fundamental accounting.	Deals primarily with preparation of financial statements rather than bookkeeping. Includes recent developments in basic theory and relationship between accounting and income taxation.	14 lessons
Constructive accounting.	Presents accounting principles and practices as they relate to tax cases.	14 lessons
Corporation accounting.	Study of accounting phases related to preparation and examination of corporation records. Presents intermediate and advanced principles.	14 lessons
Special review accounting.	Provides a review of fundamental, constructive, and corporation accounting procedures.	14 lessons
Analytical accounting.	Deals with analysis of transactions into their double entry elements; of accounts to determine if content and values are in accordance with generally accepted principles; and of statements to ascertain earning power and financial position.	14 lessons
Individual income tax law, 1954 code.	Covers tax liability of individuals under the 1954 Internal Revenue Code and amendments. References are made to pertinent IRS rulings and court decisions.	20 lessons

[a] One or more courses had been offered in each district office, Atlanta region, by July, 1962.
[b] Generally a 2-hour classroom session was devoted to each lesson.

As can be seen from this outline, instruction in typing and shorthand was not generally included, largely because secretarial classifications were lower than the grade occupied by most affected employees. Some of this group residing in cities where free facilities existed were, however, urged to take advantage of adult evening school programs offering this type of training; where a nominal fee was involved, the Internal Revenue Service reimbursed the student. One large office set up its own after-hours course in office skills, and there is the possibility that others may follow this example.[21]

The development of staff for the data-processing center was based on the policy of recruitment from within the organization so that full utilization would be made of existent skills and experience. It is reported that four out of five persons chosen to occupy the jobs in the eight classifications associated with the operation of the new center were already on the Internal Revenue Service payroll.[22] Table 2 gives a full analysis. Selection procedures, designed by the national office,

TABLE 2

Source of ADP Employees, by Occupational Group[a]

Occupational group	Sources of Employees				
		Within IRS[b]		Another Federal Government agency	Outside Federal Government
	All sources	Affected field units	Elsewhere		
Total employment:					
Number	261	22	195	31	13
Percent	100.0	8.4	74.7	11.9	5.0
Administrators and managers	47	4	30	9	4
Management analysts	30	3	25	1	1
Systems analysts	69	4	53	9	3
Programmers	75	4	69	1	1
Schedulers and controlers	9	1	4	2	2
Console operators	18	2	8	7	1
Peripheral equipment operators	3	0	1	1	1
Tape librarians	10	4	5	1	0

Source: Riche and Alliston, "Impact of Office Automation," p. 37.
[a] Riche and Alliston, "Impact of Office Automation," p. 3.
[b] All IRS regions.

began with the Federal Service Entrance Examination, followed by a programmer aptitude test in which reasoning and arithmetical ability, memory, accuracy, and facility for carrying out minute and complex instructions were deemed especially important. Then supervisors evalu-

[21] Ibid., p. 44.
[22] Ibid., p. 3.

ated each of the candidates on fourteen aptitude and skill elements of a nature similar to those covered by the objective test situation. After a personal interview conducted by a panel, a composite rating was made, with previous education and experience bearing due weight. The applicants who emerged successful were sent to the national office for a two-month training in programming. This was in the nature of a tryout, and final appointments were made only upon satisfactory completion.

Assessing the characteristics of the personnel qualified for the jobs created by electronic data-processing as against those of persons displaced by it, one is again forced to recognize the recurrence of a familiar phenomenon. Whatever the new opportunities created by technological change, the workers whose functions are taken over rarely are the ones who can derive direct benefit. In the Internal Revenue Service, most of the new automatic data-processing jobs were filled by men under the age of forty-five, and a respectable but not overwhelming portion of the persons who went into the management echelons were forty-five and over. But of the 1,074 workers who faced job loss in the district units, 83 percent were women, and more than 50 percent were aged forty-five and over. The educational level attained by nearly all automatic data-processing personnel and by most persons in the continuing local jobs was found to be post-high-school and preponderantly college. The number of school years completed by employees in affected units was relatively lower—about 8 percent not even high school graduates, some 40 percent had completed high school, and some had taken additional work in business or other colleges.

But even in cases where retraining would have repaired some of the deficiencies of previous academic background, some employees seemed reluctant to improve their situation. Some workers were wont to proffer family responsibilities as the reason for failure to enroll in after-hours classes. Transportation presented a problem, particularly for those who participated in car pools as the usual mode of commuting. Some individuals doubted that class instruction would enhance their placement potential or provide adequate preparation for new assignment. There was a tendency on the part of lower-echelon workers to emphasize immediate personal inconvenience and to disregard the possible longer range benefits.

The experience in the Atlanta Region of the Internal Revenue Service, ably analyzed and reported by the Bureau of Labor Statistics,[23] provides valuable guidelines not only for the districts facing similar conversion, but also for private companies anticipating the

---

[23] *Ibid.*

introduction of large-scale computer operations. The report has been translated, published, and circulated by the French government as a model for use by its officials. The research findings prepared the other regions of the Internal Revenue Service for the tasks which they must address in achieving a viable transition.

THE SAN FRANCISCO EXPERIENCE

The San Francisco District, where May, 1964, was the official date for training plans to take effect, provides a case in point. The distribution of employees as of July, 1961, among the eleven cities involved was as follows.

TABLE 3

EMPLOYEES IN DIRECTLY AFFECTED UNITS

Locality	Total Employees[a]	Number[b]	Percent of Total
San Francisco Region	5,776	1,581	27.4
Anchorage, Alaska	49	—	—
Boise, Idaho	157	45	28.7
Helena, Montana	167	49	29.3
Honolulu, Hawaii	147	46	31.3
Los Angeles, California	2,091	577	27.6
Phoenix, Arizona	252	65	25.8
Portland, Oregon	440	129	29.3
Reno, Nevada	129	32	24.8
Salt Lake City, Utah	177	52	29.4
San Francisco, California	1,498	382	25.5
Seattle, Washington	669	204	30.5

SOURCE: Internal Revenue Service.

[a] About 5 percent of these employees are temporary hires.

[b] Permanent employees only.

With 1965 as the cutoff date set for transposition to the new system with Ogden, Utah, as its center, the San Francisco regional office organized its retraining program in three stages: planning, control, and execution. Most of the eleven cities in the region had reached the final step by January, 1964. A one-week depth seminar for division chiefs representing the principal collecting agencies in the region served as the initial point of departure. During the sessions, these executives were given an understanding of the procedural changes in store and the chance to see the relationship of their particular functions to the new system.

Since it is generally known that centralization brought about by integrated data-processing often threatens the authority and status of persons in the upper echelons, these discussions were considered highly pertinent. Aware also that innovation usually generates insecurity and fear, the training director showed several films dealing with these psychological mechanisms and included as a discussion leader an Atlanta official who could share his firsthand experiences. This involvement of top managers was not a ploy to allay fears by creating an atmosphere of spurious security but rather a bona fide educational process by which these key men acquired a working knowledge of the new system. Prepared in this way, they could maintain control of their own operations and further the organization's goals. Many of them had voiced misgivings prior to the orientation seminar. Convinced that the electronic equipment and altered procedures would not only bring complication and chaos but would also erode their power, several of the men who were fairly close to retirement hinted that they would opt early leaving. The week of instruction and discussion imbued them with enthusiasm about the future and a substantial measure of confidence about the centrality of their role in achieving smooth transition. Secure in the belief that they would not be bypassed when automation took over, they were better able to help build acceptance attitudes toward the changes and to stimulate the interest of their subordinates in the challenges rather than the threat of the new techniques.

With the cooperation of these top echelon personnel, the regional training director set up a detailed planning schedule for every occupational group—or every individual if he did not fit into a larger category—involved in the changeover. The magnitude of this task can be appreciated when one studies the "career maps" indicating that by the time total conversion takes place some 2,400 persons in the region will have undergone retraining and that they will average three courses each. Some are already reported to have completed as many as ten.

Emphasis on training is no new phenomenon in the Internal Revenue Service. Changing tax laws, revisions in collection regulations and procedures, and altered methods of processing returns have put a premium on flexibility in this agency. The mounting complexity of operations in this branch of the government has made education an intrinsic part of its commitment to those employees seeking to make a career in this service. Outlined in Washington and available for adaptation at the regional level are 103 fully developed programs, ranging in content and sophistication from simple accounting to the most intricate aspects of specialized tax law. Regionally, the training director maps out and submits for approval every aspect of his projected activities more than a year in advance of actual occurrence. In the case of the changeover to automatic data-processing, the western region of the Internal Revenue Service was given about three years' lead time in which to prepare the work force.

The orientation direction was from the top down. After the managerial sector had been briefed on the new methods and procedures and their implications, attention was focused on the supervisors, the group from which were drawn the instructors for the personnel at large. This active involvement of middle management people in the retraining process deserves special mention because it suggests a promising solution to the perplexing problem of supervisors' vulnerability to office automation.[24] As might be expected, this group revealed strong feelings of uncertainty as regards the future and expressed a good deal of fear about the import of the reorganization. For them as for their superiors, sessions were devoted to a frank discussion of the anticipated consequences of the new techniques.

In groups of twenty-five these supervisors were retrained to take on the duties of instructors. Teaching methods, use of printed and filmed materials, remedial and demonstration techniques formed the intensive one-week curriculum, which was followed by two weeks at the Service Center to learn the procedural and technical aspects of the work. Added to long experience with the Internal Revenue Service, these skills will equip this cadre to perform a vital role not only as teachers during the transitional phase but as more competent supervisors later. Many of the men who came to San Francisco for this specialized training had been with the agency for as long as twenty years and brought a wealth of knowledge to the new assignment. As a morale booster, this utilization of present manpower demonstrated its worth. But its value was not to be measured in human terms alone; the return as competent leadership in their respective home districts is incalculable.

With the automated system taking over most of the routine clerical jobs, it is estimated that more than one-fourth of the employees in the western region, comprising eleven offices, will be directly affected. In addition to its impact on such obvious areas as the checking and filing, electronic handling of data will soon have wider reverberations in the Internal Revenue Service. With such activities as revenue collection, auditing, and intelligence slated for substantial growth and change because of the output of the machine, personnel at all levels are encouraged to chart their careers intelligently by taking advantage of the numerous retraining "packages."

Most of the clerical jobs pinpointed for elimination are to be found in the large centers, such as Los Angeles and San Francisco. The new

---

[24] Ida R. Hoos, "Sociological Impact of Office Automation," *Management Technology*, Vol. I. No. 2. (Dec., 1960), p. 17.

jobs at a comparable grade level are located at the Service Center in Ogden, Utah. Openings are available in card-punching, verifying, and the like. But so few employees accepted transfer that active recruitment for these jobs had to be initiated in such areas as Idaho and Wyoming. The only persons who moved to Utah from other districts were those who received promotion or could envision opportunity for certain advancement. Parenthetically, it may be noted that already some 250 employees at the Ogden Center have volunteered for after-hours training to upgrade their skills.

For the clerical worker whose job in the district was slated to be eliminated, there were several possible career paths. Transfer to Ogden is, as indicated above, not always attractive or feasible. Most of the employees affected were women—tied to a particular geographical location by family responsibilities, or bound in many cases as the secondary wage earners and not free to pursue an independent course. Brochures prepared by the Internal Revenue Service present a realistic picture, with details regarding moving, housing conditions, and life in Ogden. From the negative response to the call for transferees, it may be inferred that Ogden, Utah, had less drawing power for persons from such urban centers as Los Angeles, Seattle, and San Francisco, than Atlanta had had for residents of the smaller southern cities. It was for this reason that local recruitment was necessary.

Redundant clerical workers were urged to enroll in stenographic courses in many cases so as to improve their secretarial skills, this being a demand occupation within and outside the federal service. In the western region, use was made of ongoing adult classes. By far the greatest number of surplus employees were encouraged to learn to become tax assistors, the persons in direct contact with the public in such matters as filling out forms, interpretation of terminology, and explanation of regulations. Entrance requirements are fairly moderate for this classification and for that of office auditor, similarly recommended as an avenue of redeployment. Advanced technical training does provide an excellent promotion ladder to the ambitious, however. Opportunities in these occupations are expected to grow considerably because of the centralized electronic system. Because it is programmed with certain tolerances, the machine will reject certain entries which exceed the limits; these exceptions will require the services of specialized auditors. More intensive examination of individual returns will be made possible by automation. With a higher incidence of noncompliance brought to light, the Internal Revenue Service anticipates substantial increase in its intelligence personnel.

In almost every instance, office workers are bound to feel the impact of the computerized system. How they prepare data, the nature and flow of the print-outs, the content and pace of their work will all undergo change. Many of the clerks will remain at the same level, but they will have to learn the new procedures. It is here that the supervisor-instructors will prove their mettle. As was demonstrated in the McClellan Air Force study, the person who has grown up in the system and who thoroughly understands its workings has considerable advantage over the synthetic specialist who is sometimes brought in to carry out the new mission.

In the districts, the basic course structure consists of two hour classes in (1) Fundamental Accounting (about 22 sessions), (2) Individual Income Tax Law (about 45 sessions), and (3) Constructive Accounting (about 24 sessions), half on official time and half after work. Some recognition is given those persons who make the effort to qualify for reassignment by taking retraining even though they fail. Employees who make no effort to develop new skills or who merely drop out from the course for lack of motivation are subject to dismissal when their jobs disappear. The two main reasons listed for dropping out are (1) difficulty of subject matter, and (2) the training was provided too far ahead of the actual conversion. This matter of scheduling deserves special consideration and scrutiny in view of the generally held notion that there is no limit to the utility of lead time in preparing workers for technological change.

While the primary purpose of the retraining program was to provide opportunity for those employees whose jobs would be abolished to qualify for reassignment, all personnel interested in self-development were urged to take advantage of the courses. The anticipated changes in job content made this advisable as a tangible form of employment security. The avenues of work now relatively unexplored because of pressure of day-to-day tasks will soon be thrown open as automation takes over routines and provides greater amounts of information for tax purposes. Toward its 60,000 employees, the policy of the Internal Revenue Service has been one of redeployment by skill development. The Atlanta experience served as a feasibility study and blueprint; the western region provided more guidelines for enlightened personnel policies vis-à-vis automation. States, cities, and counties, just beginning to feel the impacts of technology, can derive valuable lessons from these practices.

The Government's Personnel Policies vis-à-vis Automation

The retraining experiences observed at the U.S. Naval Air Station at Alameda, the McClellan Air Force Base in Sacramento, and the Internal Revenue Service do not represent isolated or sporadic instances of the government's concern for employees threatened with skill obsolescence. Since 1957, the Civil Service Commission has focused attention on the personnel problems generated by technological change, especially by automation as applied to data processing. An analytical study[25] of ten agencies investigated the impact of electronic procedures on present employees insofar as their number and skills were concerned and tried to assess the implications for the work force of the future. Agency heads were asked to delineate the means to achieving smooth adjustment as they envisaged them and the obstacles which they had encountered. The recommendations in the report indicate that the government recognizes that vast personal and organizational shifts are in store and that these cannot be accomplished properly without definite manpower policies. Itself always under pressure to perform its manifold duties economically and efficiently, the federal government proposes to take steps that include humanitarianism as one of the desiderata. As was shown in the case materials discussed earlier in this chapter, such a goal is not inconsistent with good business practice; in fact, it may bring calculable returns.

Stressed as the existing areas of greatest difficulty are those related to the mobility and retrainability of personnel. The factors contributing to the unwillingness to relocate were readily apparent in the case materials. They require special emphasis in view of the Civil Service Commission's prediction that increasing automation will most certainly affect field organizations, that centralization of various functions is bound to occur, and that readiness to move with the work will become an important factor in keeping one's employment status. Reassignment and retrainability were regarded as crucial and progressively less attainable as productivity rises as a result of electronic devices; positions involving routine manual work will disappear, thus eliminating the slots into which relatively unskilled displaced clerks could fit.[26]

It was apparent from the prognostications of the reporting officials that a new and higher order of skills would be required to carry on both the computer operations and the adjunctive functions. This prediction is consistent with the findings of the present study and provides a clue to one of the most urgent questions we must face: What are the new jobs for which we must prepare our work force? On this score, the government's recommendations are somewhat limited, in that they deal almost exclusively with the development of computer specialists and with management personnel whose training will harness

[25] U.S. Civil Service Commission, *A Study of the Impact of Automation on Federal Employees*, for Subcommittee on Census and Government Statistics of the Committee on Post Office and Civil Service, House of Representatives, 88th Congress, Second Session (August, 1964), p. 11.

[26] U.S. Civil Service Commission, *Impact of Automation*, pp. 30, 31.

the synthetic intelligence provided by electronic technology for aid in decision-making.

Somewhat more intensive government-based research into the problem of utilization of human resources in the face of continued automation has brought to light the dramatic need for greater verbal skills. In what seems to be an anachronism in a time of increasing reliance on machines, it becomes apparent that while advanced technology can reproduce messages faster, disseminate them farther, and even translate them into foreign languages, communication skill still remains essentially a human trait. The vast memory capacity, information digestion, and proliferation of reports are unintelligible and useless unless they can be converted into terms applicable to the work situation. In the case studies, it was found that government officials are beginning to stress the value of clear exposition as it relates to all organizational functions. The Internal Revenue clerk displaced from her routine task by automatic data processing may not only salvage her job but improve her promotional capability by qualifying for the tax assistor's position, which requires articulateness and literacy. Under a new organizational plan, at the Alameda Naval Air Station, more sophisticated quality control is being introduced. The upgraded inspectors must demonstrate the ability to function on a more abstract level than did the mechanics who performed the work previously and must be able to communicate orally and in writing—skills for which the training department is providing foundation by setting up courses in (1) principles and techniques of quality control and (2) clear exposition. As was pointed out in the McClellan Air Force Base report, production workers displaced by mechanization have achieved employment security by acquiring the training necessary to obtain desk jobs.

The conclusion seems to be warranted that the occupations under federal civil service that will remain in the demand column even after new methods and machines have eliminated the routine office and production jobs will be those which call for a high degree of literacy. By inclusion of personnel specialists in every phase of the planning, even as participants in the feasibility study group that analyzes and proposes applications of automation, appropriate job specifications can be designed and training programs for career development initiated. The federal agencies' commitment is summed up like this. "Federal agencies have a dual personnel responsibility toward automation in the future—to assure human capability to increase the effectiveness of automation and to minimize any adverse impact upon agency employees." [27] Government officials have been very generous in sharing

---

[27] *Ibid.,* p. 34.

their experience with the changes brought on thus far by automation; the candid self-appraisal and realistic evaluations by responsible agency heads have provided much needed empirical information on the effects of electronic data-processing and other technological developments. Through its announced policies and its demonstrated practices, the U.S. government is exhibiting a determination to maintain efficiency through optimum utilization of both machines and humans.

Retraining by Private Industry

TECHNOLOGICAL CHANGE AND THE WORKER

To keep up with changing technology, the airplane mechanic has had to learn jet propulsion; the typographer must master the lino-film machine. The steam fitter must handle all sorts of new metals and materials moving from laboratory to construction site. The corporation executive must learn and apply modern management science. The doctor at mid-career must learn how to use electronics for diagnosis and treatment. The scientist has to reconstruct his fundamental concepts of physics; he must acquaint himself with the properties and behavior of elements and energy unknown when he was a student. In short, at every level of our working society, technology's impact is considerable.

Because of the rate at which new equipment, processes, and substances are making their appearance in the industrial world, one can hazard a safe guess that the pattern of any individual's work life will be determined in large measure by his ability to cope with change. A study by the U.S. Department of Labor reported that under conditions existing in 1960, a twenty-year-old employed male could expect to live about 50 years more and to work almost 43 of them.[1] Assuming that the 1960 age pattern of job changing remains unaltered during the coming 40 or so years, the estimate was then put forth that this twenty-year-old would make more than six job shifts during the remainder of his working life. These were defined as changes of employer; no effort was made to identify the possible reconstitution of tasks preceding, attendant upon, resulting from, or contributing to

[1] U.S. Department of Labor, Office of Manpower, Automation, and Training, *The Length of Working Life for Males, 1900–1960,* Manpower Report No. 8 (July, 1963), p. 2.

the move from one place to another. The report did, however, underscore the fact that during the 40 years ahead there were certain to be
many vicissitudes in the economic climate and alterations in technical
processes. "Viewing in retrospect changes that have occurred in our
industrial structure in the past 40 years enables one to appreciate the
almost overwhelming task of providing our workers with the kinds of
training and retraining that will help them to meet new developments." [2]

Hiring Practices

How private industry handles its role and responsibility in retraining its own employees for the changing requirements brought
about by automation, mechanization, new methods, and new materials cannot be examined meaningfully if divorced from hiring and
promotional practices or from the state of relations with any unions
involved. The small firm depends almost solely on personal recommendation and interview; in large companies there is heavy emphasis
on objective measures like aptitude and personality tests, with criteria
almost identical among all types of business enterprise. The clean-cut
high school graduate is subjected to the test battery, usually comprising the Wonderlic in combination with something more specifically
related to the business.

If the young applicant is hired, he usually begins in the helper
classification, where his performance during the trial period determines his survival. After that, his progress into the firm, if its work
force is organized under trade union regulations, depends on collective bargaining agreements as well as on his own initiative. Most of
what he learns will be on the job, under the tutelage of foreman or
supervisor. There will be little formal training. When technology
brings about changes in his work, responsibility for the development
of requisite skills may, under some circumstances, be assumed by his
union. On the other hand, management may prefer to provide him
with specialized instruction, particularly if he has shown promise. It
must be noted, however, that retraining on a large-scale basis for
categories of workers threatened with skill obsolescence is not as commonly found in private industry as in the Civil Service.

A survey of industry in the San Francisco Bay area, preliminary to
intensive research, uncovered the fact that while many companies conducted some apprenticeship program, either of their own or in conjunction with unions and the Department of Labor, most of their
other training focused on safety practices and management develop-

---

[2] *Ibid.*

ment. Courses in anticipation of technological change or to provide employees with new skills as a means to job security were exceedingly uncommon. The closest approximation to this was the practice of sending certain selected workers to the vendor to learn about a particular piece of equipment. The findings on the local scene are consistent with such reports as were available from other parts of the country. In New Jersey, for example, where the government canvassed 38,000 establishments employing four or more workers, two-thirds of all reported programs were apprenticeship, management, or short-term skill improvement. Accounting for more than one-half of the enrollment were employees in management, safety, and sales training.[3]

To ascertain how private industry in this region copes with the manpower problems accompanying technological change, scores of training directors in companies of all sizes and in all types of business were interviewed.[4] In banks and insurance companies, where change-over to electronic data processing has affected large sections of the work force, the questions were related to preparation and reassignment policies, procedures, and performance. In cases of companies that had closed down obsolescent operations in this region and built modern, automated plants elsewhere—not an uncommon pattern—inquiry was directed to the disposition of their local employees. Where automation of processes and relocation of facilities had occurred, the companies' practices vis-à-vis their employees were investigated; where opportunities were provided for retraining, workers' response was ascertained and the programs reviewed. Most of the firms reviewed in the San Francisco Bay area relied heavily on turnover and attrition to siphon off the workers rendered excess by technological change; the corporations that moved their locus of activities generally offered transfer possibilities only to persons in the upper-level brackets.

Turnover and Attrition

The widespread inclination to depend on turnover and natural attrition as a means to sever unwanted employees from the payroll works best during periods when job opportunities are plentiful and the given industry is expanding. It should be noted, however, that the introduction of automation and labor-saving mechanisms is a ubiquitous occurrence, affecting many persons and companies simul-

[3] Hearings before the Subcommittee on Unemployment and the Impact of Automation of the Committee on Education and Labor, House of Representatives, 87th Congress, 1st Session, *Manpower Utilization and Training* (June 6, 13, and 14, 1961), p. 40.

[4] Cf. U.S. Department of Labor, Bureau of Employment Security, *Work Force Adjustments to Technological Change* (Jan., 1963).

taneously. Other jobs are to be found only at the lower-paying levels, where age is a handicap and experience a small asset. Reduced to simple routines, most clerical duties can now be mastered very quickly and are so specialized that knowledge of them has little transfer value.

If changeover to the new system is gradual, a recognized personnel practice for relieving the firm of superfluous workers is reliance on natural attrition, where the older members or others who wish to do so voluntarily withdraw from the labor force. Implicit in the term "attrition" is the element of personal choice. Unfortunately, however, the use of this label to cover the process whereby workers are virtually forced to leave without being retired or fired has somewhat blurred the purport of its original connotation. This happened in a large bank where the introduction of electronic data processing had displaced more than 150 women operators of bookkeeping machines. Because most of them had been with the firm for some years, it is reasonable to assume that they either needed or liked the work, or both. The personnel director maintained that the bank had followed its oft-repeated policy of laying off no one, but that attrition had accounted for the disappearance of about 125 of the women.

Further investigation supplied the following information. These bookkeeping machine operators, who had worked on a nine-to-five job in the downtown business and financial district of San Francisco, had been told that the bank could employ them only if they became proficient at running the proof machine. Training would be provided free, but because of pressures of priority, the time of instruction would probably be on an evening or night shift. There was a strong likelihood that ultimate job assignment would be to such off hours because of the nature of the work flow. Geographically only a few blocks from the downtown financial district, the training location was a career's distance away. Housed in the industrial area, the proof-machine course ran on a three-shift, round-the-clock schedule. The job content of the operator is to read the hand-written sum on the face of a bank check and imprint the exact amount mechanically so that subsequent sorting and accounting can be carried out with no further human participation by the integrated data-processing system. Accuracy and speed are the prime ingredients of this occupation.

It must be noted that such routine, monotonous, and repetitious operations, performed under factory-like conditions—excessive noise, vibration, heat, pressure, and off-shift—require a completely different mental set from the one that characterizes the typical white-collar worker. The majority of the displaced bookkeeping machine operators were not prepared to accept the occupational downgrading implicit in their reassignment. They rejected the bank's offer of retraining and hunted for offices that still used old-fashioned equipment.

Some of the older women recognized the dearth of opportunity in other firms, especially since even small companies now have access to computerized accounting on a fee basis. Aware that the jobs for which they were once prepared were obsolete, this group accepted the bank's retraining offer. Nervous tension and the pressure for speed proved unbearable and some of the women left. The total situation for the 125 withdrawals was set down in the bank's record as "attrition."

Advancing technology will soon replace the proof machine with scanning devices so sensitive that they can "read" handwritten figures and even letters. Their impact, however, will be miniscule as compared to that of on-line, real time teleprocessing, which will transform the total concept of banking. Something like a universal credit card could eliminate paper checks entirely. The structure of our financial institutions faces fundamental changes, with tremendous implications for the white-collar work force.

The "turnover" brought on by the relocation of a major industry amounts more often than not to dumping onto the local labor market unskilled workers whose services are not needed in the new automated plants. In very recent years, several prominent manufacturers have closed down all but their sales-distributing operations in the San Francisco Bay area and set up new facilities elsewhere. With automated equipment to carry out production, efficiency no longer depends on a reservoir of workmen. Thus, flight from a region of comparatively high-priced labor to the enticement of tax concessions from industry-hungry hinterland towns is economically logical. Opportunity to transfer is rarely offered anyone below the supervisory level. Thus, even if an employee were willing to pull up stakes, overcome all the well-known human obstacles to mobility, and follow the job, he is denied the chance.

When asked about retraining for nonmanagerial positions in his company's new location, the personnel director of one of them reported that all hiring for the $18 million plant, equipped with every modern device and capable of substantially increased production, had been done "off the street." Using a set of criteria that did not prevail in the old plant, the company now required high school graduates who could pass a series of tests. The recruits, nowhere near the number of persons left jobless, were neither experienced nor skilled, but a short period of orientation was considered adequate preparation for their jobs.

Much of what industry does to equip its work force to carry on present assignments and to prepare for technological change comes more appropriately under the heading of orientation than of training. This is illustrated in department store training divisions, where they teach the newcomer how to fill out a sales slip, what number to dial in order to check a customer's credit rating, and the like. Courses in merchandising are offered to the ambitious, especially in the larger companies. In industry, manufacturers of automated equipment generally have programs to acquaint users with the special operating and maintenance facets of the new hardware. Producers of the machines controlled by punched tape, for example, run a two-week class for their customers. In the lower echelons of banking, five to ten days of indoctrination suffice to prepare tellers for their work. Realizing that service to customers is a prime asset in maintaining a favorable competitive position and that tellers are the most frequent point of contact with the public, new and heightened interest is being directed to proper preparation for this position. In fact, this is one of the occupations where programmed teaching has been applied and experience shared.[5]

Use of Programmed Teaching Devices by Industry

Programmed instruction is the learning situation in which lessons on tape, film, or conventional print take the place or extend the activities of the teacher. The "program" leads the student through a set of specified responses arranged in an order such that the trainee will learn what the program is intended to teach him. The course may be housed in a machine that allows the sequence to be moved forward or backward, with answers against which the student checks his own performance. That the program and not the mechanical device is of utmost importance has been stressed by authorities who recognize that the public, commercial manufacturers or publishers, and even some educators persistently try to create the impression that the machine is primary.[6]

The New York Trust Company office of the Chemical Bank reported that eight months were devoted to preparation of a programmed training course for tellers at a cost of $18,000, which covered consultants' fees, materials, production, duplication, binding, and the machine for showing slides. Using this method, which provided 1,600 frames eliciting 2,400 responses, the training department taught the recruits the fundamentals of the teller's job in $16\frac{1}{2}$ hours, as compared with the 17 to 20 hours required by traditional techniques. Undoubtedly, many other firms have developed courses of this type for their own employees with varying degrees of success. An authori-

---

[5] Donald R. Alverson, Jr., "Programmed Instruction and Teller Training," *Training Directors Journal*, XVII, 7 (July, 1963), pp. 18–20.

[6] Wilbur Schramm, *Programmed Instruction Today and Tomorrow* (New York: Fund for the Advancement of Education, 1963).

tative evaluation of programmed teaching has yet to be achieved, although there are scattered reports.[7]

In the San Francisco Bay area training departments, a number of kinds of mechanisms are used as teaching aids. This technique was applied experimentally with promising results in a class for electricians undergoing updating and upgrading, as was reported in the previous chapter. Positive also was the experience with a programmed course in elementary mathematics, designed as a remedial measure and used at the U.S. Naval Supply Center in Oakland, California. Free from the embarrassment of competition with subordinates, employees even in the supervisory echelons responded with enthusiasm to the depersonalized autoinstructional situation. At this and other locations, both in government installations and private industry, the use of films for inculcating safety habits, training in sales and personnel relations, and developing leadership and managerial talent is becoming more extensive. Programmed techniques represent a wide spectrum of professional quality, running the full gamut from the *Encyclopaedia Britannica's* highly regarded materials to those of opportunists, the veneer of whose sales talk lies thin over the inadequacy of their product. In some cases, their service could easily be duplicated and probably improved on for a fraction of what they charge their customers for a glossy, latter-day version of a stereopticon and slides.[8] In the San Francisco headquarters of a large corporation developing its own key-punch operators, a small room has been set aside for an elaborate setup of this type. The $5,000 projector can do little more than a magic lantern of yesteryear, except that its speeds can be regulated by a hand-sized control unit. The types, films, instructors' manuals, and other accessories must be paid for separately. Not included in the expense are two card punch machines rendered unproductive by allocation to the classroom, and the salary of the teacher, a young woman who previously worked as a verifier in the automated data-processing division of the company. The schedule of two weeks of programmed learning, with the teacher handling the on-off switch, and one week of supervised production on live work implies a degree of effectiveness not substantiated by the results. In one year of operation, the program which costs $5,000 exclusive of the overhead expenses and the salary of a full-time production worker, turned out only ten key-punch operators. The report of this experience is not to be construed as an indictment of all programmed instruction but

[7] "Report of the Committee on Teaching Methods—Programmed Instruction," *Accounting Review*, XXXIX, 2 (April, 1964), pp. 432–446.

[8] Ida R. Hoos, "The Personnel Administrator and Technological Change," *Public Personnel Review*, XXIV, 3 (July, 1963), pp. 152–158.

rather as a caveat for those who may mistake the sleekness of packaging for the substance of teaching.

Just as was indicated in the New Jersey study on retraining by industry,[9] private companies in the San Francisco Bay area tend to concentrate their training efforts on safety classes and the development of sales personnel and management talent. Little else of a substantive nature is known about the actual extent of training by industry. Although the Secretary of Labor has been quoted as considering private industry the nation's second largest developer of skills, exceeded only by the educational establishment,[10] efforts to identify the programs and assess their value have yielded little definitive data.[11] In a recent canvass carried out by the U.S. Department of Labor in preparation for a special study,[12] from some one hundred organizations, many of which had made technical changes that seemed to require retraining of workers, only four were found to meet simple criteria like these: (1) if it kept objective measures of the performance of individual workers during retraining, (2) if it included in the programs persons over 40 years of age as well as those younger, and (3) if it maintained personnel records showing age and educational level of the workers.

It should be noted that many firms encourage all categories of their employees to enroll in evening classes, and some have tuition refund arrangements for work-related courses; but the examples of a curriculum specifically set up by a company as a retraining measure to meet new personnel requirements created by technological change or to help update obsolescent skills are such rare phenomena that we have included in the case materials in this chapter analyses of *all* of them existent in this geographical area when this research study was begun. For background for the findings, we look to reports of retraining in other parts of the United States.

THE ARMOUR EXPERIENCE

What comes under the heading of retraining by industry frequently turns out to be a company's arrangement to guide its displaced employees to classes or courses of action outside its own sphere of operation. In other words, the organization depends on someone else

---

[9] Hearings before the Subcommittee on Unemployment and the Impact of Automation, *Manpower Utilization and Training.*

[10] U.S. Congress, *January 1963 Economic Report of the President,* Hearings before the Joint Economic Committee, 88th Congress, 1st Session (1963), Part I, p. 211.

[11] Stanford Research Institute, *Training in Industry* (Palo Alto: Stanford Research Institute, 1962).

[12] U.S. Department of Labor, Bureau of Labor Statistics, "Industrial Retraining Programs for Technological change," Bulletin No. 1368 (June, 1963).

to retrain its surplus workers for jobs somewhere else. The results of this type of effort can be seen in the experience of Armour and Company, one of the largest meat-packing corporations in the United States. When this firm closed six of its plants in 1959 and thus affected 5,000 production workers, an Automation Fund Committee was established to cope with the vast range of problems generated by this mass reduction. An authoritative report sums up the Oklahoma City experience as follows: "Perhaps because of the uniqueness of the sponsorship by a special management-labor committee and the possibility that this might be a trail-blazing experiment in finding a solution for a major social problem, much was expected of the efforts of the committee. The experiment, as it turned out, was a relatively minor effort, hastily developed some months after the plant shut down." [13]

Of the workers who were tested, 65 percent were not offered retraining because of such reasons as these: (1) the Automation Committee had authorized only $150 as the maximum training allowance; (2) the majority of the displaced men had had very little schooling, and their work experience, limited to meat packing operations, had small transfer value; (3) welding, air conditioning, auto mechanics, and such other occupations as were considered most feasible in the geographical localities affected by the shutdown were deemed to be beyond the capability of most of the disemployed. Out of the active seniority list of about 400, 52 workers received special training in 15 different subjects. The local adult education division of the public school accommodated six men and four women in such classes as reading and writing, typing, business English, blueprint reading, and electronics. Subsequently, a special course in upholstery, which enrolled 15 of the workers, was added to the list of adult education offerings. At private schools the Automation Fund paid the first $60 of the fee plus one-half of the rest, providing that the total did not exceed $150; air conditioning, auto mechanics, and beauty culture attracted 11 of the employees to these. For a group of 13 men who failed to qualify for job openings as retail meat cutters despite their years of experience with Armour, a special class was initiated. Despite the dearth of spectacular success in the endeavor, retraining proved to be more fruitful than any of the other salvage measures.[14]

Among the other conclusions to be drawn from the study of the Armour shutdown and from similar cases in the San Francisco Bay area, the one that stands out is that private industries do not as a

---

[13] Richard C. Wilcock and Walter H. Franke, *Unwanted Workers* (New York: The Free Press of Glencoe, 1963), p. 252.

[14] Edwin Young, "The Armour Experience: A Case Study in Plant Shutdown," *Adjusting to Technological Change*, eds., Gerald G. Somers, C. Edward L. Cushman, and Nat Weinberg (New York: Harper and Row, 1963), pp. 144–158.

general rule provide their workers with "job insurance" in the way of redeployment through retraining after the fashion of the federal government. This lack of activity can perhaps be attributed to the observation made earlier that training by industry is a function of the economic situation of a particular company; active training programs are likely to be maintained only where there are large numbers of jobs to be filled and when the local labor pool cannot provide persons with adequate preparation for them. The research into worker response to retraining points up an interesting corollary. As cutbacks in personnel occur, voluntary enrollments and attendance in classes drop off sharply. This behavioral phenomenon suggests the possibility that prime motivation to participate in courses comes from perceived advantages in the way of enhanced employability or promotion. When this "carrot" is withdrawn, perseverance fades. Some of the training lessons, learned during an era of company expansion, may have relevance to the overall problem of work force adjustment through retraining. It is for this reason that we look with special interest into the one San Francisco Bay area company that reported a large-scale and continuing education, training, and retraining program.

THE LOCKHEED MISSILES & SPACE COMPANY

This division of the Lockheed Aircraft Corporation, located in Sunnyvale, California, some 40 miles from San Francisco, expresses its concern for employee training in the following statement.[15]

The way a company utilizes its assets makes a big difference in its progress. Trained and experienced personnel in all fields are our company's most valuable assets. In the past seven years technological advances have challenged the capabilities of the aerospace and electronics industry. We must adjust to rapidly changing conditions. The coming decade will see more changes in our industry. Lockheed is moving forward on all fronts: propulsion, guidance, communication, structures, computer research and development. In the year ahead, we see substantially greater competition, continuing expansion, and growing complexity of our work—all these point up the need to do everything we can to develop employees who can handle greater responsibilities in both technical fields and management.

By way of encouraging employees to improve their qualifications, the company (1) grants partial reimbursement for courses satisfactorily completed at accredited educational facilities, (2) rearranges schedules to allow for participation in classes held during working hours, (3) initiates related educational and training programs to meet the specific

---

[15] Lockheed Missiles & Space Company, Industrial Relations, Education and Training, *Education and Training Programs,* Foreward to General Bulletin 1963–64 by H. J. Brown, Executive Vice President, p. III.

needs of the company, (4) provides a reduced work schedule in certain specific instances so that individuals may complete their studying toward a degree, and (5) permits leaves of absence for attainment of advanced degrees. There are two major divisions under employee training. The first, titled "company training," includes both formal instruction utilizing the courses conducted by the company and departmental, on-the-job teaching of a more informal and somewhat more specifically work-related nature. The second, called "project training," is identified closely with the specific contractual task at hand. The development of skills related to such individual assignments may be conducted internally or by subcontract with outside institutions. The catalogue of offerings ranges from vestibule indoctrination of common office procedures to graduate-level seminars for the Space Systems Division engineering staff. Not listed in it but important because it illustrates that flexibility has been achieved along with institutionalization is a special course dealing with the problems of crimping and the insertion and removal of pins and sockets in connectors. A high rejection rate of crimped contacts had indicated some skill deficiency along the production line. From February to June, 1964, 287 employees completed the training course. As the training department perceives such lacks, or line management identifies them, appropriate classes are set up. The courses taken by employees are "added to their jacket"; this record is taken into account when changes of status occur. Although seniority plays some part both in the order of layoffs and in rehiring, the worker who has demonstrated industriousness in training enjoys specific benefits. The company records indicate the magnitude of training operations during the past several years (Table 4). It should be noted that these figures reflect only formal activity in the plant located in Sunnyvale, California, and under the supervision of the Industrial Relations Department. Not accessible but certainly very significant is the informal, on-the-job instruction which is constantly in progress throughout the company. Lockheed does not, however, engage in formal apprenticeship programs. Because of the unsettled pace of work, a trainee could be brought to the very threshold of journeyman status only to be fired for lack of work.

Due to the mercurial nature of the space industry, where international, national, and regional considerations govern the letting and cancelling of contracts, there are wide swings in the size of work force required. With the completion of major projects, there may be a cutback of as many as 10 percent of the employees—2,000 displaced at times, who range from engineers to laborers. Even though his own staff is affected by general reductions of this magnitude, the manager of training sees no erosion of the basic training function. On the

TABLE 4

LOCKHEED MISSILES & SPACE COMPANY TRAINING[a]

1962		
Total training hours		267,241
Company time	146,688	
Employees' own time	88,231	
Nonemployee training[b]	32,322	
Satisfactory course completions		17,126
1963		
Total training hours		221,335
Company time	122,968	
Employees' own time	88,975	
Nonemployee training[b]	9,392	
Satisfactory course completions		
1964		
Total training hours		131,850
Company time	84,351	
Employees' own time	44,499	
Satisfactory course completions		9,691
1965 (estimated through December, 1965)		
Total training hours		135,241
Company time	72,705	
Employees' own time	62,536	
Satisfactory course completions		8,890

SOURCE: Mr. T. E. Lyons, Manager, Education and Training, Lockheed Missiles & Space Company, Sunnyvale, California.

[a] These figures do not include the activities of the two additional but separate training departments which concentrate on the specific operations related to missile or space vehicle hardware. Not calculated in the totals are the numbers enrolled in adult evening high school and junior college classes. It is reported that in 1962 there were 2,095 college course enrollments and in 1963 there were 2,246.

[b] Nonemployee training hours were derived from the program for soldering, open to outsiders who wished to qualify for this type of work with the company. This practice was discontinued in 1963.

contrary, lulls of this kind appear to provide an opportunity for evaluating policies and improving this aspect of the organization in preparation for the next upturn. He regards the quiet period as the proper time to put into operation some of the lessons learned during the growth era.

Identified as a major problem is the fact that a substantial amount of training effort has had to be devoted to remedial teaching. Mathematics and trigonometry have to be taught not only to the high school graduates but also to many who have taken technical courses in junior college. Improvement of communications skills is urgently needed at all occupational levels. Many of the courses designed to cope with these inadequacies are perforce of an ad hoc nature, set up for a given group under particular circumstances.

The "crash" and discrete nature of much of the project training underscores the need for communication from the line supervisors. When there have been no clues as to what is in store in the way of new equipment, processes, and products, the training personnel have been hard put to plan appropriate programs. A lack of input from the line is particularly serious in an industry where varied customers (such as the National Aeronautics and Space Agency), new concepts, and new specifications put a premium on up-to-the-minute know-how; even six months is considered a fairly long skill life in some areas of the company. Lack of guidelines has frequently prevented the training department from helping interested employees design long-range career development plans. When information has been wanting as to what specific skills would be required, this division has been hampered in its attempts to provide occupational guidance to individuals and in its efforts to devise coordinated curricula consistent with future job opportunities.

Accustomed to the dynamic nature of the aerospace industry, the training manager of Lockheed explored the possibility of offering courses at various levels for their former employees. By this means, displaced workers could maintain, increase, or refurbish their skills in preparation for the time when this or some other company began hiring again. It was anticipated that persons in occupational groups in oversupply, such as mechanical engineers, might benefit from specialized classes that would qualify them in the relatively open fields of electronic and electrical design. Evening programs were under consideration for those who might have found interim employment but were motivated toward self-betterment.

This company's interest in continuing to provide training services to its displaced personnel, whether it stems from outright humanitarianism or from the perceived advantage of developing a reservoir of skilled help, is noteworthy.

It may be a reflection of a labor condition peculiar to the aerospace industry, where sharp ups and downs occur. Unable to make long-range predictions, the firms engaged in this kind of contracting lay off thousands and then, six months later, are forced to recruit vigorously. The manpower available will probably lack the precise skills required, especially since this is an industry characterized by rapid technological change. Hence, the fairly marked emphasis on the training function. Under the mid-1966 conditions of a fairly tight labor supply, the company is encountering severe shortages but only in highly specialized areas, such as programming and cryogenics. And even these jobs could probably be filled if it were not for the industry's propensity toward "hoarding." Many firms maintain larger technical staffs than they utilize, simply for insurance purposes, and advertise that they will even pay a bounty for qualified personnel. At lower skill levels, no such situation exists; in fact, despite the much-publicized boom in business, Lockheed Missiles & Space Company has not taken back as many workers as were laid off in the most recent cutback.

For all categories, in the present environment of economic prosperity, the training department (still minus several persons it lost in the retrenchment) is pursuing the practice of offering courses both at the plant and outside. The director reports that the present employees seem to evince more receptive attitudes toward self-development; he considers that campaigns alerting workers to the dangers of obsolescence may be taking effect. Sharper, more realistic vocational orientation in some of the local junior colleges may be a factor in attracting after-work participation. In fact, members of Lockheed's education staff helped design the curriculum for electronics technicians at one such institution. Also, with funds from the Vocational Education Act of 1963, the company provides subsidies for up-dating opportunities during summers to vocational arts teachers from nearby schools.

The most profound lesson to be learned from the Lockheed experience deals with workers' attitudes toward training. The fact that men dropped out from courses even before they lost their jobs indicates the extreme degree of volatility of motivation. Herein lies a major problem and one encountered in other retraining efforts. Research into the much publicized retraining of 69 men by the Xerox Company underscores the fact that morale was low and trainee attitudes generally poor.[16] In this situation, as in the Lockheed case, the company's readiness to reassign laterally, if not promote, and to absorb workers who have been retrained is a strong determinant of workers' acceptance attitudes and behavior. So is a sufficiently promising market elsewhere for the new skills. If retraining is to succeed, there must be a tangible return in sight.

If employees are not receptive and there is poor communication within an organization, it can complicate the operation of a training program no matter how carefully it is conceived. This is illustrated in the case of the tracer lathe operators at Kaiser Aerospace and Electronics Corporation in Oakland, California.

THE TRACER LATHE OPERATORS' PROGRAM AT KAISER AEROSPACE AND ELECTRONICS CORPORATION

This division of Kaiser Industries is engaged in missile work and includes the tracer lathe as part of its equipment. Somewhat similar

---

[16] Felician F. Foltman, "Xerox Corporation—a Case Study in Retraining," *Management of Personnel Quarterly*, I, 5 (Autumn–Winter, 1962), p. 18.

to the commonly used engine lathe, this machine can turn out un-usual configurations without constant resetting. Since there is a con-siderable degree of skill-transfer from engine to tracer lathe operation, officials of the company hoped to retrain present employees. In fact, it was anticipated that this opportunity for slight upgrading, plus the addition of another skill, would help solve the excessive rate of turn-over among tracer lathe operators. A termination rate of 95 percent among those hired during the previous year had caused management considerable concern because of the high cost of recruitment, reference checking, personnel record processing, shop supervisors' time, and negative balance in the tax account vis-à-vis the California Unemploy-ment Insurance Code. The basic source of trouble appeared to be intrinsic in the nature of the work, which involved plastics and car-bon and was therefore dirty and messy. The company had installed all possible countermeasures, but it had succeeded only in alleviating and not eliminating the problem.

The assumption was made that since employees were already aware of these environmental conditions and reconciled to them, they would not be so prone to take flight. Thus, the 55 machinists were notified of the opportunity to acquire training on the tracer lathe; they were not required to undergo tests of any kind. Their present rate of pay would continue, with a ten cent hourly increase plus considerable overtime when they became proficient; acquisition of a new skill could be regarded as an asset. The prospect of pay while learning and a guaranteed job and better wages later seemed likely to have such great appeal that management was concerned lest a morale problem be engendered among persons not included. But of the five men who responded, only one filed an application, and he showed so little promise that he was advised to stay on his old job.

Efforts were made to recruit tracer lathe operators in Detroit, Cin-cinnati, and Los Angeles—areas where such equipment was used. No applicants were found in Detroit or in Los Angeles. Cincinnati provided some possibilities; out of these, 13 were qualified and avail-able. Only three actually reported for work at the Kaiser plant; none stayed. One proved incompetent; one was homesick because his wife in Ohio refused to join him; and one failed to show up regularly and was fired.

These fruitless attempts at recruiting qualified tracer lathe operators convinced Kaiser officials that steps would have to be taken to create their own work force through training. This decision, it may be noted, was reached with some reluctance, since previous experience with on-the-job instruction had pointed up such drawbacks as interference with production schedules and some foremen's inadequacy as teachers. The active cooperation of a local community college made it possible for the company to design a curriculum consisting of a combination of classroom and practical work. The first phase of the program consisted of three weeks of classes at the school campus—eight hours daily, five days per week. On the recommendation of plant supervisors, the college set up a special course of study that included mathematics, characteristics of metals, and engine lathe theory. Since the school owned no tracers, shop practice was done on engine lathes. The company supplied carbide cutting pieces for use in the tool geometry course. The union participated by allowing a training rate of 20 cents per hour under the minimum and of referring several prospective applicants. Classified as machine operators, the students received an hourly wage of $2.69 while at school. During the second phase, which called for four weeks of training at the plant, the men received approximately the same amount but were reclassified as tracer lathe operator trainees, the journeyman scale being $2.98 to $3.35.

It was recognized by the school and the company that this program would not develop fully competent production machinists, who must have proficiency in running a wide variety of equipment such as the milling machine, the shaper, the planer, the drill press, and the engine lathe. But this project did provide an opportunity for men to acquire the rudiments of a salable skill, the base of which they could expand by further training.

Little publicity was necessary to attract recruits to the program. The files already contained applications for many kinds of jobs. These plus referrals from the State Department of Employment totalled about 100. The initial screening point was previous employment, regarded as essential because of its value in setting habits of regular attendance, responsibility, and the like. Specific machine shop experience outweighed school in importance. After elimination of men whose personal or business references were unsatisfactory, the remaining 65 potential candidates were tested for general intelligence (Wonderlic Form B) and mechanical aptitude (Science Research Associates Mechanical Aptitude). The interview that followed served the dual purpose of eliminating the less promising and salvaging those who seemed to display promise despite doubtful performance on the tests.

Typical bases for disqualification turned out to be (1) lack of experience, (2) extreme nervousness, (3) lack of alertness, (4) test scores satisfactory, but not suited to machine shop work, (5) much absenteeism, (6) prone to complain about working conditions and fellow employees, and (7) temporary summer employment seekers.

Seventeen were finally selected, and the school phase of the program proceeded in an orderly fashion following the schedule set up by the company and the teacher. During this portion of the training, the morale of the group was high; the young men worked hard and expressed enthusiasm. There were no dropouts and very little absenteeism. Despite differences in performance and rate of progress, all 17 trainees moved into the next phase, where they were placed in different parts of the shop and on different shifts.

In the shop phase, however, difficulties began to emerge. A firm teaching schedule was impossible since conditions were clearly governed by work flow. The company would have liked to provide more experience on the milling machine, but the high cost of parts to be worked on made such an endeavor prohibitive. At times, because of a dearth of suitable work, trainees had simply to be kept busy doing interim tasks or even sweeping floors. It might be noted that, whether by supervisors' intent or by chance, the jobs least related to training generally went to the less proficient workers. Thus a circularity occurred: the more able students were given more opportunity to pursue the trade and thus to achieve success faster. Those with less capability could not progress as rapidly and were denied the possibility of catching up. Some never did attain the level of full tracer lathe operator. There is strong evidence that some supervisors were slow and even reluctant to reclassify men out of the trainee and into the operator category.

A summary of the status report of the trainees just under 11 months after the program was initiated showed four full-fledged tracer lathe operators, five men employed by the company in other capacities, five laid off (some having opted dismissal in preference to downgrading because of lack of work), and three moved or quit. The loss for the group stood at 47 percent.

While the classroom phase of the project was still in progress, the company, anticipating that its need for tracer lathe operators would not be filled by the 17 students, decided to hire into the second phase, for on-the-job training, men whose previous experience qualified them for such placement. Whether because the program had received local publicity and applicants had been attracted or because some other company had finished a contract, there seemed to be a supply of potential workers who could bypass the preliminary instruction and learn right in the shop. Of the 22 men who were trained in this fashion, only five emerged as tracer lathe operators. Two others remained with the company, but in a different capacity. The rest left or were fired.

This industry-sponsored training program provides basis for certain observations and conclusions which bear directly on meeting some of the problems of structural unemployment by retraining workers. With respect to selection of applicants, it has become the fashion in personnel circles to place heavy reliance on objective measures of personality traits and aptitudes. Employment services, public and private, as well as individual firms, are inclined to regard the test battery as the scientific means to building the most efficient work force. The findings of this research study indicate that more crucial than the test result were certain subjective elements that were allowed to come into play. For example, several applicants with marginal scores were accepted because of the way they conducted themselves during the interview or because of some telling experience in their past record.

One of the most successful trainees, for example, would not have qualified on the basis of test performance. He had worked as a cook in a restaurant and then as a laborer carrying lumber. But some years before, he had won a prize for designing and making a pair of and-irons. He expressed an earnest desire to return to machine shop work and seemed genuinely interested in the program. During the classroom phase, his performance was outstanding; he completed the course early and was one of the first graduates to achieve full tracer lathe operator status.

With respect to anticipating local labor market conditions and projecting manpower needs, this company's experience points up the realities and difficulties. The company initiated its training program at a time when 63 tracer lathe operators were at work in its shop. With the probability of continued high turnover, there was an expectation that at least 100 would be needed. The following year showed a temporary rise to 94 so employed and then a drop back to 58, five fewer than when the projection was made. Apparently, the need for tracer lathe operators had declined considerably. This shrinkage of demand within just one year points up the extreme difficulty of obtaining the secure information needed in order to set up training and retraining programs that can provide participants with at least a modicum of assurance that their efforts will lead to employment. What becomes evident is that, even with the best of intentions, companies find it almost impossible to set forth their requirements firmly enough to justify expenditure of funds for training.

In the wider context of preparing the labor force to cope with and to take advantage of technological changes still to come, accurate assessment of trends and reliable forecasts are a sine qua non. In its report to the Governor of California, for example, the Commission on Manpower, Automation and Technology gave first priority to the development of "a continuing, coordinated and adequate program of labor market information." [17] The case just discussed depicts a single

---

[17] State of California, Commission on Manpower, Automation and Technology, *Report to the Governor and the Legislature*, Report No. Commat-64-1 (Dec. 31, 1964), p. 33.

company's pioneering effort to estimate and prepare for its future needs in just one occupational category, over a relatively short period, and under fairly constant technological circumstances. If we may accept the outcome as reasonably representative, then we are forced to the reluctant conclusion that with the existing state of the art, sound predictions for many occupational categories, over a significantly long period, and under widely varied and rapidly changing conditions of technology, are practically unattainable. A certain future just cannot be predicated on an uncertain present. And it is quite apparent that our knowledge of the labor market provides only the most general kind of guidelines for vocational direction.

The frequently baffling dimensions of workers' resistance to retraining become apparent when one studies this company's efforts. Noted earlier was the reluctance of employees to participate in the program even when it was evident that they had nothing to lose and could conceivably stand to gain. This resistance to change encountered under such benign circumstances—no threat of job loss and no major technological innovation—becomes a considerable roadblock when an industry converts in a substantial way to new equipment and methods. It has been observed that older workers are prone to reject classroom retraining that may involve tests and grades because of (1) the possible threat of revealing their ineptitude, (2) fear that they have lost their ability to learn, or (3) unfavorable memories of earlier school days. But none of these standard drawbacks can be invoked in analyzing this company's experience since the retraining for engine lathe operators was on-the-job. An interesting contrast to this employee reaction was the one shown in the Naval Air Station instrument mechanics' program, described in Chapter 2, where the trainees were constantly on the lookout for upgrading opportunities, filed applications and took tests for every possible promotion, and enrolled in a wide variety of classes ranging from the job-related to the cultural.

Officials in government, industry, and schools are always searching for a key to the complex of factors that motivate and make for perseverance on the part of enrollees. The record of the men who went through both phases of the tracer lathe program is significant in this context. Not one dropped out; all completed the school-based portion. Of the group no longer employed by the company, only three left voluntarily. The other five chose termination as the alternative to temporary downgrading. These results seem to indicate that for the younger worker, at least, a definite job waiting at the end of training is a powerful factor in insuring participation. Moreover, the lower rate of turnover among the group that underwent complete training indicates a measure of loyalty and degree of commitment that helped the company achieve one of its permanent objectives—stabilizing the work force by reducing turnover.

AMERICAN CAN COMPANY

The experience of the American Can Company demonstrates that private industry can under certain circumstances conduct effective on-the-job retraining in much the same way as was accomplished by the federal service (Chapter 2). Recognizing that the production mechanic is one of their key workers and that in this highly competitive field revolutionary changes in materials, equipment, and basic concepts of packaging are in progress, the American Can Company has set up training guidelines for its fifty or more plants situated all over the United States. The data provided here are derived from the Oakland, California, factory where some local variations occur in the implementation of the master plan. The training agreement with the United Steelworkers of America, the specific manuals, and, of course, the philosophy underlying the effort are the same throughout the country.

The Oakland plant program for upgrading and updating the production mechanics, of whom there are about 80 in a work force totalling close to 600, is a combination of classroom and shop instruction. The project, known officially as "Improving Performance of Skilled Employees," was initiated in October, 1962, and utilizes facilities both at the shop and at the local junior college. A committee made up of such company officials as the plant manager, master mechanic, and safety and training superintendent meets once each month to discuss details. Workers are given no choice about participation; according to their seniority rating, they are assigned to training, which takes place during working hours and at their regular wage. Instruction begins with a two-week session in a classroom at the plant. Here, the trainees are taught to use the detailed manuals that have been prepared to acquaint mechanics with the structural and operational characteristics of numerous pieces of equipment. The rest of the 4,000 to 5,000 hours of training are spread over a period of time, perhaps as much as several years. With the manual serving as the foundation, practical on-the-job acquaintance with the machinery is developed under the supervision of the foreman, the assistant foreman, and the experienced mechanics. The role of the training supervisors appears to be tied in somewhat more with record keeping than with the behavioral side of the program. This is a deficiency already perceived by management, but significant corrective steps have not yet been taken.

All persons assigned to this performance improvement project must attend the blueprint-reading and mathematics courses. These were

originally set up at the local junior college for the company's apprentices and later opened to specially selected journeymen. (This is to
be discussed below.) The students attend one-and-a-half hour classes
in these subjects twice weekly. The men selected for this program
have sufficient seniority, possess the educational background, and have
displayed the competence to justify management's confidence in them.
The men who complete the training are good candidates for reassignment to new equipment in another part of the plant as it gets into
production. Regarding their production mechanics as the key occupational group in their work force, the company, with union approval,
intends to concentrate on updating them so as to maintain "efficiency
of operations, quality, and service, in order to improve and maintain
our competitive position in the container industry." [18]

Related Schooling Program

Like many other manufacturers, American Can Company faces
keen competition at the same time that changing consumer demand
is affecting its product, and advancing technology is creating new
machines and methods. Similarly, this one has among its work force
a considerable number of men who have attained seniority but who
lack the educational background to cope adequately with incoming
equipment. These employees work as machine feeders and warehousemen, and are familiar with only limited aspects of the process; they
are many degrees removed from the level of competence called for in
today's maintenance mechanics and production machinists. It was with
this group in mind that the company expanded its related school
program, designed primarily for apprentices. Certain selected journeymen would now take courses at the junior college. During the three
hours per week of instruction in blueprint reading and mathematics
they would receive their regular wage. The men understood fully that
no promotion was in sight; the prime purpose of the program was to
equip them to do their present jobs better. It was generally understood, however, that there was a strong element of job insurance involved. The men who could absorb knowledge and apply it to their
work would develop versatility—would be better able, therefore, to
keep up with changing technology. Consequently, they could expect
to be more secure in their chance for continuing employment.

Although the company, for obvious reasons, would have preferred
to make its selection of trainees on the basis of ability, the union

[18] Agreement between American Can Company and United Steelworkers of
America, dated and effective October 1, 1962, pp. 55–56.

contract required that seniority be the prime desideratum. A jointly approved, company-devised qualifying examination has served, however, as an effective screening device. This is a five-part test, assessing (1) mechanical aptitude as evidenced by recognition of tools and equipment, (2) perception, (3) mathematics, (4) reasoning power, and (5) balance as to alignment of equal objects. Most of the men who are qualified for this retraining are journeymen with a range of experience from four to 20 years. The average age of participants is estimated at thirty-five. Acceptance of the opportunity for related schooling is not mandatory; about two-thirds to three-quarters of those who are notified of their eligibility take the test. Those who show no interest are permanently barred from entry to the training; they are frozen at their classification level except for the step increases and promotions that automatically come their way if they perform satisfactorily. A strong correlation is noted between previous educational level attained and response to this skill improvement offer. The more schooling a man's record shows, the more likely he is to take advantage of the classes. Especially predominant among the workers who turn down the plan are older men who realize that they lack the academic background needed. The company continues to regard many of them as valuable employees because of their long experience and good record. Since physical examination also forms part of the screening process, there is some question as to how many of the older men would have been admitted. The criteria for selection appear to be realistic in view of the small percentage of dropouts.

Because the new equipment calls for a higher order of skill and because workers must develop broad-based flexibility rather than narrow specialization, the American Can Company has submitted its hiring practices to realistic scrutiny, and it has made some fundamental changes. From now on, all applicants must have completed at least high school. No one will be considered unless he has been pretested for general and specific aptitude by the State Employment Service. These steps are being taken with a view to raising the calibre of the work force and, consequently, the capacity for more retrainability. That the firm is committed to the policy of updating and upgrading their employees is clearly indicated in all of its personnel practices, from the careful screening at the entry point, through the systematic development of workshop manuals, to the arrangement for on-the-job, off-the-job, and related school training. Whether the company develops regional centers for specialized instructional purposes or continues the comparative regional autonomy of the present, there is still an overall integration of activity that permeates the organization from headquarters down. This is in sharp contrast to the policy of the firm whose training program is examined next.

TRAINING AS CONDUCTED BY COMPANY X

Company X is important in its industry, which combines construction and service. With annual contracts and sales amounting to over $199 million and a substantial gross profit, this firm is one of the leaders in its industry. Its hourly wage work force amounts to about 3,500 men. The western regional area, embracing nine states, has close to 500 of these workers. Since the union-negotiated wage scale is based on the five highest paid trades in the area, the journeyman mechanic receives about $5.00 per hour; helpers are on a 70 percent pay rate and learners get 50 percent. Most of the hiring is done by the construction superintendent, the criteria being good physical condition, satisfactory grades on the Wonderlic Personnel Test and on a mechanical aptitude test devised by the company. Previous schooling per se is outweighed by related work experience. The men are further evaluated for their potential to advance from construction into service and maintenance and then into adjusting, where the prima donnas of the trade are to be found. Since crews are subject to layoff when construction is completed, there is more assurance of permanent employment in service, although the pay rates are the same. It is estimated that in the western area about 80 men, usually in the learner or helper class, are laid off annually. Those who have done particularly well may be kept for other assignment, but there appears to be very little mobility between regions, each functioning autonomously as regards hiring and training.

New recruits are generally brought in by friends and relatives of employees. Each is assigned to a mechanic, who determines his capabilities, teaches him, and helps him prepare for the union examination for upgrading, which he will take in two to four years. On the job, a crew consists of one mechanic and one learner or helper. Operating under the assumption that an employee is a liability before he is an asset, the company has a tuition refund plan under which workers who have been on the payroll continuously for more than three months are encouraged to take after-hours courses, in person or by correspondence. Refunds, based on 75 percent of tuition, registration, and laboratory fees, may go as high as $250 a twelve-month period for completion with passing grades of a program approved by the firm. Only about 5 percent of the work force has taken advantage of this plan.

These unsatisfactory efforts have strengthened the philosophy under-

lying the company training policy, namely, that on the job is the best
place to learn. This was first established in 1954 when the industry
introduced significant technological changes. Under the field education program set up at that time, each of the ten geographical zones
of the company's operations got a supervisor who devised methods and
prepared educational materials to supplement the journeymen's individual efforts. Management thinking strongly reflects the notion that
retraining can be accomplished by sending out the neophyte with an
experienced man, so the field education program is kept small and
regionally isolated, with no defined curriculum.

To understand this deliberate inhibition from within, one must
take into account the developmental history of the company. Within
the past century of its operations it has swallowed up 250 other firms.
Its main competition comes from small rivals, any of whom may emulate its ambitious example, and all of whom are likely to use the
knowhow forthcoming from a widely publicized training program.
Management feels that printed course outlines and materials would
serve their competitors' needs. It is concerned lest, by a big program,
the company would be training men for the whole industry.

Within the regional divisions, a field official who is also responsible
for safety instruction sets up evening classes run by supervisors of
experienced foremen paid at the rate of time and a half. The men
attend two evenings per month for about nine months, with no extra
compensation or promise of reward. Average enrollment in the San
Francisco and Los Angeles areas is about 50; Seattle reports 20. Since
no selection procedures are used, the students cover an enormous
range of interests and capabilities; some of the maintenance men just
cannot cope with the new modern equipment and fail to grasp the
content of the instruction. It is virtually impossible for the group
leader to set the proper level of instruction.

Because this company still clings to a paternalistic philosophy, much
within its organization is like a family. Informal organization far
outweighs formal; there is evidence of a marked impatience toward
procedural and structural matters. Training is relegated in a very
personal way to individuals isolated in their own regions and expected to cope in an ad hoc fashion with whatever problems may arise.

This lack of a well-defined training orientation on the part of an
important firm appears as an anachronism on the industrial scene.
Both the technological and the behavioral sciences are undergoing
rapid development with more mutual stimulation and opportunity
for exchange of benefits than has perhaps been recognized. Whether
an outstanding corporation such as this one can long continue to take
advantage of the one without applying the other is a matter for
conjecture.

RETRAINING FOR QUALITY CONTROL

A situation where the exacting demands set by technological advance brought about a retraining and updating program for its workers was encountered in the Western Die Casting Company of Emeryville, California. This family-owned plant, founded in 1910, has a payroll of about 75, two-thirds of which is on an hourly rate and the rest on a monthly rate. In the manufacture of die castings, new combinations and proportions of metals and alloys, along with modernized equipment, have brought some changes in production methods. But far greater is the effect on the end product. Castings for submarines, supersonic jet airplanes, and spacecraft are infinitely more precise than those used on the conveyances of yesteryear.

The owners, wont to say that "the more you toss into the reject barrel, the more money you lose," recognized the urgency of improving quality control. Failure to meet rigid specifications had resulted in the return of an entire shipment and boded ill for future contracts. It was quite apparent, upon investigation, that many of the workers did not understand the nature of their operations and that an error in measurement of 0.0025 inch meant little to them. Most of them were women who had been hired during the Second World War. Their long years of seniority would not have protected them, however, because under union terms they could have been fired after three warning reports. Since wholesale dismissal would not have led to better quality of work, the firm decided to improve its workers. With the cooperation of the local junior college, a training program in inspection procedures was developed. Taken into account were the job requirements for both in-process and lead inspectors. The instructor was paid by the company; twice-weekly classes ran for one and one-half hours for ten weeks and covered such subjects as arithmetic, blueprint reading, statistical quality control, and measuring.

Opportunity to enroll in what came to be known as the "Inspection School" was offered to all hourly workers. Inspectors were to be paid at the straight time rate for attending. Ruling out the maintenance people and the die casters as not likely to be interested, an estimate of about 30 potential students seemed reasonable. The first class attracted 18, but the group soon stabilized at 12, of whom 9 were women. Only three were employed as inspectors and, therefore, eligible for compensation. Others were production workers, machine operators, and gate breakers, willing to face their own deficiencies and try to overcome them. One man, a diecasting machine operator who is an American Indian, took the course even though it could not improve his top-graded occupational status; he simply wanted to learn more about his job.

The relatively advanced age of the females is particularly striking. It must be recalled that these women were hired during a period of serious labor shortage. The company reports that for the past ten years it has adhered to a policy of employing only men for the shop, for only wartime conditions could conceivably have opened such occupations to women. The work is demanding physically; the place resembles a foundry with cement floors and walls, hot metals, and clangorous operations. The women doing production work wear goggles, heavy boots, and huge protective aprons. The average hourly rate is about $2.60, with a range from $2.473 to $2.828.

When the training program was being planned, the employees extracted the promise from the owners that no one from management would attend the classes. In fact, they even stipulated that salesmen, some of whom had expressed an interest in learning more about their product, were to be excluded. These restrictions were attributed to a lack of self-confidence on the part of the enrollees; they were afraid that the school situation would reveal their shortcomings and inadequacies. Similar fears had kept many of the 30 who had been regarded as potential trainees from attending and may have been the cause of some dropouts. A review of the course content, reported in diary form by the chief inspector, provides some justification for the trepidation of those who lacked a favorable orientation toward schoolwork and homework. Although conducted with a minimum of formality, the sessions were very businesslike and covered the fundamentals so that students learned why and how to maintain a high level of quality control.

This retraining program is a unique example of a company's effort to provide its work force with skills to turn out an improved product. The thinking of management was that if their castings could not meet strict specifications, contracts would be lost and the business would be closed down. Regarded from the workers' point of view, the situation was clear: if they were not qualified to do the inspections required, they faced replacement by others who were more competent. With the exception of one retirement and one physical disability, which have removed two of the graduates from the company payroll, the entire group is functioning satisfactorily. To be sure, only minor upgrading has occurred, but this was not the purpose of the program. Consequently, union efforts to reclassify the workers at a higher scale have failed. What has been achieved is job security and a large measure of employer-employee confidence and goodwill.

ROLE OF INDUSTRY IN RETRAINING

The examples of retraining discussed in this chapter are not typical; they represent isolated and, in some cases, one-time efforts. But, it must be reiterated, they were the only industry-initiated programs to be found in the San Francisco Bay area at the time this investigation began. Subsequent follow-up indicates no significant alteration in the situation. From the kind and number of projects then in existence, it was learned that for private companies training and retraining below the managerial level were determined almost exclusively by current labor market conditions as related to the firm's immediate personnel needs. The degree to which private enterprises are projecting their manpower requirements vis-à-vis technological change cannot be ascertained. Like Company X, where fear of competitors kept training confined to small, ironclad units, many firms regard a formal retraining program of their employees as giving a clue to their future production plans and, hence, to a highly confidential matter. Not only might business rivals benefit, but also unions —for whom such information would provide points on which to bargain. As will be seen in the following chapter, the initiative for forecasting technological developments and preparing their membership for them has come from certain labor organizations.

These research findings, substantiated by further investigation,[19] support the thesis that, except in instances of short supply, industry develops few retraining projects. Orientation and indoctrination appear to be more common areas of focus for industry's efforts. Lack of commitment to employees with respect to revitalizing obsolescent skills is one of the realities of the marketplace. Industry invests in such measures only when it cannot draw upon some labor pool to fill its needs; this is the pattern in 1966, when manpower shortages in some sectors constitute a serious brake on progress. At such times, when demand for workers exceeds supply, programs are initiated, but they are likely to be limited in scope. The focus is usually adjusted closely to the particular company's requirements at a given time. This was the training and retraining method, necessitated by crisis, used during war years. The narrow skill base thus provided has proved to be extremely vulnerable to later technological change. Among the semiskilled workers now being displaced by automation are those whose knowledge and proficiency are limited to one operation or one piece

---

[19] State of California, *Report to the Governor,* p. 20.

of equipment. The danger of repeating time-worn mistakes is compounded by the fact that today's rapidly expanding economy is absorbing persons who have relatively little education and experience. The kind of work world with which they will have to cope requires a lifelong commitment to learning. Motivating such persons to develop and maintain this kind of orientation may become a prime responsibility of employers. It is altogether likely that companies will also have to build into their programs training for the leisure that compulsory retirement and shorter hours promise.

One of the reasons for the paucity of retraining programs for displaced workers is that, by and large, industry assumes little responsibility for such persons. Some firms, to be sure, have supplementary unemployment benefit arrangements that may include provision for financing of courses, but there is little evidence of company-sponsored reemployment for the retrainee. Research has shown that many of the disemployed opt receipt of a lump sum instead of the tuition proposition.[20] None of the San Francisco Bay area companies that closed their local facilities had any ameliorative measures. When the old plant was abandoned, so were the workers. When a contract expired, so did the payroll. In the latter instance, Lockheed's plans for classes for laid-off employees represented a dramatic departure from established personnel practice.

In discussing with executives the lack of information about technological innovations in specific industries and their potential effect on manpower requirements, we encountered a great deal of uncertainty. Although increasingly sophisticated decision-making has become possible through electronics, little progress has been reported in the practical application of operations research to this very urgent problem.[21] And yet, until systematic manpower planning is achieved, industry itself cannot take the necessary steps or provide others with guidelines for the retraining of the work force to achieve maximum technological development with adequate safeguards against economic injury to individuals.

Summarized briefly, the findings on industry-sponsored retraining efforts suggest the following. 1) There may not be a need for disemployed workers, or the discrepancy between the skills they offer and those required is too great to allow for salvage operations. (2) Training directors cannot anticipate skill changes and set up appropriate courses because of lack of communication within the organization. (3) Com-

[20] Thomas Kennedy, *Automation Funds and Displaced Workers* (Boston: Harvard University Graduate School of Business Administration, 1962).

[21] Charles C. Holt, Franco Modigliani, John F. Muth, Herbert A. Simon, *et al.*, *Planning Production, Inventories, and Work Force* (Englewood Cliffs, New Jersey: Prentice-Hall, Inc., 1960).

panies, usually unwilling or unable to predict manpower requirements, rarely take steps to prevent skill obsolescence through retraining; such programs as are undertaken stem from immediate needs. (4) The value of retraining has been demonstrated in times of oversupply as well as in times of a shortage in labor. As technology advances, more sectors of the work force will be affected and necessity for retraining will increase. Industry can serve the entire economy by assuming a responsible policy toward its employees and committing itself to a continuing program of manpower adjustment.

[4

Union-sponsored Retraining Programs

INTRODUCTION

Protection of their membership against the hazards of the workplace and from the difficulties brought on by old age and loss of health and strength has long been the tradition of the labor movement. In many unions, these matters are almost tantamount in importance to wage and hour considerations. Within recent years, many unions, concerned with the impacts of technological change, have expanded their collective bargaining demands to include not only the routine health and welfare programs and pension provisions but also supplementary unemployment benefits. The United Mine Workers of America have a Welfare and Retirement Fund, which helps those miners still unemployed, but it contains no provisions for severance pay, supplementary unemployment benefits, or retraining costs for displaced workers. More a booster for the underemployed than an aid to jobless musicians, the Music Performance Trust Fund has been devoted to a promotion of the use of live music. The West Coast and the New York Longshore Funds emphasize job security primarily. Largely a research instrument, the Armour Fund underscores the vital necessity for remedial education and has been effective in focusing attention on the skill gaps between automation's victims and the demands of the job market. The Ladies' Garment Workers' Supplementary Unemployment Benefits Fund cushions the impacts of job displacement. The 1961 plan set up jointly by the Kaiser Steel Company and the United Steel Workers of America calls for equitable sharing of economic progress made possible through technological advance; it involves no retraining pro-

102

visions. Automation funds are a relatively new institution, limited to a few unions; there is the possibility that they may assume a meaningful role in adapting workers to change.[1] For the present, their effectiveness is limited and they so far have not significantly implemented retraining of their membership as a means to continued employment.

The testimony of labor leaders before Congressional committees has for years emphasized mechanization's severe inroads on jobs;[2] the research staffs of the various unions have made extrapolations from existent data that show a decline in the blue-shirt workers and, at the same time, a sustained rise in output. Despite the pessimistic outlook, however, labor's official position with respect to the introduction of labor-saving machines is not of the sabot-throwing variety. There is general recognition that automation can, if handled properly, have aspects of boon as well as bane for the wage earner. And in finding comfort in the long-run projections, trade unions, like other sectors of the economy, subscribe to the notion that tomorrow's technology, by mechanizing the heavy routine tasks, will call for a better-educated, upgraded working force. To be sure, there is neither unanimity about nor unreserved support for the idea that skill requirements will go up. In many instances the computerized control of processes has been seen to deemphasize the role of the human operator.[3] But, by and large, the hope persists that the economy of the future will provide jobs for the qualified and the competent. This optimism is implicit in the union push toward more vigorous apprenticeship standards and training regulations.

Most union officials interviewed in this study were wont to refer to their apprenticeship programs as the sum total of their training efforts. Actually, formal apprenticeships account for too small a portion of the workers to reflect a true picture of what the unions are thinking, doing, or hoping to do about training. For a realistic assessment of union policies, practices, and programs, it has been necessary to search far beyond the courses and classes that go into preparing the neophyte for a given trade.

Union-management agreements that provide for training employees during working hours at company expense and prevailing rates of pay now appear in some major contracts. The Ford Motor Company and the United Auto Workers have amended their apprentice-training pro-

---

[1] Kennedy, *Automation Funds and Displaced Workers.*

[2] For example, Statement of George Meany, President of AFL-CIO to Sub-Committee on Economic Stabilization, Joint Economic Committee, 84th Congress on Instrumentation and Automation (Dec. 12, 13 and 14, 1956), pp. 188–191.

[3] James R. Bright, "Does Automation Raise Skill Requirements?" *Harvard Business Review*, XXXVI, 4 (July–August, 1958), p. 98.

gram to include older seniority employees.[4] The Metropolitan Lithographers Association and the Amalgamated Lithographers of America established retraining for craftsmen displaced by improved methods of production.[5] Similarly, the Western Union Company and the Commercial Telegraphers, Armour and the Amalgamated Meat Cutters and United Packinghouse Workers, and the American Can Company and the United Steel Workers of America have included clauses providing for training of workers whose jobs are discontinued.[6] There is little evidence of the initiation of specific courses. The prevailing pattern seems to be an allowance that the recipient can apply as he wishes.

As in the case of research into any human endeavor, it has been important to observe the standard caveats. Newspaper headlines are not necessarily translated into action. What is given forth as an authoritative statement before national television cameras and for the press may influence the local region only minimally. Like most other large-scale organizations, unions have many layers of authority and much democracy, to say nothing of autocracy. Consequently, a high-ranking official may make a widely-publicized pronouncement about shift into high-geared training effort, while the local will continue to follow its own pattern. A positive and aggressive training plan developed at the national level may run one of several different courses: it may be adapted for local use, modified to suit the needs of a particular area, or ignored altogether.

Noteworthy among national and international unions that have established training programs for their journeymen are the United Association of Journeymen and Apprentices of the Plumbing and Pipefitting Industry, the International Brotherhood of Electrical Workers, and the International Printing Pressmen and Assistants' Union of North America. Through an employer contribution of two and one-half cents per man-hour worked, the plumbing and pipefitting union maintains training headquarters in Washington, D.C., and carries on extensive programs at the local level. Because it provides a typical example of the implementation of this program in an urban setting, one of these projects has been selected for intensive research in this study and will be reported later in this chapter. The International Brotherhood of Electrical Workers Skill Improvement Program was initiated by the international union as a pilot project in 1959, when

---

[4] Ken Bannon and Nelson Samp, "The Impact of Automation on Wages and Working Conditions in Ford-UAW Relationship," *Automation and Major Technological Change,* Industrial Union Department, AFL-CIO (April 22, 1958).

[5] International Association of Machinists, Research Department, *Meeting the Problems of Automation through Collective Bargaining,* (Dec., 1960), p. 18.

[6] *Loc. cit.,* pp. 19 and 20.

that organization recognized unilaterally that craftsman upgrading was required along with the apprenticeship training financed through the National Electrical Contractors' Association. The development of a countrywide curriculum and its operation in the San Francisco Bay area, as it pertains to the local scene, will be discussed in detail farther on in this chapter.

The program sponsored by the International Printing Pressmen and Assistants' Union of North America centers about the Technical Trade School at Pressmen's Home, Tennessee, founded by that organization in 1911. Except for distributing the 107 correspondence course lessons emanating from this establishment, the locals of this union run only specialized courses in local public trade schools. What is of particular interest in the study of retraining in the San Francisco Bay region is that this union was among the first in the United States to take advantage of funds from the Manpower Development and Training Act for advancing the skills of journeymen. The programs thus financed were based in the labor market area on which this research focuses. The findings on their operation are reported in the context of our discussion of MDTA on-the-job training, later in this book.

For some unions that enjoy a long history of training activities, the present push of technology may require merely an enlargement or extension of existing programs; other unions are not so fortunate. Despite their tradition, they cannot cope with the extremes of changed consumer demand and accompanying new processes and materials, which virtually eradicate the need for their members' skills. This was the experience of textile workers in a local plant turning out carpeting and upholstery for automobile interiors. The industry now favors plastic materials. With no prospect of jobs in related occupations into which skills might be diverted, the union saw its members drift into other occupations or onto relief. There are other unions in which training might help cope with change, but where no program has been attempted. For them, retraining became a reality only when the Manpower Development and Training Act provided the impetus and the money. These will be discussed more fully later.

Numerous interviews and a fairly comprehensive survey provide basis for questioning the hypothesis that the extent to which a given union will concern itself with retraining depends on the vulnerability of its membership to technological displacement. Also subject to question is the hypothesis that, other things being equal, the union with the highest dues structure and richest treasury will be the one to take forward steps in providing training for its membership. It is apparent, however, that the support by the local officers of a union for such programs of training will be determined largely by their own acceptance of the notion that training really pays off. The quantitative measure for the benefits is two-fold: (1) will the training provide the members with skills that will keep them employed and, consequently, dues-payers and/or (2) will it assure the union of jurisdictional rights over the newly-emerging and, perhaps, disputed job categories? These basic conditions having been satisfied, the myriad details regarding relationships with employers come into focus. In some instances, funds for training are established through the collective bargaining agreement. The printing pressmen and the pipefitters, both of which will be discussed later in the chapter, have run their schools on money contributed jointly by industry and labor.

Whether and how the union utilizes the public school system for updating and upgrading journeymen is a matter of interest. Some of the experiences of unions warrant special attention because they indicate strengths and deficiencies in the vocational schools. By assessing these institutions from the viewpoint of organized labor, the research findings underscore some of the fundamental problems confronting trade schools and community colleges and, consequently, add a dimension to the case analyses in Chapter 1.

In at least several respects, there are marked similarities between industry and union training efforts. In the first place, both are inclined to regard the apprenticeship program, for all its limitations, as substantial evidence of training activity. Also, both are wont to lean heavily on their middle-level workshops and seminars to justify the claim that they are keeping the work force up to date. Not uncommon are union-sponsored classes in such subjects as "Human Problems and the Job," "The Foreman and Interpersonal Relations," "Grievance Procedure-Handling." These may take the form of a concentrated series of seminars or may extend over a period of several months as weekly meetings. Often, they are developed with the cooperation of a local college or university. The "certificate of completion" indicates satisfactory fulfillment of requirements but carries no assurance of promotion.

The area of similarity most important from the viewpoint of the economy at large and the taxpayer in particular is the use of public school facilities for training. Unions, like employers, have been encouraged to develop curricula at the local trade schools. As was noted above, some have done so with a high degree of success; others have followed this practice but are voicing discontent over the outcome; still others have expressed their dissatisfaction by setting up their own, independent programs. What has been learned from these experiences raises interesting questions about vocational education responsibility and policy.

With respect to membership participation in training and acceptance of training, a number of questions arise. How are trainees selected? Do they apply on their own initiative or must they be persuaded to enroll? Is the receptivity of the unemployed or underemployed greater or less than that of their more fully occupied brothers? Are there differences among unions with respect to enthusiasm of response from members? What are the factors accounting for such differences? To what extent are workers impelled by fear of technological displacement? To what extent are they repelled by fear of tests and the classroom situation? Is there any evidence that belonging to a union provides a worker with greater access to means of skill salvaging?

As can be seen from the wide range of problems and policies, no general statements regarding either union commitment to their rank-and-file members with respect to retraining or workers' response to such efforts would be meaningful. An inventory of how many national or local trade unions offer courses or at what level and with what response might provide statistics and tabulations, but such aggregate figures would mask the important human factors so often misnamed mere details. This empirical investigation of union-sponsored training endeavors was intended to achieve perception in depth.

The rationale for applying intensive research effort to the particular programs included here—for marine cooks and stewards, ships' radio operators, steamfitters, and electricians—was that these were the only cohesive curricula in the San Francisco Bay area conducted under the sponsorship of organized labor. Trade unions carry on a wide variety of specialized courses for apprentices and journeymen, generally at public schools, but these are usually discrete and dispersed, and likely to vary in content and structure. It is worth noting that at the time of the survey, the cases now presented here were not a sample but the universe of coordinated retraining programs financed by union funds.

MARINE COOKS AND STEWARDS

In June, 1955, when the Marine Cooks and Stewards Union was certified, there was general recognition that although pot-washers and messmen were plentiful, waiters, stewards, and cooks were in short supply. By 1957 the union's request for a school to upgrade members and to attract outsiders had been approved by the shipowners. Their contribution to a welfare fund made possible a training and recreation center which has also served as a retirement home. The organization chart of the training school (May, 1958) indicates the structural relationships as well as the continued cooperation anticipated between union and industry (Table 5).

TABLE 5

ORGANIZATION CHART (MAY, 1958)
MARINE COOKS AND STEWARDS TRAINING SCHOOL

Board of Trustees
Union-Management
Government Official

BOARD OF EDUCATION
Co-Chairman

(Union President—Steamship Lines Director)
6 members from Industry   6 members from Union

		Industry Committees		
Administration	Educational	Enrollment	Financial	Public Relations
Chairman	Chairman	Chairman	Co-Chm.	Chairman
(Industry)	(Indus.)	(Union)		(Indus.)
2 mem.	4 mem.	3 mem.	3 mem.	1 mem.
(Indus.)	(Indus.)	(Indus.)	(1-Indus. 1-Un.)	(Indus.)
2 mem.	4 mem.	2 mem.	3 mem.	1 mem.
(Union)	(Union)	(Union)	(Indus.)	(Indus.)
				2 mem.
				(Union)

MC&S Training School Staff
(All Union)

Director of Education
Instructors

Chief	Baker	Butcher	Hotel Section

The training facility's tie-in with the recreational and retirement programs bears special emphasis. Situated in a rural area outside Santa Rosa, about fifty miles from San Francisco, the school is intended to simulate conditions on board ship. The students are assigned three to each room in the living quarters, so as to learn to live in close proximity as they must while at sea. Besides classroom work, they have practical instruction, and the vacationing union members and their families as well as the pensioners are the "passengers" on whom they practice their skills.

Classroom discussion begins with personal grooming and appearance and moves to shipboard conduct. This part of the curriculum forms the basic orientation and is the sine qua non for successful adjustment both to shipmates and to life in the confined community of the vessel. Dining-room procedures, from the setting up of sidestands to the best way to vacate a table diplomatically, are designed to prepare waiters for their work, while guidelines to galley duties and deportment, even to the injunction not to fight with cooks, are laid down for behind-the-scenes efficiency. The instructors are former shipboard personnel who have had long experience in their specialties. For the past eight years, 50 men at a time have gone through the course in the hotel or the cook section either for entry or upgrading.

While all members of the union are eligible to advance from one station to the next by seniority, the union has encouraged their taking the six weeks' refresher course at the school as a means to assuring that they will qualify for upgrading in the face of possible competition from outsiders. It is recognized by both management and the union that certain key posts, such as fancy pastry chef on a luxury liner, are likely to be filled by promoting the man in the assistant's job and that the training at Santa Rosa can hardly create in a tyro the art, skill, and experience called for in such a job. The schooling can acquaint a man, trained perhaps in a deluxe European or American hotel, with shipboard protocol and practice, but it must be noted that the top posts, occupied by persons who have developed a good reputation are very stable, with little turnover. The greatest benefit is to low- and middle-level members of the union for whom acquisition of a new specialty may mean upgrading. The six weeks' refresher is designed to accomplish this purpose.

During the ten years of the school's existence, more than 2,000 men have been enrolled; an estimate of 200 per year is an approximation, since upgraders move through at varying rates of speed. The fact that nearly two-thirds of the students have come from outside the industry is deplored by union and management spokemen alike. The membership's lack of interest and failure to take advantage are attributed to the following reasons: (1) Unemployed members who enrolled in the school were not available for employment and, hence, forfeited their Unemployment Compensation; (2) for family men, residence at the school imposed the hardship of additional separation from wife and children, already necessitated for long periods by the seafarer's way of life; (3) the often-encountered adult reluctance to expose himself to schooling was probably intensified by the comparative confinement of this "campus."

The course was later made mandatory for entrance into the Marine Cooks and Stewards Union. Initial application must be made at the headquarters, where past experience, education (formal and trade), and references comprise the important selection criteria. About 10 percent of the men who are prescreened at the union hall are referred to the joint labor and industry committee for interview. This procedure means that every potential entrant has the union stamp of approval before he even meets the management representative. Only those who have convinced the union that they "can become useful members" are allowed to try the next hurdle. Because only 50 can be accommodated at the school at one time, there is always a substantial backlog; often as many as 1,500 men are waiting.

Completion of the training, whether for the newcomers or those desiring upgrading, does not necessarily imply complete goal attainment. It is quite possible that a man may demonstrate that he is incapable of graduating in the category he desired. Unless he has conducted himself improperly and exerted a bad influence, however, any enrollee is allowed to finish with a rating of some kind. The director of education, a union man, recommends the classification in which the graduate will enter the industry ultimately. The first assignment, usually for about six months, is to some low-level work, such as porter, dishwasher, or janitor, just so that a familiarity with the environment may be acquired. For the older members who attended the school for upgrading, a joint reclassification board reviews their papers, performance records, and teacher's recommendation, and approves whatever change is appropriate.

Both union and management recognize the need for the program. Even though the shipping industry has undergone drastic changes and faces more as technological advance and shifting consumer preferences have impact, there has been a fairly consistent demand for trained personnel. In 1957, when actual classes began, the industry needed qualified men for two distinct types of service: for passengers on luxury liners, and for the crews of cargo vessels. For the 600 vacationers on a cruise, a complement of at least 300 in the steward department is essential, and the companies vie with each other to achieve the ultimate in Sybaritic living. At present, the number of ships involved in luxury vacation traffic has declined substantially.

Our society seems to be enjoying much affluence but comparatively little leisure. Great numbers of people are traveling; travel is no longer for the privileged upper class alone. The American tourist is to be found in the farthest corners of the globe, and he is, more often than not, a wage-earner in the middle-income bracket. But it is likely that he travels by airplane, for a three-week economy tour can circle the globe. Dwindling passenger lists have forced the steamship owners to curtail the number of large vessels and promote the use of their mariner ships, which pay their way by carrying cargo but have accommodations for 12 persons. On these, adequate service can be provided with only 14 men in the steward department.

With containerization of cargo and mechanization of freight-handling, much less time is spent at the dock-side. The speed of the new container vessels has cut the normal crossing of the North Atlantic to the continent of Europe to five and one-half days. Thus, fewer ships are needed for moving cargo. It is suspected that there may already be a sufficient supply of trained personnel to man them. Moreover, crew size is being dramatically reduced by electronic innovations: the new freighters are designed to run with only a captain and three deck officers aboard. Such classifications as firemen and radio operators are threatened by automation, and even the galley can be run by push button, with plastic dishes disposable over the side taking away the messman's job. Modification by Congress of the existing Safety of Life at Sea regulations could cause drastic reductions in personnel to take effect within the very near future. The next step, an electronically controlled submarine, to carry cargo under the sea, is not far away. Technologically as possible as the unmanned space capsule, this underwater transport of goods would be fast, cheap, and safe and would provide an ultimate solution to the labor problems that have always plagued this industry.

The speed at which technology will advance and the extent to which changes will be introduced and will make their impact felt in the offshore as in the longshore occupations depends largely on negotiations and agreements still to come. But on one matter there is dispute from neither party: so long as there are people playing or working on the ships, alimentation will continue to be a major concern. For the passengers, the menus and calibre of service will still be a prime desideratum in booking passage. As one shipping official put it, "No amount of radio, television, and magazine advertising can counteract the bad impression created by cool coffee or a tarnished pot. Our passengers buy status; they pay a great deal for the first-class voyage. We've got to keep them satisfied."

As for the crew, stories about high adventure at sea to the contrary notwithstanding, long voyages become routine and life, dull. The director of education at the school for marine cooks and stewards said that food was practically the only source of variety and interest in an otherwise boring existence. Dissatisfaction with the meals is likely to be translated into discontent and low morale, unfriendly relations with fellow crew members, and poor performance of duties. This underscoring of the far-reaching importance of food in the pattern of a sailor's life is borne out in the shore patrolmen's reports that appear in the trade newspaper. These list the ships they visited and the problems and details they handled. Not uncommon among the items entered are complaints about food; one entry notes that "a bellyrobber steward was unloaded by the company." [7]

With this recognition of the importance of food, there is agreement on the part of the shipowners and the union that the training pro-

---

[7] *West Coast Sailors,* Official Publication of Sailors Union of the Pacific, San Francisco (March 20, 1964).

gram serves a useful function to old members and new entrants alike. To be noted is the indirect service that accrues to the benefit of society in that members of all minority groups have been welcomed into the occupation, selected and trained on a basis free of racial prejudice, and encouraged to improve their status. Despite the possible changes in travel styles, there is reason to believe that there will be a demand for trained marine cooks and stewards, at least for the near future. During times of international tension, such as United States involvement in Vietnam, when troop movements overseas become necessary, every large ship carries a staff of about 325 to provide the necessary service.

AMERICAN RADIO ASSOCIATION

Another offshore union, extremely vulnerable to technological change and determined to protect its jurisdiction, is the American Radio Association, AFL-CIO. "If we don't get schools going, we'll be outside looking in the window," was the firm statement of their vice-president. The radical changes will bring in their wake a major jurisdictional struggle, and when that time comes this union wants to be the logical heir to the job by virtue of having a well-trained membership. Besides the reduction in total numbers of vessels afloat and changes in their type, the adoption of electronic communications devices has had a strong effect on the quantity and more markedly the quality of manpower required. Radio teletype has outmoded the dot-and-dash expert. Through the use of high frequency equipment, U.S. Naval stations in Japan and Guam send out weather maps for the whole Pacific Ocean, with barometric readings, wind direction, and prevailing conditions clearly indicated. Facsimile devices on board the receiving ship make such reports possible within fifteen minutes after they are requested. Operation and maintenance of the new instruments will require updating of skills.

Assessment of the radio operators' retraining program must be preceded by consideration of the criteria for entry into the occupation. High school graduation is mandatory; junior college completion is desirable. Attendance in a specialized radio school is required as is a license by the Federal Communications Commission to operate radio equipment on a ship. In addition, a Coast Guard license, because it is issued on the basis of character rating, is necessary. The aspiring radio operator will not be allowed to sail on a freighter until he has acquired six months of sea-time as an assistant. Only the passenger liners have this category, and, as has already been shown, these are becoming fewer. Consequently, there is a substantial bottleneck, with a backlog of men waiting. This, however, is well within the policy of the union,

90 percent of the membership having voted that the optimum ratio be three men for every two jobs.

Heretofore, a man who had sailed for three weeks could take advantage of the school. But the work period had to be lengthened to six months because the radio operator who was eligible for training was also qualified to receive welfare plan benefits. This constituted a serious drain on the fund, which comes from the owners and provides almost complete medical and hospital coverage for all members. Since it is from this source that the money is drawn to finance the training program, the union proffers the not-too-far-fetched conclusion that the men themselves are, in fact, paying for the training. If the school did not have to be financed, there would logically be more of a reserve in the welfare fund.

As regulations stand, any union permit card-holder now waiting for a job will be asked to attend the school before he can become a full member. This is a matter over which management's support has been sought so as to cope with the Taft–Hartley and Landrum–Griffin regulations, which are regarded as curbing the union's right to screen applicants as thoroughly as is necessary. In its efforts to maintain the aforementioned balance between men and jobs, the union is quick to get rid of the malcontents and to encourage early retirement. A new program to induce men of fifty to withdraw at half pay was proposed but did not receive an enthusiastic reception. "It is hard to make our people retire," said one spokesman. "The work is quite easy and the life is pleasant. Many of these men are without strong family ties, have a real attachment to life at sea, and want to keep working." It may be noted parenthetically that the wage level is about $1,000 per month with a 60-day annual vacation.

Apparently, this union has run into the resistance to retraining encountered in almost all the other groups studied, except that the degree of reluctance may be somewhat intensified here. The last serious demand for the ship radio operators came during the Korean War, in 1950. Since then, the number of vessels has been decreasing while the tonnage has been on the rise. Because of new methods of cargo movement—containerization, bulkhandling, and unitization, as well as automated dockside loading equipment—turn-around time has been cut. Consequently, the individual ships can do more work and travel faster with more cargo. This, of course, has affected the number of radio operators entering the union. The age distribution of present membership is reflected in the growth pattern. Assuming that the average age of the men who joined during the Korean War was about twenty-five, it is likely that the majority of the present members are over thirty-five.

As was found in all of the other retraining efforts included in this research project, resistance to schooling grows with the years. Long-entrenched antipathy to the classroom situation may have a strong deterrent influence. Moreover, enrollment is predicated on completion of certain required correspondence courses. For some members, the curriculum thus covered serves as an impetus to further education, for it exposes deficiencies in mathematics and physics. These men are likely to be in the 35–40 age group. Others, usually the older operators, experience frustration when confronted with the new principles to be learned; they are defeated by realization of their inadequacies; they shun a situation in which they are placed in competition with their juniors. But the union feels strongly that all its one thousand members should be updated so as to become fully acquainted with radar, to know how to maintain test circuits, and to handle electronic equipment competently. To this end, it carries on a constant educational campaign. But certain other obstacles to enrollment are apparent. Unless a man is assigned to a regular run, he is subject to layoff at any time. Shipping being an unpredictable business, he could miss a job opportunity while in training. Even though a potential student has the choice between the New York or the San Francisco location, school attendance entails sacrifice: (1) investment of own time; (2) substitution of boarding house or hotel life for family home life—however tenuous—in such distant cities as New Orleans or Galveston.

Impressed with the example of British shipowners, who pay their radio operators for a 12-month furlough for updating purposes, the American Radio Association is trying to persuade the employers to provide some sort of per diem stipend as an inducement to retraining. Under consideration, too, is the establishment of a preference list with priority for jobs, especially those involving the new type of equipment, given to the operators with the higher degree of skills. Implicit in such a measure is the problem of violating seniority rights, a matter which could stir up angry protest from the membership. But the union recognizes that the need for more education is so urgent that school attendance must be made attractive by tangible reward. In a showdown the union would defend retraining over seniority as a criterion for selection for the new posts.

The curriculum of the ARA Technology Institutes for Maritime Electronics in New York and in San Francisco includes these subject areas: (1) basic fundamentals of electronics and receivers; (2) radio transmitters and special circuits; (3) radar and direction finders. In the process of formulation is a course in advanced communications systems, with teletype and electronic navigational equipment a major focus. Each resident class runs daily from nine to four for one month. Since the enrollment is about six to twelve men, instruction is very personal. In view of the great differences in background and ability, parts of the classwork may be review for some of the students but much of it is entirely new. At their laboratory stations, the men are matched so that they can work at a comparable pace. The instructor noted that men who had attended trade schools or who had related hobbies were the most promising. All of them performed better at the workbench than with the theoretical, textbook tasks. Completion of the two less-advanced courses, designated "I" and "II" in Table 6,

TABLE 6

RESIDENT TRAINING GRADUATES OF TIME [a]
(TECHNOLOGY INSTITUTE FOR MARITIME ELECTRONICS)

Course	New York	San Francisco
I Basic Electronics & Radio Receivers	524	438
II Radio Transmitters & Direction Finders	398	320
III Radar	237	260
Totals	1159	1018

CORRESPONDENCE COURSES

From the beginning of the program, the New York section received, graded, and returned 8,339 lessons, the San Francisco section, 4,060.

[a] SOURCE: American Radio Association, AFL-CIO.

leads to technicians' ratings. Mastery of the radar course leads to a classification of Marine Electronics Officer, which carries a 5 percent increase in salary. The preceding is a summary of the American Radio Association Training school graduates for the year ending March 31, 1966.

SKILL IMPROVEMENT TRAINING FOR STEAMFITTERS

It has been estimated by the U.S. Bureau of Labor Statistics that between 1960 and 1970, 224,000 additional plumber-pipefitter journeymen will be in demand.[8] If it continues at its present rate, the apprenticeship program can be expected to supply only 17 percent of the needed workers. The local labor-market survey for Oakland, California, contains no seriously conflicting evidence, but further inquiry into conditions in this area provides information on impor-

[8] Rennard Davis, "Retraining the Unemployed," *Monthly Labor Review*, LXXXIV, 10 (Oct., 1961), pp. 1074–1080.

tant trends in the trade.[9] Responsible union leaders have recognized a pressing need for advanced journeyman training in view of competition from (1) young apprenticeship graduates adept in the latest techniques and (2) members of other crafts working with new material, equipment, and methods over which jurisdiction has not yet been firmly established.

In 1955, the United Association of Journeymen and Apprentices of the Plumbing and Pipefitting Industry enlarged its training program so as to assist locals in furthering their own efforts. A model classroom located in the union's Washington, D.C., headquarters was furnished with an impressive array of training equipment, including plastic-welding instructional materials and courses suitable for adaptation to local needs. An International Training Fund, established by agreement between the union and the National Contractors' Association, has been developed through an employer contribution of two and one-half cents per man-hour worked. This amounts to over one million dollars per year. Part of the money is allocated to the operation of a special summer session at Purdue University for instructors in the trade. Last year more than 500 teachers from all over the country were sent to the one-week sessions in the inert-gas shield arc welding, steam trap operations, steam and refrigerator cycles, principles of pneumatic controls, plastic pipe welding, lead work, hydraulics, water contamination, water-supply systems, and safety controls for heating and cooling systems. These subjects are all taught by industry-provided instructors. Staff members of the Purdue Industrial Education Department teach basic scientific theories and acquaint the students with the new visual and other teaching devices. The total cost, estimated at about $80,000 per session, comes out of the jointly-managed Training Fund as do the salaries and equipment for courses conducted at the local level.[10]

Recognizing the significant changes in techniques and equipment in their trade, Local 342 in Oakland, California, was one of the first dozen in the United Association to take advantage of the training money. Its membership comprises about 1,000 men—700 employed in refineries and other parts of the oil industry, 90 apprentices, 75 metal tradesmen, and the rest in uptown steamfitting and refrigeration. For many of these workers, there have been radical changes in job content. For example, the competent journeyman of a decade ago needed to know how to make special fittings. Now elbows and other pieces come to the job premanufactured and ready to be put together. This

---

[9] State of California Department of Employment, *Manpower Resources of the San Francisco–Oakland Bay Area,* Research and Statistics Section, Coastal Area (May, 1963).

[10] Davis, "Retraining the Unemployed," p. 1078.

deemphasizes a certain skill, but changing technology brings new demands. With the vast assortment of different metals, alloys, and plastics, welding techniques have been greatly affected.

Acetylene welding used to be most commonly used. This was largely superseded by the electric method. At present, heliarc equipment is generally favored, but automatic welding is close at hand. Using what is called the "short arc" or the "submerged arc," one machine now does what it took six men to do previously. The setting up of the equipment has undergone no drastic change, but the time of operation has been dramatically reduced. It is the higher productive capacity of these processes that is cutting down the need for workers. And the men do not have to possess a great deal of skill. One of the members of the Skill Improvement Committee said, "Men can go right to the machine from the farm." In 60 days, they can develop a high degree of competence. Youth, rather than experience, appears to be an asset. "The new machines require young men; they're not as cautious as the old-timers and are willing to learn."

Hiring patterns in the industries served by this union reflect and probably generate this preference for younger men for the work associated with the advanced technologies. One major California oil company, which used to maintain forty-five as the top hiring age limit, subsequently lowered it to thirty-five; at present, no one over twenty-six need apply. For reasons of safety based on physiological factors, some age restrictions seem justified. Because heliarc welding requires a steady hand and exceptionally good eyesight, men over forty-five are not encouraged to learn the trade; it is deemed more suitable for the under-forty group. Despite its hazards, however, heliarc welding was indicated to be the favorite in a membership survey conducted by the Skill Improvement Committee. About 1,000 return cards, requesting that training course preference be indicated, had been sent out prior to the development of the program. The popularity of heliarc welding is readily understandable: (1) certain phases of it are clearly useful to any steamfitter, (2) instruction is of a shop nature. Other kinds of teaching are likely to cause embarrassment because they may show up inadequacies not so apparent on the job. "Older men are afraid of paper and pencil," was the general consensus.

Applicants for this training must await their turn, since the union's program is limited by the amount of available equipment at the public school where the classes are held. At present, there are seven machines, two owned by the school, four lent by the steamfitters, one by the ironworkers' union. Pipeline welding, basic welding, acetylene and cutting torch, and heliarc instruction are available here, the union having supplied practically all of the materials and apparatus. Enrollment is restricted to members of this union. The teachers, paid by the Bureau of Vocational Education under terms of the Smith–Hughes Act and through state-appropriated average daily attendance funds, are union members with a proper credential. Two different classes are being conducted, one from seven to ten o'clock Friday evenings and the other Saturday mornings from nine to twelve o'clock. Entry into the program is allowed all union members, regardless of age, but if a man cannot pass the test after about 40 hours of participation, he is asked to relinquish his place to someone else.

Three of the programs are conducted, exclusively under union auspices, at the Central Labor Council Temple. The first meets one evening per week for a two-and-one-half hour period and covers blueprint reading and mathematics, trigonometry being stressed because the men require some knowledge of angles. The second is a weekly two-hour evening class in isometric drawing. This has to do with a dimensioned sort of delineation as compared with the flat representation seen in most blueprints. Familiarity with isometric plans enables the steamfitter to envisage height and depth relationships. In some cases he must replot, in greater size and detail, parts of the original blueprint. Apparently, men competent in this specialty are in great demand and move out of the blue-shirt category to a desk job, which seems to carry a considerable degree of prestige in the trade. The most recently formed evening class, one in refrigeration, attracted more students than the 20 benches in the Labor Temple classroom could accommodate. The union and the instructor look to natural attrition to correct the standing-room-only situation.

After an unsuccessful one-year trial, an advanced program, which was supposed to provide instruction in panel boards and calibration, has been shelved. This is of particular note because the proposed two-year curriculum would have prepared journeymen to handle industrial control equipment. Since the success of flow-process manufacturing depends on proper synchronization throughout the system, men with special training are needed now and will be in greater demand as automation is introduced into more industries and takes over more phases of production. But out of the entire union membership of over 1,000 with roughly 400 to 500 employed as instrument men, not more than ten are known to be experts at calibration.

The Skill Improvement Committee is acutely sensitive to the urgency of providing properly qualified journeymen to fill these jobs or risk forfeiture of jurisdiction, but so far only the fifth year apprentices have been exposed to this type of curriculum and then only in the classroom setting. On-the-job training opportunities have been sparse, largely because the employed men have guarded their own bailiwick against possible invasion from these newcomers. The hope for an elite program that would attract the most capable of the young journeymen has vanished; most of the rank-and-file members are quite satisfied with the high wage they receive when working and reconciled to the layoffs they are subject to because of lack of versatility. Some form of welding may appeal to them because it is so free of schoolish stigmata, but the pencil-and-paper tasks repel all but the very brave.

Evidently, the skill committee has bowed to the exigencies of the present and has not persevered in a far-sighted program of alerting the members to imminent technological change. This is to be regretted since the union, with its training fund and experience, is in the unique position of being able to forecast technical shifts and to do something about them. Other unions included in the survey made preliminary to this research study were in a considerably less advantageous position, with no training fund, mass displacement, and no foreseeable occupational trends as guidelines for skill conversion.

Registration in the ongoing classes runs about as follows: eight in pipe-welding, 14 in heliarc, 10 in isometrics, 14 in blueprint reading, and 25 in refrigeration. The age distribution of enrollees is from approximately twenty-five to forty-five, with men in the lower ranges likely to undertake the more technical subjects and the older journeymen partial to learning-by-doing, as in welding. The Skill Improvement Committee felt that there was an increase in membership response when they moved some of their courses from the public evening school to the Labor Temple, where union sponsorship is more clearly defined, perhaps. This may be attributed to the familiar pattern of resistance to school. In addition, journeymen may be of the persuasion, right or wrong, that the course given by and for members under the union's roof will be tailored to fit them better and less cluttered with the frills of academia.

Two distinct advantages to having their own program were underlined by the Skill Improvement Committee: (1) they could choose the teacher according to their own specifications, regardless of official credential stipulations; (2) they could set up courses for any number of students, no matter how small. Trade-related courses in the public school system require a minimum of fifteen registrants. Nonetheless, the union continues to use the public evening schools for the major part of the training for both apprentices and journeymen and does not appear at this time to be pursuing a plan to set up its completely autonomous, self-contained training facility. The initial step, the purchase of a lot, was accomplished, but whether deterred by costs or by the complexity of running an educational institution with a volunteer board made up of well-intentioned but amateur members, the union has not taken further steps in the direction of an independent setup.

No explicit upgrading is in store for the men who undergo retraining, there being no differentiations in classification. The return comes in the form of assured and steady employment; the more phases a man can handle capably, the greater will be his opportunities for jobs. The smaller contractors, who are extremely competitive, put a heavy premium on such versatility. Thus, the all-around worker is in a favored position. For younger men who have been receptive to education, the rewards will come in the form of eligibility for the "glamour" jobs in the trade, those associated with the self-regulating mechanisms that make possible the magic of automation. Encouraged toward and given the opportunity for proper training, this group, indeed, could be the new elite of their union, the ones who benefit from technology and are not the victims of it.

UNITED ASSOCIATION OF JOURNEYMEN AND APPRENTICES, PLUMBERS AND GASFITTERS

Worthy of mention in this context is the Journeymen and Apprenticeship Training Program of the United Association of Plumbers and Gasfitters. During the recent past, this union withdrew all of its courses from the local public schools because of what appears to have been some dissatisfaction with the relationship. It was alleged that the trend in the community colleges is toward an academically oriented curriculum leading to the degree of Associate in Arts. Many of the required courses were considered by the union to be neither pertinent nor trade-related. That there was a lack of agreement on the ultimate role of such schools in the total system of vocational education was evidenced in a school report on a group of students who had been referred for special instruction by the State Employment Service. "The one conclusion that seems to be dictated by the information available . . . is that (the school) is not serving these people in its junior college function of providing broad occupational curricula, but rather is serving the traditional short-term occupational training function it has provided in years past." [11] Moreover, it was indicated that in some localities there was inadequate communication between educators and trade-advisory committees made up of union and industry.

With an initial grant of $12,750 from the International Fund of Journeymen and Apprentice Plumbers for capital equipment and supplies, the union erected its own building and organized a training program whose support comes through the Mechanical Contractors' Fund. The employers pay two and one-half cents per hour worked, for the instruction, and five cents for building and grounds. Because the money comes from negotiated agreements, union spokesmen consider

---

[11] Oakland, California City College, Laney Campus, "Progress Report on Retraining Students" (March 29, 1963), p. 4.

that the membership actually pays for the training; this amount would otherwise appear in their pay envelopes. It may be noted that the teachers still have to meet the credential requirements of the public adult schools and, indeed, receive part of their salary from them. In the new locale, the union seems to regard this as making for improved community relations. The arrangement also accrues to the benefit of the local school district, which thus becomes eligible for reimbursement from the State for student attendance.

That the union did not achieve autonomy with respect to teachers evidently has continued to cause problems. In one reported instance, an instructor, who was a systems engineer and not a plumber, was so lacking in the rudiments of the trade that he could not sustain the interest of students in the traditionally most popular subject, blueprint reading. Enrollment dwindled to such a small fraction that the course was temporarily withdrawn.

For the program, which got under way in September, 1964, three general instructional levels were established: (1) pre-apprentice; (2) apprentice; (3) journeyman upgrading. Programs for the latter include blueprint reading, code supervision, isometric one-line pipe-drawing, trade mathematics, and control and service of technologically advanced systems. To ascertain the membership's need, 800 questionnaires were circulated. Among the 280 replies, blueprint reading was first choice and code supervision second. The director of the union's school considered this response indicative but not definitive, for behavior on registration day would be the acid test of whether these men were serious in their intent to enroll or merely temporarily swayed by publicity about the threat of obsolescence. Actually, a substantial proportion of those who enrolled were not the members who had indicated interest but rather a totally different group—civil service workers who had just come under the jurisdiction of this union and who evidently were somewhat more conscious of the importance or need for self-improvement.

For the union's 1,300 journeyman members, the school offers three upgrading classes. Drawing and blueprint reading requires one evening per week, as does welding. The class in controls takes two evenings. A course in supervision and expediting had to be dropped in midseason for lack of attendance. Whether the instructor or the curriculum was to be blamed for the failure is to be ascertained through questionnaires by the director of the school so that improvements can be instituted. Because this class was intended for them and had attracted the better educated among the members, the expectation had been that motivation and participation would have been exemplary. Educating the rank-and-file to the importance of upgrading is regarded by the union officials as a most difficult task. Flyers, brochures, announcements in labor journals, notices on company and union bulletin boards, and publicity through the employers' association constantly remind the men that the all-round journeyman gets steady employment while others float. Diversification broadens the skill base and thus provides security. But so far, this message has elicited only mild response, with less than 8 percent of the members attending classes.

At the end of its second year, the school also has 127 students in the full-time apprenticeship program. The waiting list includes an additional 150 qualified applicants, but the two-year delay before entry causes considerable attrition and turnover. The preapprenticeship program is lagging, with no jobs in sight for the 19 enrollees. By contrast, in June, 1965, the entire class of 32 were placed in the trade. Apparently, the local building industry is not enjoying the economic prosperity of the country at large; the pace of activity is slow, contracts far from abundant, and the outlook dim.

INTERNATIONAL BROTHERHOOD
OF ELECTRICAL WORKERS

With its ubiquitous representation in the construction industry, at power plants, in every branch of transportation, on telephone and railroad jobs, and even in tree surgery, the International Brotherhood of Electrical Workers with a membership of 800,000 has experienced technological change on many fronts. Determined to keep their journeymen abreast of the latest developments, from new welding techniques to theories of radioisotopes, the union set up an office of Skill Improvement Training in August, 1959. As a result of its survey of local needs for craftsman training, the union began to develop a program in industrial electronics unilaterally, before joint financing arrangements could be worked out with employers. The two-year curriculum that was organized called for a three-hour evening class weekly, four semesters of eighteen weeks.

Next in order of priority was the establishment of a program for utility workers employed at nuclear power plants and for members whose jobs involved the use of radiography and radioisotopes in industry. The course in industrial atomic energy uses, hazards, and controls was the result. But even more important than teaching materials and lesson plans was the development of a corps of competent instructors trained to conduct these specialized courses wherever needed. Teacher-training institutes have performed this function with a considerable degree of success.

Along with the broad-based curricula, some short, intensive courses were set up to provide soldering techniques for installation and servicing of electronic components in both industrial and military establishments involved in missile work. The primary objective of the five three-hour sessions—one evening a week—was to give the workers the technical information and additional practice helpful in the use of resistance soldering equipment and the numerous types of connecting devices associated with the missile industry. The director of Skill Improvement Training reported that during a period of six months 8,000 men completed the training and that all the construction sites were thus manned with "fully trained and fully qualified mechanics."[12]

At present, union records show that the two-year Industrial Electronics Program has graduated some 10,000 members, with annual enrollments growing as more locals join the 350 which have offered this training. There are more than 5,000 graduates of the Industrial Atomic Energy course. As to the short, specialized one- and two-year updating programs, the official estimate is an annual enrollment of between 75,000 and 100,000 persons.[13]

The IBEW training endeavors are supported in several ways. At the national level, matching funds are donated by the union and the National Electrical Contractors' Association. The total, for both apprentice and journeyman programs, amounted to $100,000. In the individual cities and regions, the electrical contractors contribute about one-half of 1 percent of their gross payrolls for this purpose, an amount sometimes matched by the union locals. The formation of the National Electrical Training Directors Association and institutes to qualify instructors in industrial atomic energy have done much to prepare a corps of competent personnel for service to the districts. More than 500 men have attended teacher-training classes, and it is planned to repeat the sessions "until such a time as we have a sufficient number of persons trained to conduct programs for all our people who are in need of this training."[14]

The programs mentioned above are but a few that may be implemented at the local level by committees made up of union and management representatives. The national office supplies outlines and course materials where requested. In San Francisco, the coordinator for training for IBEW Local 6, with a membership of about 1,200, emphasizes that "journeymen must progress educationally or die by the wayside." Since reclassification into higher grades is based on successful performance on tests given every two years, the more ambitious members have an incentive for self-improvement.

---

[12] Letter to the author from Joseph E. Taylor, Director of Skill Improvement Training, International Brotherhood of Electrical Workers, dated March 16, 1962.

[13] *Ibid.*, dated December 8, 1965.

[14] *Ibid.*

Present conditions in the industry, however, have contributed to a certain measure of complacency among electricians. Despite ups and downs in construction activity there has been virtually no unemployment among the members; the occasional strike or layoff between jobs is regarded as the irreducible frictional minimum. The electrical trade has also reaped an abundant harvest from the impressive array of appliances in the home with their concomitant need for extra wiring, outlets, switches, and adjustment. Scarcely noticed is the gradually increasing demand, in new commercial and industrial buildings with complicated electrical and electronic systems for production and data-processing, for a very high level of skill and versatility. Recent graduates of the apprentice program, because of stringent qualification standards and updated courses, are likely to meet the upgraded requirements. Many of them can aspire to the job of foreman within five or six years after attaining journeyman status; it is from their ranks that the full-time, year-round posts of maintenance personnel for electronic installations will most certainly be drawn.

Because the past decade has provided substantial job security, older workers have not been greatly concerned about the marketability of their skills. They are content to work ten months out of the year, threatened with no immediate or drastic obsolescence, and they are not particularly likely to be receptive to the idea of further schooling. The training coordinator for the union tries to combat this apathy by a continuous campaign, which emphasizes the trend toward specialized work in electronics. Successful completion of courses is acknowledged by official certificates issued by the national office. These in fact must be submitted before a journeyman can take the reclassification examination.

Classes are held in a local public high school and, therefore, meet the requirement of a minimum of 15 students. The combined enrollment of apprentices and full-fledged electricians "keeps the seats filled." Thus, although the school department must by law admit any qualified applicant, persons who do not belong to the union have little opportunity to enroll. After some experimentation, it was found that one weekly evening class of two and one-half hours was preferable to two sessions that were an hour and a half long. It was virtually impossible to get workers to come twice a week. Moreover, there has been growing recognition on the part of the union that traditional methods of instruction may be unsuitable for the mature worker and may, perhaps, be one of the deterrents to participation in training programs.

With the dual purpose of (1) identifying the factors that promote or impede the retraining of electricians and (2) assessing the effectiveness of new teaching devices in attracting enrollees, holding their interest, and encouraging them to continue into advanced courses, a research study was undertaken several years ago under the joint sponsorship of IBEW Local 617 of San Mateo, California, the National Electrical Contractors Association, the College of San Mateo, and the California Bureau of Industrial Education.[15] The precise findings, which substantiate the thesis that autoinstruction in conjunction with a live teacher promotes a higher degree of student satisfaction, have meaningful implications for adult retraining generally. What is specifically relevant to our considerations is that a union would concern itself with a project of a methodological, rather than a practical, nature. This effort carries forward the IBEW's determination to keep its membership in tune with technological change and to provide industry with fully trained and highly skilled workers.

CONCLUSIONS

The above examples of union-sponsored retraining may be regarded as "critical incidents" in trade union involvement in updating and upgrading the work force. The cases we have discussed cover the sum total of such projects in the San Francisco Bay area at that time and are representative of union training endeavors elsewhere in the country. In other labor market areas, the emphasis will vary with the concentration of industry. In the San Francisco Labor Council, which includes well over one hundred locals affiliated with practically every national and international union on the roster, only a few can claim credit for training programs other than those for apprentices or those effectuated by the Manpower Development and Training Act.

No clear-cut rationale for unions to embark on retraining appears evident. There is, for example, no instance of pressure from membership to provide instruction as a protective measure against obsolescence or technological displacement. Quite the contrary. Even in the most threatened trades, unions have had to stage aggressive educational campaigns to generate support and interest. As can be seen from the number of trade-related courses that have been started but had to close for lack of continued attendance, fear of underemployment or unemployment was not enough of a motivating factor to sustain perseverance. It may be appropriate to note here that it was not until the Manpower Development and Training Act came

---

[15] David S. Bushnell, "Training of Journeymen Electricians: An Experimental Study," paper presented to the 24th Annual Conference on Industrial Education, San Diego, California (March 8, 1962).

forward with appropriations that some unions took discernible steps in the direction of retraining their journeymen.

Only in the case of selected unions can labor market conditions be considered a reason for training. To begin with, it is extremely difficult to arrive at an objective assessment of the number of bona fide openings from employers and of available supply of skilled workers from unions if either side has reason to slant the report to its own purposes. For example, a union persuaded the government to put a firm stop order on any MDTA program for the training of power sewing-machine operators in the San Francisco Bay area. While employers have indicated a persistent need, the unions maintain that the supply of workers is adequate and that additions would glut the market and depress wages. The needle trades are characterized by a high degree of seasonality, and the clothing industry itself is highly volatile. Most small companies operate on a close margin of security; they are likely to collapse if business is poor, and they are relatively mobile geographically. As a result, there seems to be little basis for substantive labor market projections. According to informal union estimates, there may already be more than two thousand power sewing-machine operators working under sweatshop conditions behind painted store windows in San Francisco's Chinatown.

The pros and cons of utilizing public school facilities came into sharp view during this study. Almost unanimous was the criticism among unionists of the requirements of credentials for teachers. From their point of view, the thoroughly skilled tradesman was by-passed in favor of a less qualified man who had, however, gone through the necessary motions of acquiring a certificate. The school officials are wont to justify their standards by pointing out that competence at the work place does not automatically make a good instructor and that equal in importance to knowledge of the trade is the technique for transmitting it to others.

Some union people have become disenchanted with the trade schools because of what they claim is an unnecessarily and inappropriately theoretical and academic approach to occupations, where the purely pragmatic would suffice. A tendency to urge enrollees to acquire at least an Associate in Arts degree has drawn forth acrimonious comment from union spokesmen who maintain that this approach is wasteful of time and resources and that it is likely to alienate the student, particularly if his scholarly ambitions are tenuous. The classic, albeit undocumented example, was of a young man whom the union sent to a community college to learn to do prespotting for the cleaning and dyeing industry; he was purported to have had to submit to an elaborate curriculum, which covered such subjects as color coordination. That there is a lack of firm educational policy besetting the junior colleges cannot be gainsaid. The latter serve both as a terminal point and as a stepping-stone to institutions of higher learning. Cosmetology for the girl who wants to become a hairdresser and chemistry for the girl who aspires to transfer to a university are taught almost side by side. It appears to be true that even while improving their academic status, the junior colleges have welcomed the opportunity to set up trade-related courses. This need not be considered an indictment, but an endorsement of duality of purpose. The junior colleges have inherited and must face a multiplicity of problems created by the established school system. Despite superficially cordial relations between union representatives and school administrators, there exists a good deal of distrust. One union spokesman implied that when schools are asked to set up a course, they generally request quantities of equipment, which they then use to train the general public and thus flood the market. The latter contention seems somewhat exaggerated in view of the firm requirement that the enrollee be working at the particular trade—under union regulation—in order to be eligible to attend the class.

Dues structure has no apparent relationship to a union's proclivity toward training its membership. Some of the largest locals with the highest fees maintained token arrangements at best until the advent of the MDTA supplied them with funds earmarked for journeyman updating and upgrading. It is almost tautological to observe that those unions where collective bargaining clauses provided a specific fund were the most training-oriented. Certainly one would hesitate to distinguish here between which was cause and which was effect. But in no instance was there evidence that the rate of dues per se had any bearing on a union's position with respect to training.

Basic to the research was the question as to whether the public at large or even union members in particular can look to organized labor for help in coping with technological change through skill improvement. The empirical data support the thesis that the single most important determinant of a union's policy vis-à-vis training is its sphere of authority, present and anticipated. Just as the preservation and expansion of jurisdictional sovereignty define union government,[16] so to a remarkable degree do they define educational policy and practice at every level from apprentice to master mechanic. What subjects shall be taught, who may learn them, where they shall be presented, and by whom—all these matters are ultimately handled with reference to the union's current and projected areas of control. There appears to be no real contradiction between the

---

[16] Paul Jacobs, *The State of the Unions* (New York: Atheneum, 1963), p. 268.

unions' public declaration of disappointment over members' apathy on the one hand and the policy of controlled intake into retraining programs on the other. Almost without exception, the union is arbiter of who among their rank-and-file may benefit. With respect to the elite, upgraded, technologically advanced jobs of the future, the economics of scarcity is the favored policy.

[5

Retraining of the Underprivileged: The Neighborhood House Story

During the recent past, the attention of the American public has been forced to turn to the social, economic, and educational deprivations of minority groups, especially the Negroes.[1] The revolution now in progress has been compared to the industrial upheaval of the 1930's; it has been suggested that on its outcome may depend social peace in the United States for generations to come.[2] Even though there appears to be gradual improvement in the position of the American Negro since the beginning of the Second World War, a high rate of unemployment has persisted. It ranges anywhere from two to ten times that of the current level for white workers, depending on the source of the figures and their interpretation.

Testimony before the 1963 Senate hearings on equal employment opportunity indicated the need for more searching analysis of data on income and occupational distribution of the nonwhite and the white population. Several of the conclusions bear directly on the considerations in this chapter. It was pointed out, for example, that "pronouncements regarding economic progress which are confined

---

[1] Many of the figures cited in this section refer to "nonwhite" persons, of whom 92 percent are Negro, since data for all nonwhite persons are up to date and comprehensive. Only in the 1950 and 1960 censuses and in a limited number of special studies is information on Negroes as such identified. In the North, Negroes represent 96 percent of the nonwhite population; in the South, 98 percent. The statistics on Negroes in the western United States include Hawaii and, therefore, indicate that Negroes represent less than half of the nonwhite population for that area. The data on Negroes in California are, however, somewhat more precise than for the region as a whole.

[2] U.S. Department of Labor, Office of Policy Planning and Research, *The Negro Family* (March, 1965), p. 3.

129

to acceleration concepts and percentage change obscure the real predicament—Negroes are losing ground rapidly in gaining dollar parity with whites."[3] Several other hypotheses were put forth during the hearings, including one that the extent to which Negroes have been making progress is not nearly as important as their future advance and the factors contributing to or hampering it. If, as is generally believed, technological change is altering skill requirements and eliminating large numbers of jobs at the low end of the occupational ladder, the nonwhite sector of our labor force stands to be the most heavily affected.[4]

Unresolved is the question whether the basic problem stems, from the Negro's reluctance to participate in and contribute to the affluent society,[5] or from the technological revolution that is engulfing the jobs traditionally providing him entry into the labor force, or from the bigotry that has barred him from employment opportunity. Perhaps he could not reach the top of the occupational ladder for lack of an education; perhaps he could not attain a proper education because he lived in a slum where schooling was poor; or perhaps he could not reside in a neighborhood that had good schools because he was barred by restrictive covenants or could not afford the high rent or purchase price. The vicious circle has persisted and the mixture of circumstances has varied, depending on the social and economic climate. The effectiveness of ameliorative measures is likewise determined by prevailing conditions.

It is for this reason that, after examining the statistical and descriptive data on the status of the nonwhite population on a national and a regional basis, it is appropriate to examine the social climate of an extremely segregated Negro community and to study the experience derived from Neighborhood House, a noteworthy rehabilitative retraining project for young men. The materials will serve as a background for consideration of the Job Corps, a federally-sponsored residential program for youth "whose lives have been so underprivileged that they have little chance of becoming productive

---

[3] Vivian W. Henderson, "The Economic Status of Negroes in the Nation and in the South," *Testimony before the Subcommittee on Employment and Manpower of the Senate Committee on Labor and Public Welfare*, 85th Congress, 1st Session (July 24, 25, 26, 29 and 31; August 2 and 20, 1963), p. 441.

[4] *Ibid.*, p. 445.

[5] It must be noted that the discussion in this section is directed primarily to the "disadvantaged lower-class group among the Negroes and not to the stable middle-class, which is becoming progressively more successful, and where there is a higher premium on education and achievement than at a comparable level of white society." U.S. Department of Labor, Office of Policy Planning and Research, *The Negro Family* (March, 1965), p. 6.

citizens without a change of environment." [6] Although intended for entrants into the labor force, the program contains many of the elements of the Neighborhood House philosophy. There is little substantive information yet about the accomplishments of the Job Corps, since it has been in existence only since 1965; but it is of interest to note the emphasis on basic education and the techniques for helping the Corpsmen acquire positive attitudes toward work and the necessary habits. Application of the same remedial approach are to be seen in "Operation Self-Support," the prevocational activity of the Employment Section of the Alameda County Welfare Department.

STATUS OF THE NEGRO NATIONALLY AND IN THE SAN FRANCISCO BAY AREA

Education

Despite notable progress in civil rights, education, occupational distribution, housing, and earnings during the Second World War and the following years, the major part of the Negro population has not succeeded in breaking the self-perpetuating pattern of poverty, substandard living, poor schooling, and limited access to jobs. It is generally known that during the past decade a marked improvement in the educational level has been achieved by nonwhites; illiteracy, as measured by five years of formal school attendance, has virtually disappeared. The median grade completed has advanced by two years to 9.6. Close to twice as many Negro youth graduated from high school as a decade before.[7] There is a continuing trend toward a narrowing of the gap in the number of school years completed by the white and the nonwhite population (Table 7). This varies regionally. In the San Francisco Bay area, for example, the median school years completed by persons twenty-five and over stands at 10.3 for the nonwhite and 12.1 for the white sectors.[8]

Promising though these trends may appear to be, there are several underlying and sobering considerations. (1) It is only by comparison with a very low base that the picture seems bright. (2) Availability of an increasingly well-educated labor force has pushed hiring

---

[6] U.S. Department of Labor, *Manpower Report of the President* (1966), p. 104.

[7] U.S. Department of Labor, *Manpower Report of the President* (1964), p. 97.

[8] State of California, Department of Industrial Relations, Division of Fair Employment Practices, *Negro Californians*, San Francisco, June, 1963, p. 34.

132   RETRAINING THE WORK FORCE

requirements upward.[9] (3) Mere figures on school grades completed
are far from definitive. Variations in the quality of education are
so wide that there is serious deficiency not only among graduates
of predominantly Negro high schools but also in Negro graduates
of almost any high school—northern or southern, urban or rural.[10]
Formal education, instead of compensating for environmental deprivations, has been shown in some instances to compound them.

TABLE 7

MEDIAN YEARS OF SCHOOL COMPLETED BY PERSONS 25 YEARS OLD AND OVER
AND 25 TO 29 YEARS OLD, BY COLOR AND SEX, 1940 TO 1959

	Male		Female	
Date and age	White	Nonwhite	White	Nonwhite
25 years and over				
April, 1940	8.7	5.4	8.8	6.1
April, 1947	9.0	6.6	9.7	7.2
October, 1952	10.1	6.8	10.8	7.4
March, 1957	10.7	7.3	11.3	8.1
March, 1959	11.1	7.6	11.6	8.4
Increase, 1940 to 1959, in years completed	2.4	2.2	2.8	2.3
25 to 29 years				
April, 1940	10.5	6.5	10.9	7.5
March, 1957	12.3	9.4	12.3	10.3
March, 1959	12.5	10.9	12.4	11.0
Increase, 1940 to 1959, in years completed	2.0	4.4	1.5	3.5

SOURCE: U.S. Department of Commerce, Bureau of the Census. As presented in
U.S. Department of Labor, *The Economic Situation of Negroes in the United States*,
Bulletin S-3, Revised 1962, p. 28.

Initial verbal disadvantage has been seen to persist and act as a
brake to such an extent that, at every testing point from the third
through the twelfth grade, pupils' scores in prevailingly Negro and
Puerto Rican districts of New York were consistently below grade
level.[11] It is significant to note the strong correlation that has been
found between income groups and composite elementary achievement scores, with the differences in favor of higher income groups

[9] U.S. Department of Labor, *Manpower Report of the President*, (1966), p. 80.
[10] U.S. Department of Labor, *Manpower Report of the President* (1964), p. 98.
[11] Marjorie Smiley, "Research and Its Implications," in U.S. Department of
Health, Education, and Welfare, Office of Education, *Improving English Skills
of Culturally Different Youth*, Bulletin OE-30012, No. 5 (1964), p. 41.

increasing from grade to grade.[12] By the time the student reaches senior high school, curriculum division on the basis of performance has institutionalized and perpetuated the lag almost beyond remedy. For this reason, young people from lower socioeconomic classes who persevere and receive the high school diploma are probably not much better educated than those who dropped out, and not as well educated as their fellow graduates who are white. In 1962, 46 percent of the nonwhite youth aged eighteen through twenty-four who had attended high school had failed to complete the four years, as compared with 25 percent of the comparable white group.[13]

In many urban communities throughout the country, there is evidence of a growing appreciation of the feedback from educational opportunity to the economic and social situation of the minority members. In California some cities have developed special compensatory programs designed to correct early handicaps, not only for Negro youngsters but also for Mexican-American and other groups who have been affected by the prevailing pattern of racially segregated housing.[14] Berkeley, where some 20 percent of the total population is Negro and where Negro children account for 32 percent of the school enrollment, extended the principle of its integrated community high school in September, 1964, to the junior high school level to try to overcome some of the obstacles generated at that stage. The redistribution involved a considerable transfer of youngsters from one area to another and brought them together from the schools representing the city's sharpest contrasts in background—not only contrasts in ethnic origin and socioeconomic status, but also academic rating. Since the amalgam is experimental and in its early stages, little can be said about its prospects for achieving an improved education for the minority population. It would be well to note that the outcome may be significant as well in other parts of the country where similar efforts are in progress. In addition, the results could influence the pattern of adjustment for such groups as the Mexican-Americans, the magnitude of whose growth in this area due to natural increase and immigration has received little public attention because of the more immediate urgency of the need to solve Negro-white tensions.[15]

If one were to hazard an a priori and superficial observation on

---

[12] Patrician C. Sexton, *Education and Income* (New York: Viking Press, 1961), p. 26.

[13] U.S. Department of Labor, *Manpower Report of the President* (1964), p. 97.

[14] Paul Bullock, "Employment Problems of the Mexican-American," *Industrial Relations*, III, 3 (May, 1964), pp. 37–51.

[15] Wilson Record, *Minority Groups and Intergroup Relations in the San Francisco Bay Area*, University of California, Institute of Governmental Studies (Berkeley, 1963), p. 1.

this effort to counteract de facto segregation in a school system, one might suggest that the social effects have been more immediately discernible than the educational. Except for minor personality clashes, which could have been misinterpreted as racial incidents, there has been no evidence of hostility. Contrary to the dire predictions of citizens who tried to unseat the school board for initiating this change, the longer bus trips now required seem to have created no serious hardship, and there has been no wholesale exodus of white residents to the suburbs. Just how the redistricting will affect the teaching and learning situation has yet to be demonstrated. Neither the contention that such a mixture would adversely affect the high achievers nor the hope that it would spark the ambition of the less-motivated has yet been substantiated. But the reorganization serves as undeniable evidence of the community's determination to attain balanced racial enrollment in its schools. This goal, it must be noted, can be accomplished only if the population retains its present proportions between Negro and white. It would be impossible in cities like Washington, D.C., where the residents are predominantly Negro and surrounding suburban areas almost exclusively white.

Employment

Educational attainment is inextricably woven into the pattern that determines employability, employment, and, where necessary, retraining and reemployment, so it is important to examine the data on schooling in the light of the Negro's status in the world of work. The high dropout rate mentioned in the foregoing section might have been attributed to the discouraging occupational outlook. Until very recently, differentials in unemployment rates indicated that by completing high school a white student could significantly reduce the probability of being unemployed, while the nonwhite graduate improved by very little his chance for getting work. The marked decrease in the relative numbers of unskilled and semiskilled jobs traditionally open to entrants into the labor force means all of today's youth are encountering difficulty in securing employment, but the young Negro population is disproportionately represented among the jobless. National figures show that in late 1964, one out of every twelve of the young white men no longer in school was not in the labor force; among nonwhites, the fraction was reported as one out of every eight.[16]

The Negro student evaluating his chances for profiting by an education can derive little comfort from the statistical record. Figures

---

[16] U.S. Department of Labor, *Manpower Report of the President* (1966), p. 90.

from the 1960 census suggest that up to that time, at least, the lifetime earnings of the average nonwhite college graduate would amount to less than those of the white man who had not gone past the eighth grade. This situation prevailed not only in the South, but to a lesser extent in other parts of the country.[17]

As can be seen from the accompanying tables, the unemployment rates are disproportionately high for nonwhite persons—for reasons

TABLE 8

UNEMPLOYMENT RATES BY AGE, COLOR, AND SEX, 1957 AND 1963–1965

| Item | Total, 14 years and over | 14 to 19 years | 20 to 24 years | 25 years and over | | |
				Total	25 to 44 years	45 years and over
ALL PERSONS						
Men						
1957	4.1	11.3	7.8	3.2	3.1	3.4
1963	5.3	15.5	8.8	4.0	3.9	4.0
1964	4.7	14.5	8.1	3.3	3.2	3.5
1965	4.0	13.1	6.3	2.8	2.7	2.9
Women						
1957	4.7	10.1	6.0	3.9	4.5	3.2
1963	6.5	15.7	8.9	4.9	5.9	3.9
1964	6.2	15.0	8.6	4.6	5.5	3.7
1965	5.5	14.3	7.3	4.0	5.0	3.0
NON-WHITE						
Men						
1957	8.4	17.5	12.7	6.8	7.5	6.0
1963	10.6	25.4	15.5	8.2	8.8	7.5
1964	9.1	23.3	12.6	6.9	6.9	6.9
1965	7.6	22.6	9.3	5.4	5.6	5.2
Women						
1957	7.4	18.9	12.2	5.5	6.4	4.1
1963	11.3	33.1	18.7	8.0	9.9	5.4
1964	10.8	30.6	18.3	7.5	9.3	5.0
1965	9.3	29.8	13.7	6.4	8.0	4.1

SOURCE: Department of Labor, *Manpower Report of the President* (March, 1966), p. 25.

of less adequate preparation, earlier work force participation, discriminatory hiring, and the like. Table 8 shows the national figures,

---

[17] U.S. Department of Labor, *Manpower Report of the President* (1964), p. 107.

and the disadvantage of the nonwhites is evident at all age levels, although the differentials vary somewhat.

The unemployment rates of Negroes in California, as shown in Table 9, follow the national pattern. The consistently high incidence

TABLE 9

UNEMPLOYMENT RATES, BY AGE AND SEX, CALIFORNIA, 1960 [a]
(Percent)

| | Male | | Female | |
Age	White	Nonwhite	White	Nonwhite
Total 14 years and over	5.5	10.1	6.3	9.8
14 to 17 years	11.6	22.0	11.3	18.9
18 to 19 years	13.0	22.3	10.1	19.7
20 to 24 years	8.1	16.1	7.6	15.1
25 to 34 years	4.3	9.4	6.4	10.1
35 to 44 years	3.8	7.9	5.7	8.4
45 to 54 years	4.9	8.7	5.5	7.3
55 to 64 years	6.3	9.7	5.3	7.5
65 years and over	7.9	10.8	5.4	6.9

SOURCES: U.S. Bureau of the Census. State of California, Department of Industrial Relations, Division of Fair Employment Practices, *Negro Californians* (San Francisco, June, 1963), p. 27.

[a] Unemployment as a percent of civilian labor force, 14 years and over.

of joblessness at every age level suggests that the recent advance in education shown by Negroes has not been reflected in their work experience. It is likely that longer years of schooling are part of our national ethos and, if it is reflected to equal degree in all of the subcultures of our society, minority members have gained little on their disadvantage at getting jobs. In some sections of the country, where communities have responded to fair employment practice legislation, civil rights pressures, or their social responsibility, there is evidence of discrimination in reverse. Employers frequently give preference to the Negro applicant especially in situations of high visibility, such as retail selling. Because of this new version of "unfair competition," hidden hiring and nepotism are likely to increase. The white college student on vacation seeks the same unskilled job as the Negro high school dropout. Rather than run the risk of prosecution for violating the Fair Employment Practice Act, an employer avoids publicizing an open job through channels and fills it through personal contacts.

In the San Francisco Bay area, rate of Negro joblessness is double that of the general population, a ratio that has persisted with only minor fluctuation during the past decade. The fear has been expressed that the discrepancy will increase as automation takes over more of the unskilled and semiskilled jobs.[18] The State Department of Employment's collection of racial information on new unemployment insurance claims, a practice begun in July, 1963, provides valuable clues to the occupational distribution of the minority work force as compared with the majority work force. Scrutiny of new unemployment insurance claims collected during the last half of 1963 showed that 9 percent were filed by Negroes, although Negroes constitute only about 5 percent of the labor force covered by the Unemployment Insurance Code. Mexican-Americans filed approximately 12 percent of all new claims, although they form only 8.3 percent of the insured labor force.[19]

For the Mexican-American worker, concentrated like the Negro in blue-collar categories and vulnerable to technological change, employment projections indicate little variation from the present path, which lies somewhere between that of the Negro and the "Anglo." While he has not encountered discrimination as rigid in the area of skilled and clerical work, he—like the Negro—is represented hardly at all in the high income professional classifications.[20] Obscured at present by the Negro problem, the Mexican-American situation vis-à-vis education and employment has received little more than token attention in the San Francisco Bay area. As was pointed out earlier, since their numbers are increasing rapidly in the northern part of California, it may be prudent to include this minority when plans are made to ameliorate the lot of the nonwhite residents of this region. As has been seen in the Los Angeles experience, neglect of this minority group can engender a complex of social ills of significant import.[21]

Whether the cause of the Mexican-Americans will derive ultimate benefit from the attainment of equal rights by Negroes or be hampered by it is a matter of interest but not of direct concern in this research study. Empirical data available at present provide little ground for prediction. What is certain is that the low educational and economic status of this large minority group puts them in the category of the deprived, and that the findings with respect to the

---

[18] Wilson Record, *op. cit.*, p. 15.

[19] State of California, Employment Relations Agency, Department of Employment, *Inventory of Antipoverty Programs Involving Employment Security Administration,* Sacramento, California, June 30, 1964, p. 21.

[20] Paul Bullock, "Employment Problems of the Mexican-American," *Industrial Relations,* III, 3 (May, 1964), p. 43.

[21] Testimony of Dionicio Morales on "Employment Problems of Mexican-Americans in California," *Hearings before the Subcommittee on Employment and Manpower of the Senate Committee on Labor and Public Welfare,* 88th Congress, 1st Session, Part 4 (August 6, 7, Sept. 10, 11 and 12, 1963), pp. 1257–1265.

retraining of these nonwhites will pertain to them as much as to the Negroes.

Just as the Negro's unemployment seems to have roots in deficient and inadequate schooling, so does his occupational distribution. As can be seen in the accompanying national and state tabulations (Fig. 2, Tables 10 and 11), employed Negroes are concentrated in low-

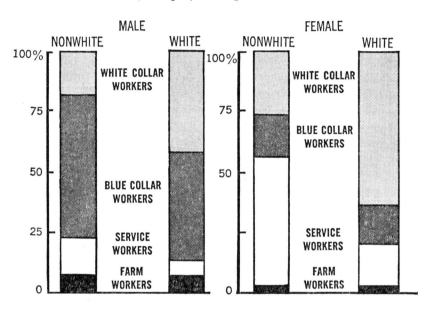

Fig. 2. Proportion of white and nonwhite workers in various occupational groups, March, 1965. (Source: U. S. Bureau of the Census.)

skilled and poorly paying jobs. Men are heavily represented among the laborers and women among household domestics. The poverty syndrome is reflected in the fact that Negroes are associated with occupations which carry low status, poor pay, and limited prospects. Not only in comparison with the white population, but even with other nonwhite groups, the Negroes were found to be in the least desirable jobs.[22] Figures showing the occupational distribution of Negroes in California indicate a configuration similar to the one that is shown nationally—scarcity in the upper echelons and marked concentration among the service, laborer, and other unskilled categories.

With respect to wage and salary income, and despite some lessening of the gap between them and the white labor force during the Second World War and the Korean conflict, the Negro workers continue to

[22] U.S. Department of Labor, *Manpower Report of the President*, Table II-7. "Negroes as percent of all nonwhite employed persons by major occupation group and sex" (1960), p. 273.

TABLE 10

Employed Persons, by Occupation Group and Color and Sex: Annual Averages, 1955, 1961, and 1964

Occupation group	Percent distribution						Nonwhite as a percent of total		
	Nonwhite			White					
	1955[a]	1961	1964	1955[a]	1961	1964	1955[a]	1961	1964
Total employed:									
Number (thousands)	6,438	6,936	7,480	56,561	59,860	62,877	—	10.4	10.6
Percent	100.0	100.0	100.0	100.0	100.0	100.0	10.2	—	—
White-collar workers	12.0	16.4	18.7	42.1	46.7	47.3	3.1	3.9	4.5
Professional and technical	3.5	4.6	6.7	9.8	12.3	12.8	3.9	4.1	5.8
Managers, officials, and proprietors	2.3	2.5	2.6	11.1	11.6	11.5	2.3	2.4	2.6
Clerical workers	4.9	7.7	7.6	14.2	15.6	16.1	3.8	5.4	5.4
Sales workers	1.3	1.6	1.8	6.9	7.2	6.9	2.0	2.5	3.1
Blue-collar workers	41.8	39.1	40.4	39.0	35.3	35.8	10.9	11.4	11.8
Craftsmen and foremen	5.2	6.1	7.0	14.1	13.7	13.5	4.0	4.9	5.8
Operatives	20.9	20.1	20.3	20.2	17.3	18.1	10.6	11.9	11.8
Nonfarm laborers	15.8	12.9	13.0	4.7	4.3	4.2	27.6	25.7	26.9
Service workers	31.6	32.8	32.2	9.0	10.6	10.9	28.6	26.3	26.0
Private household workers	14.8	14.5	13.5	1.8	2.2	2.1	48.8	43.4	43.6
Other service workers	16.8	18.3	18.7	7.2	8.4	8.8	21.0	20.1	20.2
Farm workers	14.5	11.7	8.7	9.9	7.3	6.0	14.3	15.7	14.7
Farmers and managers	5.0	2.9	1.9	6.0	4.2	3.5	8.6	7.4	6.3
Farm laborers and foremen	9.5	8.8	6.8	3.9	3.1	2.6	21.8	24.8	23.8

Source: U.S. Department of Labor, Bureau of Labor Statistics. Data are from the regular monthly Current Population Survey.
[a] Based on an average of January, April, July, and October; data have not been adjusted to 1957 definitions of employment and unemployment.

TABLE 11

OCCUPATION OF EMPLOYED NEGROES, BY SEX, CALIFORNIA, 1960

Major occupation group	Male		Female	
	Number	Percent	Number	Percent
Total employed	173,311	100.0	115,694	100.0
Professional, technical, and kindred workers	7,629	4.4	8,762	7.6
Farmers and farm managers	844	0.5	33	a
Managers, officials, and proprietors (except farm)	3,973	2.3	1,517	1.3
Clerical and kindred workers	13,500	7.8	16,370	14.1
Sales workers	3,096	1.8	2,014	1.7
Craftsmen, foremen, and kindred workers	23,090	13.3	1,146	1.0
Operatives and kindred workers	38,038	21.9	16,865	14.6
Private household workers	1,026	0.6	31,503	27.2
Service workers (except private household)	28,359	16.4	23,938	20.7
Farm laborers and foremen	3,347	1.9	440	0.4
Laborers (except farm and mine)	30,907	17.8	1,247	1.1
Occupation not reported	19,502	11.3	11,859	10.3

SOURCES: U.S. Bureau of the Census. Table adopted from State of California, Department of Industrial Relations, Division of Fair Employment Practices, *Negro Californians* (San Francisco, June, 1963), p. 21.

a Less than .05 of 1 percent.

demonstrate the adverse effects of poorer education, higher unemployment rate, concentration in the lower-paying, less steady jobs, and the wage discrimination that has prevailed in many occupations and industries. The national median income in 1963 for Negroes 14 years old or older was $2,400 for men and about $1,000 for women, as compared with about $4,800 for white men and $1,400 for white women. In the thirteen Western states median income for Negro males was $4,160 and for Negro females, $2,134; for the same period, the figures for white males showed $5,208 and for women, $1,474.[23] The lower earnings for white women indicated their labor force participation pattern rather than their disadvantage.

Because of riots in the Watts section of Los Angeles in the summer of 1965, the President appointed a task force to investigate conditions in that area. The special census survey revealed some telling statistics: median family income (adjusted for price changes) stood at $4,700,

[23] U.S. Department of Commerce, Bureau of the Census Current Population Reports, *Population Characteristics*, Series P-20, No. 142 (Oct. 11, 1965).

and it had dropped from $5,100 in 1959. Similar declines were seen in the three Mexican-American neighborhoods in East Los Angeles.[24]

Recently, thanks to the various pressures of the civil rights movement, mounting delinquency rates, and rising unemployment among youth, efforts have been made to put meaningful punctuation into the long sentence of required schooling. Supervised study halls, more counseling service, college volunteer tutors, and "sandwich" programs combining paid outside work and class attendance have been initiated to keep youngsters in school. Whether such endeavors will contribute to the attainment of a better education and enhanced opportunities for labor force participation cannot be predicted at this early date. The fact that problems are being identified and corrective measures being applied provides basis for hope that the young people still in school will emerge better prepared to compete for jobs.

Those who look to the educational process to break the involutional cycle of poverty often insist on more vocational training for young people in order to (1) keep them interested in their schoolwork and (2) turn them out ready for gainful employment. But there is much work to be done on the value structure of our society inside and outside school walls, and on the calibre of curriculum, equipment, and teachers before these goals can be achieved. The image of the vocational track as a dumping ground or custodial service for the dull, the unmotivated, and the behavior problem will not fade easily.

A key role will have to be played by counselors, who vary enormously in function, commitment, and ability. In some schools the primary duty of arranging schedules keeps them from contact with any but the most exceptional students, the stars or the troublemakers. Frequently the counselor is a fugitive from the classroom with a certificate earned by taking extra courses. This combination of over-involvement with paperwork and lack of knowledge about the rapidly changing world has reduced the counselor to a mere functionary at a time when there is a need for alert, well-informed, dynamic persons. Not only should they be able to help interpret the realities of the marketplace but they should also serve as guides in the increasingly depersonalized school system. A heavy reliance on objective tests and automated programming which rule out consideration of individuals' options and requirements is having the effect of reducing students to mere data. Instead of serving as a tool to free counselors for more creative activity in their role, the system has regimented them still further.

At best, the school alone cannot be expected to provide remedies

---

[24] U.S. Department of Commerce, Bureau of the Census, Current Population Reports, Technical Studies, *Special Census Survey of the South and East Los Angeles Areas Nov., 1965,* Series p-23, No. 17 (March 23, 1966), p. 1.

for all ailments. That it is a pressure point in the circulatory system of the social body cannot be gainsaid. That it is not the only crucial area is obvious and a truism, of course. The proportions in which it may best fulfill its functions in training, teaching, and educating are far from clearly established. Perhaps improvements in the system will have an impact in the future. They may affect the children of the unskilled, untrained, and unemployed, but they can do little to solve the persistent problems of those who at present cannot qualify for gainful employment.

THE NEIGHBORHOOD HOUSE JOB UPGRADING PROJECT

The North Richmond Community

Illustrative of a professional effort to enhance the employability of a group of young Negro men by remedial measures is the one in operation at Neighborhood House in North Richmond, California. This is a unique endeavor, the forerunner of efforts in other parts of the country to reach alienated and unemployed youth and to provide them with prevocational help.

A subcommunity that sets into sharp perspective the deprivation of the long-time unemployed is that segment of North Richmond, California, included in the unincorporated portion of the Census Tract 65. This is the only area in West Contra Costa County where the many Negroes emigrating from the South during the Second World War to work in the shipyards were able to buy property. The lots cost $800 to $900 each, on a $10 down, $10 per month basis. Many of them had to be filled. The residents often put up temporary packing-crate dwellings because they were unable to qualify for loans, but they gradually turned these into homes by dint of weekly purchases of lumber and supplies as the pay checks came in. A mass exodus of these first settlers took place at the end of the Second World War, and residents continued to leave in subsequent years as employment opportunities in the Richmond shipyards declined. Total population has remained the same, however, due to immigration of other Negroes either from the South or from other parts of the San Francisco Bay area. But another factor is contributing to the decline of the area— the effectuation of a county master plan calling for heavy industrial zoning, which froze property values and discouraged improvement.

Long designated a blighted area by the county, this community is isolated from the Negro community at large. It is cut off physically by wide bands of heavy industry and skirted by double sets of railroad tracks. The crossings are so likely to be blocked by freight cars that residents of the area have a special dread of fire. They are dependent on surrounding communities for protective services since theirs is an unincorporated area with no city government, so they listen first for the train whistle and then for the siren of the fire engine. They have seen houses burn while the equipment waits across the track. Over the years North Richmond has developed a reputation for vice, crime, and delinquency, but it is aggravated no doubt by the participation of miscreants from neighboring communities. In their nightly roving in quest of excitement, such visitors could usually count on this area for activity. Feelings of isolation must certainly be fostered by the paucity of public transportation available. The buses take a time-consuming, circuitous route to meet their sparse schedules, and commuters must allow extra hours to reach their destination in other parts of the San Francisco Bay area. Thanks to pressure from community action groups, more service has been provided for the school children, but the off-shift worker or the person who must travel by night is at a severe disadvantage.

This separation has brought about a psychological alienation that contributes to feelings of rejection and inferiority. North Richmond is typical neither of the urban nor the rural slum, though some of its characteristics are to be found in other ghettoes throughout the country. They must be taken into account in order to understand fully the problems of the young men served by the Job Upgrading Program at Neighborhood House and other slum-dwellers for whom special remedial measures are needed.

In 1964, the Household Enumeration Survey covered the 1,580 household units in this area with 1,472 or 93 percent, of the families responding. The data reported are based on the first 1,000 households, occupied by 3,846 persons. Negroes represent 95 percent of the population, the age distribution of which indicates that the median is sixteen years and that almost one out of every five males is in the forty-five-or-older bracket.[25] Unemployment among males eighteen years of age and over is 40 percent, with a rate of 85 percent estimated on the basis of the 1960 census of total number of youth in the community and requesting job assistance from Neighborhood House, the social agency where our research is centered. The answers given to the question, "Are you employed?" are as shown in Table 12.

The data on annual income for the North Richmond tract list

---

[25] Joseph F. Whiting, *The Multipurpose Home Visitor Program* (Contra Costa County: March, 1964), pp. 22 and 24.

TABLE 12

EMPLOYMENT STATUS OF RESIDENTS OF NORTH RICHMOND[a]

	Male		Female[b]	
	Number	Percent	Number	Percent
Employed				
Yes	516	60	252	25
No	337	40	754	74
No answer			5	1
Total	853	100	1011	100

SOURCE: Joseph F. Whiting, *The Multipurpose House Visitor Program* (Contra Costa County, March, 1964), p. 24.

[a] 18 years and older, N = 1864.

[b] Although there may be some question as to how many of these women were available for employment, it is interesting to note that 46 percent of this group indicated a desire for help in finding jobs.

39 percent of the families as receiving under 4,000, 53 percent in the $4,000 to $7,999 group, and 8 percent in the $15,000-and-above bracket. This places the average at about $4,555, but the figure is not very meaningful. Welfare payments and such income as veterans benefits, aid to the families of dependent children, and Social Security could account for up to $3,900 annually. Social workers familiar with the area agree that the $4,555 figure masks the true plight of the Negroes living in the North Richmond ghetto because the Census Tract includes a relatively well-to-do section where the residents are on an entirely different socioeconomic level. The estimate is that close to half of the residents of the area under study are on some kind of public relief and that actual wage and salary income is probably under $3,000.

Similarly, the reported average of 10.2 years of school completed fails to portray the true facts. Consistent with the data provided earlier in this chapter on the education of Negroes, scrutiny of the 28 percent who attained a high school diploma points up the fact that this group has not acquired sufficient preparation to compete successfully with white high school graduates. Reading and arithmetic skills are deficient, vocational courses in auto body shop and woodworking have failed to provide adequate training. In fact, the situation of second generation unemployment, aggravated by absence of any success model, has alienated the young people in this region from the world of work to the point that they require, in addition to remedial schooling and specialized training, attitudinal readjustments and the development of acceptable job habits before they can qualify for even the minimal level occupations.

Development of the Job Upgrading Project

In 1959, with the help of a $38,000 grant from the Rosenberg Foundation and the Lucie Stern Fund of San Francisco, Neighborhood House, a community center, which had been established in 1950 by the American Friends Service Committee, originally as a delinquency control center, set up a project for the out-of-school, out-of-work boys residing in North Richmond. The aim was to organize a program of positive orientation toward work, of guidance and training, and of supervised job experience that would help them qualify for stable and satisfactory employment "with possibilities for growth and development in responsibility and citizenship." [26]

Cooperating actively in this endeavor were the California State Employment Service, the California Youth Authority, and the Richmond School Department. The original grants from the Rosenberg and Stern funds were supplemented by help from the Ford and the Crown-Zellerbach Foundations.

Within recent years, the Job Upgrading Project has received substantial assistance from the Office of Manpower, Automation, and Training, "to provide for selection, testing, vocational and supportive counseling, remedial education, institutional and on-the-job training, and employment placement of unemployed persons sixteen years and older living in North Richmond." [27] The present two-year contract provides $350,000 for this purpose and makes possible some services to girls and women. Its original dimensions have also been extended by activities under the Office of Economic Opportunity, some Job Upgraders having participated in the Neighborhood Youth Corps. In addition, as part of its contractual obligation to prepare unemployed or underemployed clients for the competitive labor market, Neighborhood House conducted "Project Growth," an experiment in the use of domestic labor in agricultural work.

The five steps in the program to get young men oriented toward work and on a job were as follows:

Steps and Upgrading Experiences	*Comments*
1. Motivation	
A. Group	
1. Neighborhood House Youth Activities Program, Richmond Continuation School	Run by Richmond Public School Department

---

[26] North Richmond Neighborhood House Job Upgrading Project, "First Quarterly Report" (June 30, 1960).

[27] U.S. Department of Labor, Office of Manpower, Automation and Training, Contract No. 82-04-22.

Steps and Upgrading Experiences	*Comments*
B. Individual 1. Determination of personal needs for job achievement and current employability	Starting with the intake interview, all pertinent information on each Upgrader is kept on file

2. Socialization and Work Personality Development
  A. Personal problems
    1. Crisis situations
    2. Family problems
    3. Referral assistance
    4. Resumption of schooling
	These matters are handled through counseling and guidance individually and in group sessions

B. Vocational problems
    1. Work permits
    2. Social Security registration
    3. Counseling and vocational planning
    4. Job information
	With a State Employment Service employee working right at Neighborhood House, Job Upgraders could obtain forms, permits, and the like without delay. The close physical proximity between the employment agency and the Neighborhood House staff enhanced communication to the benefit of all persons concerned

C. Improving basic communication skills
    1. Reading and writing
    2. Speaking for answering "Help Wanted" advertisements
    3. Handling telephone calls and interviews
	Remedial classes at various levels are taught at Neighborhood House

D. Revising attitudes and developing personality
    1. Racial identity and hostilities
    2. Social problems
    3. Manners and dress
    4. Work attitudes
	Unstructured discussions, "bull sessions," and role-playing are some of the methods used

3. Developing work habits
  A. Experiencing actual job requirements
    1. Punctuality
    2. Lasting eight hours
    3. Taking and following orders
    4. Working alongside peers
	Wherever job slots could be found, the young men were given the opportunity to develop these habits. Some went through Supreme Services, others were assigned through the neighborhood Youth Corps or work-study programs

B. Experiencing self-reliance
    1. Responsibility
    2. Initiative
	At this stage, counselor encouraged a more independent job hunt

C. Experiencing the regular job 1. Generalizing previous lessons	The counselor's supportive role continued here because of the young men's need for sustained encouragement

Steps and Upgrading Experiences	Comments

4. Training for employment and placement
  A. Development of potentialities
    1. Formal training programs
    2. Apprenticeships
  B. Job placement
  C. Follow-up
	Examples of this kind of training are evening school programs, on-the-job arrangements under MDTA, and union-approved pprenticeships. The latter category has been the least well represented, but local unions are making some effort to improve the situation

5. Employment and career development
  A. Applying upgrading philosophy
    1. Personal advancement
      a. Taking advantage of on-the-job training
      b. Seeking promotions
    2. Social concern
      a. Adopting other Upgraders and "little brothers"
	As under 3.C., the staff continues its interest in each Job Upgrader into the "post-graduate" stage

An operational description of the Job Upgrading Program shows the personal side of the endeavor.

The Job Upgrading Program is centered around group and individual counseling. As young men register, they are assigned to a group with which they meet once or twice a week. The groups spend much of their time studying problems associated with their status, practicing employment interviews, filling out sample applications, and using audiovisual aids in conducting group discussions of therapeutic value which allow expression of feelings—often deep-seated feelings of hostility, bitterness, and despair.

Because we wish to serve a cross section of the out-of-school, unemployed youth and not to limit ourselves to those who are the most highly motivated, we recruit the boys in their homes, on the streets, in the pool halls, and other places. If a boy is depressed and thus does not have the emotional energy to meet with the group at 8:30 a.m., a staff member goes to his home, awakens him, and brings him to the meeting.

Slowly, in minor but significant ways, a structure is established for the boy. This is necessary if these young men are to meet the demands of the employers. Few of them have had to meet any type of schedule since leaving school. At home they eat when they please, rather than with the family. Because there is no need to get up in the morning, there is no need to go to bed at a reasonable hour.

Because these boys have been failures at school, in their own homes, and in the community, it is necessary to give them minor assignments or goals at which they can succeed. Among these are filling out applications or blanks and obtaining social security cards, but even with a simple task like this some of the boys have had to be accompanied to the employment office because we realize they might panic at the window. For many of the boys,

this is the start of self confidence and the first task in which they have succeeded in years.[28]

The scope and depth of socialization at the preemployment stages
is made poignantly clear in this excerpt from the November, 1963,
Monthly Report.

In the counseling area around personal problems we are seeing the same
pattern as can be expected each year at this time. "Christmas is coming and
the goose is getting fat." All youth will have an increasingly difficult time
finding holiday employment. The competition is too keen. An old saying
around the Center and the J.U.P. is, "Too bad; some old lady will lose her
purse, some man with too much Christmas spirit will lose his billfold, and
some family their gifts from the back of their car. After all, you know, a
fellow has to have Christmas one way or another. It's the American way of
life." [29]

The original group consisted of thirteen young men ranging in
age from seventeen to twenty-two. All but three of them had been
known to the Probation Department. Four of them were fathers. Out
of the eight who had attended the local continuation school, three
had graduated. The five others were dropouts. Only two of the entire
group had accumulated as much as one year's work experience. That
the characteristics of subsequent enrollees remained fairly consistent
can be seen from examination of interim reports. By January, 1961,
24 young men had been enrolled in the Job Upgrading Program.
Of these, five had finished high school; two had reached the ninth
grade; one, the eighth; the others had gone as far as the eleventh or
twelfth. Ranging in age from sixteen to twenty-three, only seven
had had as much as six months' work experience; nine of the others
had never held a job. Only a small portion of their number was bondable. At least 16 of the group were known to the Probation Department. The number of fathers among them had increased to nine.[30]

All of the enrollees were so far removed from the realities of work
life that the early program levels of the project, those described in
the foregoing outline as (1) motivation and (2) socialization and work
personality, concentrated on elementary but basic fundamentals. Much
of the staff members' time, for example, was spent in going to the
boys' homes in the morning to get them out of bed. The discipline
of a regular schedule was foreign to their habitual ways; they were
used to sleeping until noon, "because it helped pass the time." Even
though the morning sessions at Neighborhood House opened with

[28] Neighborhood House, *My Job Likes Me.*
[29] North Richmond Neighborhood House Job Upgrading Project, Monthly
Report (Nov., 1963), p. 1.
[30] Neighborhood House, Job Upgrading Progress Report No. 2 (Jan. 1, 1961)

the serving of hot coffee and doughnuts, the daily reports indicate that listlessness and lethargy were not easily dispelled. During the two-hour "bull sessions," which centered around the problems of where and how to go about getting a job, there was considerable discussion of the factors that contribute to or impede success. How a person should look and act when he applies for work, proper job attitudes, realistic aspirations, acceptance of responsibility, and good work habits—these were the steps preliminary to those of group instruction and individual tutoring.

Vocabulary building, simple arithmetic, and practice in filling out application forms made up the major portion of the educational level of the program. As an impetus to the boys to use the resources of the California State Employment Service, registration at that office was made a requirement for membership in the Job Upgraders. This in itself was a major hurdle, for one must recognize the extent to which the North Richmond residents had been alienated from the rest of the community. Many of these boys were not used to "crossing the line" into the city proper, especially for such businesslike purposes; they approached the State Employment Service with fear and perhaps some hostility, which was their defense mechanism against possible discrimination. As their self-confidence developed, however, most of the Job Upgraders not only registered every month at the State Employment Office but even took the general aptitude tests. Communication with that agency became considerably easier and closer cooperation was established in September, 1962, when the State Employment Service assigned one of its workers to Neighborhood House on a part-time basis. This resulted in a greatly improved interchange of information, about job opportunities in one direction and the very special problems of applicants in the other.

Liaison with the State Employment Service

Because of his intimate association with all facets of the Job Upgrading Program, the State Department of Employment representative often found himself caught between the professional demands of the agency he represented and the exigencies of the particular clientele he was trying to serve. This conflict of roles is reflected in one of his monthly reports.

In this atmosphere of social work, surrounded by social workers, it is probable that a department representative will assimilate some social work thinking. How much he assimilates depends on how social work-minded he is. The department representative often finds himself sounding like a social worker. This happened recently. A young man who was suspected of being a sneak thief was at the step of Stage 3, where he should be moved into Su-

preme Services. After all, he is only *suspected* of theft. We have those in the
program whom we know have been *involved* in crimes. This is thinking more
like a social worker than a department counselor. A department counselor
would have to say that this young man is not ready until he shows that he
can be trusted. The department representative must bend toward the boys
in this situation. He must have faith in the boys even when they do things
to destroy that faith. After all, we are working with a group of young men,
75 percent of whom are known to the Probation Department. We also will
receive far more confidential information. The less we know about a person,
the more lenient we will naturally be in our decision; the more we know of
his background, the less lenient we will be. To explain this, if we don't
know a person has a record, we would refer him to a bondable job. The
more we know of his background, the less likely we are to refer him when
we find out about any facts in his past which are detrimental. If he looks
good, we refer him unless we have information which tells us differently, and
certainly in this situation, we have more information all the time.[31]

An item in a subsequent report underscores the need for flexibility
and understanding on the part of the employment worker.

Something which is always prevalent . . . is the crisis need. All the young
men have real need for work, but there seem to be more crisis needs in this
area. Certainly it is because of the environment. A young man is given
a traffic fine to pay off. He does not have anyone to turn to for money if
his father is unemployed or if his family is receiving welfare. He has only
his counselor or his probation officer to turn to. Many times the young men
have approached the department representative for loans. In only rare cases
will he lend anything. He will usually refer them to a prevocational counselor with the added statement that jobs are the prime concern of the counselor.
These crisis needs bring an added pressure to placement. At this time there
are two young men who need jobs outside the community or they will be in
trouble. One young man needs money for bare subsistence, another for rent,
still another to pay traffic fines, and at least three must find work or face loss
of probation. These crisis situations often tax the counselors' ability to be
objective and force them into being quite imaginative in their approach.
When the counselors have two or three crisis cases at one time and possibly one job, it becomes a very difficult situation. It is difficult to decide
who will be referred and as difficult explaining to the others why they were
not referred.[32]

The case of G. S. has been selected as typifying the many ways
the employment worker gets involved in dealing with seriously vocationally handicapped youth. This young man was eighteen, an eleventh grade dropout of immature and youthful appearance. By dressing

---

[31] Report of California State Employment Service, "Neighborhood House
Project" (Nov., 1963), p. 2.
[32] Report of California State Employment Service, "Neighborhood House Project" (Jan., 1964), p. 3.

and acting even younger, he resembled a fifteen- or sixteen-year-old and reduced his chances of referral to jobs. The most obvious physical deterrent to his getting placed was his hair, which he allowed to grow long and bushy; it was apparent that he had not had it cut in several months. Both his prevocational counselor and the employment worker had discussed this matter with him frequently. After his interest in work had been somewhat whetted by a few casual jobs, he was told that no permanent placement would be forthcoming until he had his hair cut. He balked at this suggestion and ceased coming in to the employment office. Although accepted as a member of the work team, he showed no inclination to change for some time. He made no effort to communicate with the employment office.

Then gradually a change began to occur. His hair was cut; it was still rather long, but neat. He dressed more carefully; the clothing he chose was less flamboyant. To complete his high school education, G. S. had enrolled in evening classes. These promising developments, along with satisfactory performance on the work team, were reported by the prevocational counselor to the State Employment Service representative, who then asked G. S. to come in for referral to a full-time permanent job as a doughnut packager.

When G. S. reported, there were no case aides or prevocational counselors available to take him out to the job. At these times, the department counselor must be very flexible in his routine. He must not be tied down to a desk or a schedule or routine. He must be able to individualize his efforts and make the placement of one man of prime importance. If he has to dress, drive, help the man in any way, then this is what he must do. G. S. was very nicely dressed with white shirt, tie, suit, but his clothes were a little disheveled. The department counselor helped him straighten his clothes. Drove him to the job. He got the job. He had no carfare to get home, so carfare was given to him. (Only in an emergency like this will the department counselor lend money which he is reimbursed by Neighborhood House.)[33]

Work Experience

Well aware of the limitations of employment prospects for the young and inexperienced, especially those who are poorly equipped educationally, socially, and emotionally to compete for jobs, and who are further handicapped because of color, police records, and the like, Neighborhood House faced the urgent need for a period of supervised work to serve as a bridge between the job preparation phase and entry into open competition for jobs. The fact was recognized that

---

[33] Report of California State Employment Service, Neighborhood House Project (Feb., 1964), p. 4.

even if openings were found in industry, premature placement of the Job Upgraders could result in unsatisfactory results such as increased reluctance on the part of the business community to hire any young Negro workers and an undermining for the individuals concerned of the self-confidence so painstakingly built.

Two separate programs were set up to help development of work attitudes and habits: (1) the work team and (2) Supreme Services. The work team was a project designed both to provide a resource for training and experience and to involve some parts of the North Richmond community in a self-betterment plan through property improvement and education. Such jobs as yard cleaning, outside painting, and furniture moving are sought, various contributions having made these and other services possible. The Richmond Automobile Dealers' Association provided a truck, the Richmond Police Department supplied numerous work tools plus a trailer for hauling trash, and the local sanitation company came forward with permission to use local dump facilities without charge. The team consists of two to five men and a work trainer. They work ten hours a week and receive a grant of from 75 cents to $1.25 per hour, depending on their previous experience and the difficulty of the job.

Upgraders assigned to the team had done practically no work and had been identified as needing a group situation to develop interpersonal relations in the setting of a job. It was felt that some of the problems inherent in orientation to work could be solved in this environment, which was structured by the team supervisor rather than by an employer. To this extent, this represented a sheltered situation where specific matters of authority, issuance of orders, and standards for satisfactory job completion were the responsibility of the supervisor. Recognizing that most Upgraders have no conception of the world of work, this program provided a gradual introduction to its basic requirements.

A comment by the work supervisor, who was a volunteer, indicated the intricacy of the factors involved in developing acceptance attitudes on the part of these young men.

Working in one's own community in front of your peer group presents real problems, where this type of work has little prestige value. Appropriate incentives are needed for the Upgrader. He is particularly vulnerable to the criticism and ridicule of unemployed, unmotivated friends who see him working. The work experience background is such that Upgraders at this stage have very ambivalent feelings about work. The friends may say, "Only fools work," but the Upgrader has to weigh the rewards he gets for working against this criticism. It is the job of the work team supervisor to develop incentives and rationalizations with the prestige rewards within the work situation. We must help the Upgrader sustain and gradually overcome the ridicule of his peers. This he will do as he develops positive attitudes toward work and the work world values.[34]

The second work experience program at Neighborhood House has provided an opportunity for some of the men to apply their skill, develop work habits, and build their competence in an atmosphere more closely akin to that on a job in private industry but still somewhat structured by the instructor-supervisor. This program cannot be regarded as an institutional phase of the Job Upgraders, for not all of the members are accepted into it. In order to qualify, the men must demonstrate that they have learned the lessons of the earlier phases—that they come to work on time, wear clean clothes, and have their hair cut. The intent is that this serve as a sort of halfway house employment experience, with conditions simulating the real situation. To provide such an opportunity, Neighborhood House went into business for itself in 1962. Set up as a corporation, Supreme Services has supplied janitorial and building maintenance help of all kinds to property owners. Emphasized as its main functions are the following: interior cleaning of office buildings, schools, warehouses, theaters, banks, department stores, factories, studios, and private homes. Among its specialties are the cleaning and waxing of floors, washing of walls and doors, cleaning of windows, dusting and polishing of desks, furniture and fixtures, vacuum cleaning of rugs and wall-to-wall carpeting. Long- or short-term contracts have been made with institutions, business firms, and home owners. Wage scale arrangements, made with the Building Employees Service Union, call for a starting rate of $1.50 per hour up to a maximum of $2.50 per hour after six months of satisfactory performance.

Money from their Rosenberg Foundation and Lucie Stern Fund grants was allocated by Neighborhood House for the purchase of a work bus, equipment, and supplies. Conducted as an independent venture, Supreme Services has been run by a business manager who seeks out prospective customers, makes estimates on jobs, keeps books, and pays the men. He also supervises their 54 hours of preliminary training and acts as foreman. From the business point of view, Supreme Services has shown considerable growth. Close to paying its own way, except for the manager's salary, it provides not only training but wages to many Upgraders, and it has made contributions of cash and service to Neighborhood House. A report for the year ending October, 1965, showed a total of $26,000 in gross business, with employment for 24 men. A subsidiary business operation, called Clean

---

[34] David Eichorn, "A Project for Work Experience through Community Service," North Richmond Neighborhood House Job Upgrading Project, Monthly Report (March, 1964).

and Green with short-term jobs like lawn cutting, hedge clipping, and watering was developed one summer and employed Upgraders at about $2.30 per hour under work conditions similar to those established by Supreme Services. With a number of young men ready for placement but without prospects, the manager welcomed these openings for the various benefits to this group, like wages, extra work experience, and a continued exposure to the outside community, which would reinforce and provide added self-confidence. It should be noted that Supreme Services is not intended to limit the trainees to janitorial work; its primary purpose is to provide a realistic experience to strengthen and bolster the nascent social attitudes developed in earlier phases of the Job Upgrading Program. As a way station on the road to employability, its accomplishments cannot be assessed in monetary terms.

Job Upgraders and the Neighborhood Youth Corps

Inasmuch as the Neighborhood Youth Corps has as its objective that of developing the attitudes and behavior required for regular employment, this nationwide program has meshed with the Job Upgraders. Ideally, the work experience was expected to serve as a bridge, to enable young people of sixteen to twenty-one to return to school, undertake skill training, or hold regular jobs. The in-school program provides up to 15 hours of work per week at $1.25 per hour; part-time students can work up to 20 hours. Operated by state and local government and private nonprofit agencies under contract with the Office of Economic Opportunity, the projects put these young people into various kinds of jobs where they help meet unfulfilled public needs without displacing regular employees. One city government is cited as having found aide positions for landscaping, library, clerical, teaching, street-beautifying, street repair, conservation, cafeteria, recreation, warehouse, and janitorial work, to mention only a few.[35]

In all, 1,446 projects that provided 513,000 jobs were approved during 1965. It is anticipated that the total from fiscal 1966 appropriations will be about 356,000. Young people still in school will account for 100,000; those who have left school will claim 60,000. During the summer, 1966, special projects will involve an additional 165,000 students on vacation.[36] The primary criterion for eligibility is poverty; enrollees must come from families whose income does not exceed certain prescribed limits. This varies somewhat according to the age and sex of family members, $1,580 for one person under age 65 to

---

[35] U.S. Department of Labor, *Manpower Report of the President* (1966), p. 102.
[36] *Ibid.*

$5,090 for a family of seven or more in a nonfarm location.[37] Because resources adequate to permit enrollment of all needy youth exceed present budgets, the Neighborhood Youth Corps has given first preference to those least likely to succeed without a saturation of services. Consequently, priority factors are poor academic achievement, unfavorable attitudes toward work, physical and mental handicaps, and delinquency or criminal records.

By these standards, the Job Upgraders as a group were eminently qualified for enrollment; as individuals they could claim varying degrees and combinations of disadvantages. The first contract called for a 13-week program for the summer, 1965, and had 24 openings. This was followed by another, initially involving 29 persons but ultimately dropping to 15. Indifferent performance and absenteeism were given as the main causes for attrition.[38] The supervisor observed that the best record was achieved by enrollees who were assigned to posts away from Neighborhood House and, in fact, outside its immediate environs. This may be explained in part by the fact that most of the local jobs came under the heading of "beautification and street repair," about which the common complaint was, "I don't want the girls to see me sweeping nobody's streets." This criticism is more valid and basic than may appear at first glance. Low-level work assignments carry a stigma and undermine the value of a program of this kind. If the objective is to build self-confidence through a work experience, then it must be meaningful, and purposeful job assignments are essential. This is no easy task, especially since such activities would require a great deal of supervision on the part of professionals, already in short supply in almost every field. Nonetheless, self-confidence, incentive, and motivation to perform are not likely to be created by exposure to only the menial housekeeping jobs of society.

"Project Growth"

During the summer of 1965, Neighborhood House was involved in a special experimental and demonstration project in which 60 unemployed young men of low educational level and motivation were taken into the strawberry-growing areas to harvest the crop. The use of domestic labor in agricultural work has been a matter of particular public concern because of restrictions on the importation of Mexican "braceros."

Along with Job Upgraders and referrals from the California State

---

[37] U.S. Department of Labor, Manpower Report of the President (1966), p. 53 footnote.

[38] Job Upgrading Project, *Monthly Report to Office of Manpower*, Automation and Training, Division of Special Programs (Dec., 1965, Jan., 1966), p. 6.

Employment Service, recruits came through local schools, police and probation departments, county welfare offices, ministers, boys' clubs, and the like. Ultimately, two groups were formed, with divergent characteristics. The first was described as follows: "Essentially school dropouts, low literacy, disorganized, rebellious acting-out personalities. Almost all had juvenile delinquency records, most were on probation or parole." [39] The second group had less serious juvenile records; many were still in school but doing poorly—likely to drop out. Also included were some volunteers who had heard about the project.

In preparation for the activity, Neighborhood House counselors and representatives of the U.S. Department of Labor and of the California State Department of Employment made unannounced inspection visits to various labor camps in the Salinas Valley. The detailed examinations culminated in the report that, "compared to a State of California Prison Camp (Road Building or Forest Conservation), all the labor camps were sub-standard. And it was clear that much inspection by Federal and State officials would be needed to keep the camp at even a sub-standard keel." [40]

A four-week preorientation program had been provided in the contract, but the staff lacked sufficient lead time to prepare one. Moreover, the picking season was too close at hand to allow for many of the necessary preliminaries. Actually, only one week was devoted to indoctrination, and even during it recruitment continued. As a consequence, some men had only a day or two of the training. The content consisted primarily of films and of discussion about the work and pay. In addition to physical examinations and chest x-rays, there were physical training sessions; each group went on an all-day hike and picnic to get a taste of outdoor life. There was no individual testing and counseling, but the group meetings did help clarify the realities to be faced in the month ahead. The project staff served in a supportive capacity throughout, even to the extent of personally administering rubdowns to ease sore muscles and tired backs. They had been hired for a 24-hour-a-day, seven-days-a-week assignment.

The following account of camp life indicates some of the adjustments that the group had to make.

Camp life was characterized by: living in a crowded barrack; rising at 4:30 a.m.; walking 150 feet to the out-of-door toilet building; standing in line in the cold, moist air waiting for breakfast which was often late and served to only one line for the more than 350 youth in camp; riding to work on a "bus" made especially for hauling braceros (a cracker box on a long chassis truck, small windows near the top which allowed some light to come

---

[39] Neighborhood House, "Project Growth," Final Report (Sept. 29, 1965), p. 3.
[40] Ibid., p. 4.

in but no outward vision except of a fog-laden sky) which was dirty, crowded, and cold; working at stoop labor for eight hours, which started at 7 a.m. with dew-covered berry plants and wet soil and ended at 3:30 p.m. with a bright sun and often high wind and involved standing in line or waiting in the bus for as much as half hour for the checking-out process (seeing that the tally of crates picked during the day checked with the picker's records); and eating a field lunch of hot stew (cooled quickly by the wind), vegetables, beans, bread, milk, and fruit while squatting or sitting in the nearest available space. These were truly different conditions than our youth were accustomed to, particularly the early rising and the discipline of eight hours of hard work (about ten and one-half hours away from camp).[41]

There was a considerable amount of absenteeism because of illness, probably caused by diet and field conditions but attributable also to "low spirits due to the camp and field environment." Eighteen enrollees worked a full eight weeks; three worked seven weeks. Based on the record of these 21 men, the highest individual gross earnings were $427, the lowest, $190, and the average, $300. Evidently there was some question about the validity of what had been offered as a guaranteed $1.40 per hour minimum, for under poor picking conditions, the men could not earn more than one dollar. At some locations, the men encountered less than cordial treatment because they were in the cross fire of a battle between growers who favored braceros and the government officials who sought more utilization of domestic workers. A poor performance on the part of the latter would have had implications much greater than the picking of one strawberry crop.

The final phase of "Project Growth" was directed to post-job orientation, with heavy emphasis on remedial education and prevocational training. Even the group made up predominantly of students was included, for many of them were doing poorly. The final report shows that most of the out-of-school group were placed in employment or training programs; as for the others, one went into an on-the-job training position, and the rest returned to school—two of them to junior college. Perhaps the most telling commentary on "Project Growth" appears in the following, a typed copy of a letter sent by the in-school group to Secretary of Labor W. Willard Wirtz on September 10, 1965.

Dear Sir:

Knowing that education and training are vital to our growth and to the future of our country. From a small nucleus we have grown into a tightly-knitted organization determined to be successful in the project. Through the mail we are attemping to bring you a few of the basic background facts concerning the overall program and a small look at the way in which we

---

[41] *Ibid.,* pp. 5–6.

see this project. We see this as a chance for youths to earn money and to break out of an endless cycle of poverty, defeat, and despair and to find a new hope, dignity, and may our fair share of the good things in life. For the most of us this is our first working experience in a job which will give us our working record. Picking berries is as hard as we heard it would be. For as you well know it is stoop labor.

We found out that once you start a job to prove we are prepared for work, and could stick it out. We found out that by having a job we would not hang out on a street corner with nothing to do. We found that by having a job we have a little in our pockets and can use it to good advantage.

On our first day at arriving in Castroville we receive a lot of bad reports about this job. Some were good and some were bad but we came to make up our own minds about this project. Some of the things we had to put up with were the living quaters was not what most of the boys had expected and the food wasn't like anything in the world like most of the boys were use to. Those who ate the food got sick and the ones who didn't got sick. The showers were away from the living quaters and sometimes weren't very clean. Our first four weeks we lived to far from the berries fields. It was a good hour an fifteen minutes ride. As a result we had to get up at 4:30 a.m. The lunches in the fields were to grease and not prepare to fit the youth of America. Our relationship with other boys from other parts as the United States was wonderful and we made lots of new friends. As a result we learned a good deal about human relationship with other boys. We also learn more about our country agricultural prombles. At first were sure that the growers of Salinas did not want us there and did a lot of things to discourage us. They change our sixty-four hour of guarantee of a $1.40 an hour to 48 hours. We feel that there were too many deductions made for the type of food were getting in our first four weeks.

While living in camp we feel we should have better transportation to town. On our fifth week we move to Salinas Camp 3A where the food was marvelous and the camp was cleaner, the cooks were nice, the camp manager was nicer. We could get up later to go to work. We got up at 6:15 a.m. The weather was warmer and most of us look forward to going to work and most of us look forward to improving on our picking. Things went along smoothly we got to know our forman better, our checkers, the ranch boss, and the supervisors. We met other people from other communities and were invited by them on pinics, youth dances, and also house parties.

From this program we feel that we have become more responsible young men and we know what hard work is. If we get a better job we would stay with a lot longer.

This experience taught us to be dependable upon themselves. It also gave us a sense of responsibility. After those eight hard weeks we finally realized that this was a very worthwhile program. It also showed that our community can accomplish what it sets out for.

Yours Sincerely

Neighborhood House
A.G.W.E.P. Group
Richmond, California

Profile of an Upgrader

The average age of the Upgrader is eighteen. Usually a dropout from school, he has seen no relationship between education and the world of work. If he has stayed in school long enough to receive a diploma, this document is meaningless, since he has learned little more than those who withdrew early. At no point has there been evidence of participation in activities or school spirit. His reading, writing, spelling, and arithmetic skills are far below grade level; he finds it difficult to read and fill out the simple forms applying for participation in the Upgrading Program. Although functionally illiterate, he does not admit these handicaps, but has learned instead to keep them quite well hidden.

He is rarely affiliated with any organization—in particular, no church—although his parents are likely to attend. He is most certain to have been investigated, held, or sentenced by one of the law enforcement agencies in the community. His chances of being listed in the files of the Probation Department are three to one; that his case is active calls for odds of two to one. One in every three Upgraders is a father, probably unmarried or officially listed as absent.

The trait considered most characteristic is his impatience with time. Prone to early frustration and discouragement, he requires easily obtained successes and short steps with immediate rewards in order to persevere. Although likely to express the desire to get work, he seems to want the job on his own terms, with no conception of the realities of the marketplace in terms of dearth of openings for the inexperienced, child labor laws, and employers' attitudes and expectations.

That the typical Upgrader is not emotionally or vocationally ready even for such preliminary training as may be offered in an environment outside of Neighborhood House' sphere is shown in the experience with a course for groundsman-gardener given at a local junior college under the Manpower Development and Training Act. Of the ten referrals from Job Upgrading, six finished the eight-week class, but only one was recommended as qualified. Lack of attendance accounted for the dropping of four of the boys. One had found himself work in a sugar refinery; one, a probationer, was taken into custody for hit-and-run driving. Of the third, it was said that he lacked the proper clothes and sophistication required to cope with a community college environment. The fourth boy had shown great interest, but he did not have the ability to learn and, moreover, cut classes. A week after he was dropped from the program, he was involved in an armed robbery and arrested. Only one of the graduates from the course received a certificate of completion, and none has found employment as a gardener.

CASE HISTORIES

Several case histories selected from the Neighborhood House files may serve as a guide to understanding the dynamics of the vocational rehabilitation of the long-time deprived and alienated.

James Wilson, born August 31, 1944, is the oldest of five children living with his mother and stepfather. There is a very close family relationship, especially between the mother and children. The house is inadequate in space for a family of this size and the furnishings poor. Known to the Welfare Department in recent years, the family is not receiving aid at present. The oldest sister, who is unmarried, has a child, but there is a marked feeling of stability, understanding, and discipline from the parents.

A graduate of Richmond Union High School after attending summer sessions to make up grade credits in 1962, Jim is a well-built youth, just over six feet tall and weighing about 180 pounds. He is not a leader but is liked and highly respected by his peers.

During the spring of 1963, following his first and only working experience—a laborer's job that lasted about three weeks and terminated with the employer's illness—Jim began to present serious behavior problems. He stayed out late at night, drank excessively, gambled, and got into fights. While living in Oroville, California, where he had been sent to stay with an aunt in the hope that a new environment would be beneficial, Jim was arrested for attempted robbery and assault with a deadly weapon. This charge was reduced to assault after a counselor from Neighborhood House had convinced the Probation Department that Jim's positive adjustment in the community could best be brought about by his participation in the Job Upgrading Program. After a four-month jail sentence, Jim was on probation for three years, but upon his return to Richmond, he entered the program.

His performance on such odd jobs as gardening, furniture moving, and general laborer indicated that he had good potential. He failed, however, to impress the three employers who interviewed him for full-time openings and became so discouraged that the counselor feared that he might revert to problem behavior. It was at this point that Jim was brought into the orientation phase of the program, during which he demonstrated positive growth and motivation. For example, he told the counselor that he had never before been aware of the importance of personal grooming. He discovered that when he was dressed neatly and clean shaven he had the confidence to discuss his prison record with prospective employers.

After three weeks, Jim was adjudged ready for Step 4 in the program (i.e., full-time employment) by his counselor, the representative of the State Employment Service, and other staff members. He was referred to a job doing stock work in a furniture company and was hired as a full-time permanent employee. The follow-up record shows that Jim is enjoying his work and that the employer is well satisfied. Jim has recently expressed an interest in continuing his schooling by taking evening courses in junior college.

Lon Graham seems older than his twenty-one years. Quiet and soft-spoken, he is conservative in his dress and always immaculate. He relates appropriately and readily to many types of people and gets along well with both co-workers and supervisors. His perceptiveness as to what is expected of him in a particular job situation is unusually high. Although lack of training and experience have contributed to his failure to find work, the primary problems besetting him while in the Job Upgrading Program were of a personal nature and devolved from his inability to stay out of trouble with the police.

Lon came well recommended to the Job Upgrading Program in March, 1961, his uncle having participated and done well in it. His parents, born in Oklahoma and Texas, had settled in this area in 1941, when Mr. Graham had come to work in the Richmond shipyards as a carpenter. Lon is the oldest of their ten children. In June, 1960, when Mr. Graham became ill, Lon dropped out of school in order to help support the family. A temporary job connected with the demolition of Army camps was all he could find, and an invitation to join the Job Upgraders found him receptive, especially since two of his close friends were members. His active participation in group meetings and regular attendance brought him early assignment to a supervised work station, where he developed considerable self-confidence.

During the late summer of 1961, Lon got into trouble with the police. Along with two other boys, he was arrested for statutory rape and sentenced to two months in prison. Members of the Job Upgrading staff visited him while there and continued to work with him after his release. Under a special arrangement, by which Neighborhood House paid the employer to train and supervise a trainee and pay him while on the job, Lon was placed as a washman in a commercial laundry. His job, supervising the washing and bleaching of the various batches, was heavy and dirty, but it was also semiskilled and one for which there is a steady demand.

Lon was making a fine adjustment in the laundry when he was

arrested again, this time for participating in the burglary of a junk-yard. An offense of this type usually incurs a charge of felony, but the Job Upgrading counselor sought the help of the Court and the Probation Department on the ground that permission to develop specific vocational skill would be more valuable in Lon's overall rehabilitation than would be a stiff jail sentence. The Court allowed a plea to a lesser charge, for which Lon served 45 days and was fined $100. His return to the trainee post at the laundry was of only three weeks' duration because of a ruling by the Laundry Workers' Union that this arrangement did not comply with their regulations.

Because of Lon's good performance on the laundry job, he was selected by the staff as the recipient for a tuition scholarship provided by a privately-owned electronics school. Even though his performance on the aptitude test for electronics assembly was far from impressive, his earnest desire to get ahead was considered a strong factor in his favor. During the training, which began with the preliminary two-month course in assembly and extended to 48 weeks when Lon was moved into the technician's curriculum, Neighborhood House gave him a weekly maintenance allowance of ten dollars.

In November, 1962, Lon was arrested for driving without a license. This being his fourth such offense, he faced a compulsory six months in jail. To keep Lon from forfeiting his scholarship, the Job Upgrading staff and school officials wrote to the judge for special consideration, which came in the form of a sentence that would not affect the school schedule: Lon spent the ten weekends from January to March, 1963 in jail and attended classes in between. That he continued the schooling with no small degree of reluctance could be attributed to his urgent desire and need for a secure job with a steady income. He desperately wanted to marry his girl friend, who had recently given birth to his twin sons; he still owed restitution for one of his fines.

Although he completed the course with a B minus average and obtained a license as third-class Electronics Technician, no jobs in that occupation were available. Several temporary placements as unskilled laborer were made, however, and one of them would have been permanent if he had had a driver's permit, but his had been revoked until December, 1963. The Job Upgrading staff and the State Department of Employment worker helped Lon organize his job hunt. With their assistance, he prepared a résumé, sent it out to various employers, and mailed follow-up letters. One of the jobs to which he was referred by the State Employment Office was as laborer with a local oil company. This seemed to provide opportunity for advancement and Lon was hired on November 15, 1963. Subsequent follow-up has revealed that he is a willing, capable worker, well liked by his foreman, and that if he perseveres in his intention to take an electronics course in the evening at the local junior college, his employers may reimburse him.

The question has been raised as to whether the schooling was wasted, since Lon's present job in no way involves electronics. Seen from the point of view of his long-range occupational career, the course had positive value: it provided discipline; it broadened his educational base; it built confidence and a favorable self-image in a young man who needed to know that he could, despite numerous failures, succeed in something. His having been given a job that could conceivably have been filled by a somewhat less qualified applicant might, at first glance, be construed as an instance of underemployment. But one of the overwhelming factors in his favor, both at the point of hiring and later, has been the evidence that he could profit from training and that he was willing to put forth effort toward advancement.

THE JOB UPGRADING PROGRAM IN WIDER PERSPECTIVE

These case studies illustrate the techniques used by Neighborhood House to help unmotivated, inexperienced, and handicapped persons achieve vocational adjustment. The problems they exemplify and the methods used are representative of those recorded in the files. The success which they indicate does not, it must be noted, extend to all Job Upgraders. Some former Job Upgraders are to be found behind prison bars; others cannot negotiate the grade between Supreme Services, the supervised work stage, and adequate performance on their own; and still others revert to old behavior patterns and require additional guidance. How Neighborhood House assesses its role is embodied in the following statement.

We believe that the Neighborhood House project has produced outstanding results, given our objective of serving all unemployed, out-of-school youth, and not just the most highly motivated. We have worked in depth, seeking for job stability and advancement, not just placement. We are influencing the neighborhood to see its responsibility for boys and young men who heretofore have seemed not to have a chance. We are also influencing local institutions, and we look forward to the day when a Job Upgrading Project will no longer be needed at Neighborhood House. We are sharing our experiences with other communities interested in providing services to their unemployed youth, and we are acting as good-will ambassadors for the role of the Labor Department.[42]

---

[42] North Richmond Neighborhood House Job Upgrading Project, "A Request for a Second and Third Year for a Work Experience and Training Program for Out-of-School Unemployed Youth" (June, 1964), p. 5.

Implicit in the philosophy being applied is acceptance of the norms of the larger society; there is recognition of the fact that "white, middle-class values" of a nice home, a good car, a steady income, and decent living standards are desirable in all sectors of society. Such goals are disparaged only verbally and when they appear unattainable. Glorifying some other way of life both smacks of a sort of condescension and admits defeat in the assimilative process and the battle for vertical mobility that have contributed to American democracy. Now that massive federal resources are being allocated to the creation of a more favorable socioeconomic climate, and some measure of enlightenment is improving opportunities, the burden of responsibility falls more and more on the people themselves. Such programs as Job Upgraders, which accept the individual where they find him, direct him to the myriad of services now available, and help him with the personal counsel he needs, show promise of helping the hard-core unemployed gain self-confidence and independence.

The program at Neighborhood House cannot be regarded as one of retraining under the definition set forth at the beginning of this study. An examination of it in depth, however, has been important because of its rehabilitation emphasis. This approach to employability through the rebuilding of human confidence and readjustment to the norms of our economic society is applicable not only to the Negro youth of North Richmond, but to children of Mexican-Americans, of Kentucky miners, and of Oklahoma meatpackers. The identification of a hierarchy of objectives and the development of appropriate program levels, where each weakness is recognized and each positive adjustment built on, would serve well the needs of all segments of our population who have poverty and deprivation as their heritage. The case materials at Neighborhood House illustrate the long road that must be traveled by many of our citizens before they can reach even the bottom rungs of the occupational ladder. That this is not a situation that can be cured by crash programs becomes very apparent when one reviews even the stories of success that are included here.

The Job Upgrading Program, even with assistance under the terms of the MDTA, is certainly limited in scope, but its implications are tremendous. It forms a bridge between good social philosophy and intelligent manpower retraining policy. With due regard and respect for cultural differences, it is free of maudlin sentiment about "subcultures," which are often nothing more than a defense mechanism against discrimination and "outcastness." It represents a happy wedding of the social work and the "strictly business" approaches, in both of which are implicit the fact that dignity and a feeling of worth are prized possessions of every human being at every socioeconomic level. By its close cooperation with the California State Employment Service and the U.S. Department of Labor, it has pointed up how the resources of the government can be used to ameliorate the lot of the deprived.

Examination in depth of the Neighborhood House records has provided insight into the problem of underprivileged members of our society. Scrutiny of case after case has shown that the key factor in alienation is the inability to get work and participate in the economic life of the community. This probe in depth has shown that alienation is not just a matter of skin color; the North Richmond Negroes are segregated even from other Negroes. Sensitivity to the important existence of communities within communities makes the researcher, the social worker, and the policy-maker alike appreciate that the concept of the Negro problem has been oversimplified.[43] There are many different Negro problems that must be identified and solved, at different levels and with different techniques.

The methods developed at Neighborhood House, for helping those whom poverty and disadvantage have separated almost totally from hope, are based on sound psychological principles and can be applied in helping others break free from the shackles of their unemployability. Unique only in its conception, the Job Upgrader Program is wide in execution possibilities wherever we wish to help an alienated minority group find a meaningful definition in American social life.

---

[43] Cf. Quarterly Bibliography on Cultural Differences, Compiled by California State Library (Sacramento, California: Oct., 1964), List No. 2.

[6

Retraining of the Underprivileged: The Job Corps and Programs for Welfare Recipients

Like the Job Upgraders, the Job Corps is remedial in its orientation and intended to meet the needs of young people who are handicapped in the competition for employment. Its scope and resources are of a different magnitude, however. Financed by the Office of Economic Opportunity with "War on Poverty" funds, the Job Corps has already been allocated some $489 million, while Job Upgraders, except for short-term contracts under the Manpower Development and Training Act and grants from benevolent organizations, must constantly seek support from interested citizens and the Community Chest in order to continue. For its operations for the fiscal year starting July, 1966, the Job Corps will receive $200 million.

In its first year of existence, the Job Corps developed 73 conservation centers, with 8,000 enrollees; eight urban centers for men, with 8,000 enrollees; six urban centers for women, with 1,500 enrollees. Totals of 30,000 are expected by the end of fiscal 1966 and 45,000 by the end of the following year. The Corps has been described as "a residential training program for youth out of school and out of work, whose lives have been so underprivileged that they have little chance of becoming productive citizens without a change of surroundings." [1] Two years have been designated as the maximum length of enrollment, the typical course being of shorter duration. Participation is completely voluntary; the enrollee may leave when he wishes. In addition to living expenses, each individual receives $30 per month.

---

[1] U.S. Department of Labor, *Manpower Report of the President* (1966), p. 104.

This may be increased by $10 to $20 by virtue of special achievements or assumption of a leadership role. Besides, terminal allowances of $50 are provided for every month spent in the Corps. If the enrollee opts to allocate up to $25 per month of this accumulated total to a qualified dependent, the Job Corps will match the allotment. There is also an issue of clothing, necessary because many of the recruits arrived at camp poorly and inappropriately clad—"with nothing but the clothes on their backs." Prominent among the items provided is a smartly tailored jacket, the pocket of which is adorned by a Job Corps insignia.

Applicants must be between the ages of sixteen and twenty-one; they must come from families where poverty and unsatisfactory conditions compound the desirability of a change; they must be deficient in education and motivation; they must be jobless. At present, 5 percent are high school graduates with reading levels of seventh grade or less. An estimated one-third are Negro. Due in large part to a vigorous publicity campaign, the total number of applicants waiting to join the Job Corps is officially estimated at around 250,000. Present facilities cannot accommodate nearly this number, but an active recruitment policy is pursued. Evidently pressure on admission serves as leverage for continued support of the program in the halls of Congress.

Philosophically, the approaches of Job Upgraders and the Job Corps have much in common; both accept the individual as they find him and provide the basic orientation and education required to offset his deficiencies. In other words, there is by intention no effort to single out the most likely candidates to the continuing disadvantage of the rest. The Job Corps curriculum reflects this acceptance of all comers in its remedial reading and arithmetic courses as well as in "world-of-work" classes, which are designed to acquaint the student with occupations, their requirements, and the attitudes and habits needed for job-holding. At the conservation centers, all of which are government-operated, one-half of the students' time is devoted to these matters; the rest is given to such activities as building trails and shelters, digging ditches, planting seedlings, doing fire prevention work, much in the manner of the Civilian Conservation Camps of the mid-thirties. Vocational training as such receives little emphasis.

By contrast, focus in all urban centers is on job skill training. In fact, these have been referred to as "large residential vocational schools." All operated under contract with private corporations and non-profit organizations, they reflect a "principle of pluralism," [2] under which the sponsors are given complete responsibility for the

---

[2] U.S. Department of Labor, *Manpower Report of the President* (1966), p. 105.

TABLE 13

URBAN CENTERS IN OPERATION, JUNE 30, 1965

Men's Centers	Contractors	Activation Dates (1965)	Enrollee Capacity
California			
Parks Job Corps	Litton Industries		
Center	Beverly Hills, Calif.		
Pleasanton,	in conjunction with		
California	Univ. of California	April 26	2,000
Indiana	Midwest Education		
Atterbury Job Corps	Fdn., Inc.		
Center	(state agency)		
Edinburg, Indiana	Indianapolis, Indiana		
	in conjunction with		
	Indiana Univ. and		
	Adler Educational		
	Systems	April 27	2,600
Kentucky			
Breckinridge Job	Southern Illinois Uni-		
Corps Center	versity		
Morganfield,	Carbondale, Illinois		
Kentucky	in conjunction with		
	Univ. of Kentucky		
	and General Electric		
	Co.'s Appliance Divi-		
	sion Louisville, Ky.	May 27	2,004
Michigan			
Custer Job Corps	U.S. Industries, Inc.		
Center	Silver Spring, Md.		
Battle Creek,			
Michigan		June 22	1,500
New Jersey	Federal Electric Corpor-		
Kilmer Job Corps	ation		
Center	Paramus, New Jersey		
Edison, New Jersey	in conjunction with		
	Rutgers University	February 11	2,500
Oregon			
Tongue Point Job	University of Oregon		
Corps Center	Eugene, Oregon		
Astoria, Oregon		February 1	1,250
Texas	Texas Educational		
Gary Job Corps	Fdn., Inc.		
Center	(state agency)		
San Marcos, Texas	San Marcos, Texas	March 3	3,000
	TOTAL ENROLLEE CAPACITY		14,854

TABLE 13—*Continued*

Women's Centers	Contractors	Activation Dates (1965)	Enrollee Capacity
California			
Los Angeles	Young Women's Christian Association Los Angeles, California	June 11	252
Florida			
St. Petersburg	Pinellas County Board of Public Instructions St. Petersburg, Florida	April 6	284
Nebraska			
Omaha	Burroughs Defense & Space Group Paoli, Pennsylvania	June 29	335
Ohio			
Cleveland	Alpha Kappa Alpha Sorority Chicago, Illinois	April 29	325
West Virginia			
Charleston	Packard Bell Electronic Corporation Los Angeles, California	June 9	300
	TOTAL ENROLLEE CAPACITY		1,496

administration, from procedures to teaching techniques, and from scheduling to establishment of criteria for success. The freedom of action and autonomy resulting from this policy appear to have both strengths and weaknesses. While on the one hand encouraging innovation and experimentation, they have provided grounds for invidious comparison and severe criticism. Among the various centers for men, vocational emphasis may differ considerably; one facility may stress automobile repair while another may specialize in data-processing machine operations. The occupations listed in the official publicity include accounting clerks, automotive repairmen, cooks, data-processing machine operators, farm equipment operators, hospital orderlies, waiters, and "numerous other jobs responsive to labor market conditions." [3] For women, the subject areas are: business and clerical occupations, clothing services, various electronics technician occupations, food preparation, graphic arts, and health services. Table 13 shows urban centers in operation as of June 30, 1965, and such pertinent data as the responsible contractors, their location, and capacity.

[3] Office of Economic Opportunity, Public Affairs, "Job Corps Facts" (Washington, D.C.: Government Printing Office, 1965), O-797-093.

Because of its official tie-in with the University of California, the Parks Job Corps Center is of particular interest in the context of this study of retraining. This operation, housed at a former U.S. Army training base in Pleasanton, California, about an hour's drive from San Francisco, is one of the "urban centers"—so-called because of its skill orientation and organization rather than its location, which is actually semirural. Litton Industries' original contract was for two years and involved $13.4 million, an estimated $3,350 federal expenditure for each of the four thousand young men expected to participate.[4] Due in part to unforeseen medical and dental problems, the budgetary appropriations have proved to be unrealistic, and substantial additions have been made. Undoubtedly, with further experience, considerable revision will be forthcoming as the contract is renegotiated and others drawn up. Like all the other centers, this one is relatively new—its opening date having been April 27, 1965. The "oldest" of the centers have been in existence a scant eighteen months, so few conclusions about their efficacy could be reached even if the current facts were available. These, however, are not accessible. Actually, there is some doubt as to how much can eventually be learned about the dynamics of the Job Corps; the answer will depend to a great extent on the Office of Economic Opportunity and on the contractors themselves.

While definitive and substantive materials for the total Job Corps are as yet lacking, competent observers have examined individual camps. Their praise of the training equipment has been almost unanimous. Singled out especially for commendation have been the arrangements for electronics training and the programmed teaching devices utilized in various courses. Far less favorable were reactions to the personal and human factors—the remedial education, the attitude of teachers and counselors, and their inability to develop empathy with the students. In the shop courses, foremen and supervisors appeared unable to handle students at the low level of competence encountered. Consequently, the electronics laboratories, full of the best available equipment, were untouched because of the inability of the classes to handle advanced concepts. The lack of rapport between teachers and students was seen to result in the perpetuation of misconceptions and unrealistic objectives. A student who designated "missile engineer" as his goal had completed only one year of high school, and that in the vocational track, but he was not taking advantage of the center's program leading to a General Equivalency diploma and

---

[4] Testimony before the House Appropriations Committee in September, 1965, placed the estimated cost per person at $6,000. The actual cost in 1965 for all centers was reported in March, 1966, to the House Education and Labor Committee to be $11,251, and higher for men's urban centers taken alone.

was having great difficulty with the elementary course in electricity.

An academic session at Kilmer Job Corps Center was reported to be "as bad as most academic work that I have seen in the State Training School for Boys. Half the kids were sleeping, the other half were indifferent, and teachers were droning on and on with no involvement. They simply had not won the kids to either the subject matter or to themselves." [5] This observation is not intended as an indictment of all Job Corps teaching staff. At the center at Huntington, West Virginia, Basic Systems, a subsidiary of Xerox Corporation, is putting to use programmed techniques especially developed for slow learners under its four million-dollar contract with the Office of Economic Opportunity. The counselors who supply the human dimensions are reported to be teachers, most of whom have had experience in dealing with underprivileged youth and up to 40 percent of them are non-white.[6] Through its official liaison with the University of California (Berkeley), the Parks Job Center can call on professional educators, psychologists, sociologists, and whatever other specialists may be needed to help train staff, initiate experimentation, and conduct research.

Because the Job Corps is made up of "socially immature, ignorant, backward, uncivilized people from every area of the country," [7] the problems of remedial education and motivation are extremely varied and complex. The vocational side of the program has its problems, too. "If you bring a boy (to New Jersey) from California and say to him, 'We are going to train you as an electrician,' then I think you have the responsibility to do that. If you can't do that, you shouldn't have brought him in the first place." [8]

The question raised by some employment and youth work professionals has to do with the availability of post-training jobs. It has been pointed out that there has been a facile assumption that a successful work experience awaits the 70,000 graduates, with little regard for the possibility of a devastating and demoralizing letdown if this fails to materialize. "What I saw (at Camp Kilmer) that troubled me was . . . this assumption that Job Corps experience will lead to a job. This troubles me because it creates a tremendous amount of pressure on the kids. They believe it and so they are putting forward all the effort they can muster, and with all this effort a lot of them are not

---

[5] Robert Schrank (Director, Urban Youth Work Corps, Mobilization for Youth) in "The Job Corps: A Dialogue," American Child, XLI, 1 (Winter, 1966), pp. 23–24.

[6] "Rochester Firm Pioneers in the Management of Job Corps Centers," Industrial Bulletin (State of New York, Department of Labor) XLV, 4 (April, 1966), p. 5.

[7] James W. Corson (Center Director, Wellfleet Job Corps Conservation Center) in "The Job Corps: A Dialogue," p. 4.

[8] Schrank in "The Job Corps: A Dialogue," p. 24.

coming up to the standards required by the camp administration." [9]

The standards referred to in the foregoing comment may take the form of "rigorous, intense, and unremitting application of the Protestant ethic within the camp," [10] an approach which ran counter to the humanistic orientation of the Rutgers Advisory Committee on Camp Kilmer. While denying the alleged restrictive policy of discouraging teachers from talking to outsiders, the president of Federal Electric acknowledged that some boys had been sent to an isolation barracks and assigned to work details.[11] This "paramilitary" environment has received considerable criticism. It must be noted, however, that the heterogeneous backgrounds of the Corpsmen themselves and the fact of a confined but voluntary group-living arrangement combine to obscure the path between an orderly, structured situation and one which is strictly regimented. Always mindful of their public image, camp administrators know that the least rumble is translated by the press into a riot and that communities are hostile to the "invasion" of strangers from low socioeconomic strata. Thus, they are wont to put a special premium on keeping the kids quiet and out of trouble. Where such a policy becomes a preoccupation, counselors' duties consist mainly of finding acceptable outlets for the Corpsmen's energies. One camp has devised a system under which the staff's competence is judged almost exclusively on their ability to control their particular charges. "Accountability" is the term most frequently used, with everything from broken windows to riots listed among the critical points.

On the other hand, life in the closed community of the camp has been seen as an opportunity for modification of behavior through group processes. With a skilled counselor to guide the emergence and development of interaction that would foster desirable patterns and discourage others, such theorists argue in favor of interpersonal relations as the ideal means of control. Using as an example of the extreme opposite the prison, where docility is the summum bonum, proponents of this approach stress its long-range benefits with respect to personality development. These intangible consequences are put forward as among the major benefits to be derived from the Job Corps.

For the present, accomplishments must still be subjected to such traditional measures as dropout rate and job placements. As to the former, 30 percent is the estimate, the causes ranging from home-

[9] *Ibid.*

[10] Francis P. Purcell (Professor, Graduate School of Social Work, Rutgers University), Letter to the Editor, *American Child*, XLVIII, 2 (Spring, 1966), p. 3.

[11] Joseph A. Loftus, "Kilmer Job Corps Advisers Find 'Flagrant Deficiencies' at Camp," *New York Times* (Nov. 17, 1965).

sickness to unreasonable expectations. The accuracy of this estimate is, however, subject to scrutiny because of lack of clear articulation as between the dropout and graduate. With a constant flow of new-comers and leavers, one way to achieve flexible schedules is to establish short units of time. As a consequence, an early leaver may be classified as a graduate for having reached the end of some such period even though it is nowhere near the actual completion of the program in which he is enrolled.

Determination to preserve the success image is further displayed in the way the contracting industries interpret their training mission to the public. A full-page advertisement in a national business weekly magazine[12] shows a photograph of several ovens in front of which stand three men, a teacher in white coat and two boys (one Negro and one white), clad in crisp white uniforms. The caption reads, "ITT is teaching Mike Fontenot how to bake a cake." The text follows.

When Mike's completed his cook's training he can take an advanced course leading to a successful career as a pastry chef. A successful career—that's one big reason for the Kilmer Job Corps Center in New Jersey, operated for the U.S. Office of Economic Opportunity by Federal Electric Corporation (FEC) an ITT subsidiary.

Instruction is offered in over 30 trades, ranging from pastry baking to automotive mechanics to offset printing. Eventually Kilmer will graduate 2500 young men a year.

FEC is well qualified for the Kilmer project, having also trained thousands of men for highly technical jobs around the world. Some handle communications and instrumentation to track spacecraft and missiles. Others installed the largest communications system in Europe for the U.S Air Force. Still others operate and maintain the strategic Distant Early Warning (DEW) Line which stretches from Alaska to Greenland.

Service is FEC's business—from helping make war on unemployment to helping defend the free world.

International Telephone and Telegraph Corporation, New York, N.Y.

As is evident in the above, the company emphasizes the demonstrated capability of its own technology as a qualification for Job Center administration, and it stresses the vocational areas as the one in which it and the graduates will perform. It assumes success not only in the training process but also in placement. It implies a fait accompli in all these matters, as well as easy access to occupations where union restrictions have traditionally barred all but the most closely related to incumbent members. It leaves the reader with the impression that all this is performed in the name of "service" and

---

[12] *Business Week* (Jan. 29, 1966), p. 40.

implies a large measure of patriotic devotion, with no mention what-soever of the fact that substantial tax money is supporting the "free" enterprise.

This kind of public statement can be dismissed as "Madison Avenue propaganda," or its assumptions must be examined. As regards the in-house training capability, industry's record in the past points to accomplishments with only a certain segment of its employees. ITT did not have to teach the technicians who "handle communications and instrumentation to track space craft and missiles" to read. The situations are entirely different, and while trading on irrelevant achievements may impress the unthinking, it fails to inspire confidence in others. This type of publicity is obviously aimed to contribute to the maintenance of a "good front." But if it is given precedence over other objectives in the operation of the program, such as the teaching of marketable skills, then the value of the entire effort will be seriously undermined. The discomforting thought is that, without unbiased, properly supervised evaluation procedures, the taxpayer will never have a basis on which to judge whether his dollars were well invested or simply part of a "for-profit company's quest for a replacement of cutbacks in defense contracts." [13]

The prime question that should be addressed in any such overview of this massive effort pertains to its residential aspect. Unavoidable in conservation work, a camp life experience may actually play a salutary role in helping an adolescent make some personal adjustments. Many young people have gone into an Israeli Kibbutz for just this purpose. But to tie group-living into vocational rehabilitation is a different matter and may create more problems than it solves. The state of the art in the behavioral sciences has not yet reached the point where we can confidently set out to manipulate environments so as to attain certain goals, and no one is sure that this is desirable anyway. The custodial aspect of the Job Corps is its most costly and its most controversial. The aspects for which there has been a clearly demonstrated need are the remedial and the vocational; it is in these areas that the resources of the Job Corps should perhaps be concentrated. The Job Upgraders of Neighborhood House can serve as a model in the experimental Job Corps camp approved by the House Education and Labor Committee (May 10, 1966). This one, situated at New Bedford, Massachusetts, will contain a residential center and also a vocational school for day students, so as to give Congress a clearer conception of the relative costs and effectiveness of the two types of operations.

---

[13] Purcell, Letter to the Editor, *American Child.*

RETRAINING PROGRAMS FOR
WELFARE RECIPIENTS

The rationale for inclusion of retraining programs for recipients of public assistance lies in the fact that poverty, welfare, and unemployment are inextricably knitted together. Consequently, efforts to help poor persons on public relief rolls achieve financial independence through vocational rehabilitation become a proper subject for study here. Statistics show that one out of every four unemployed persons in March, 1964, was listed among the poor. Unemployment was more than three times higher among the heads of poor families than among heads of other families. Moreover, members of households where the head was unemployed were subject to double the rate of unemployment of nonpoor families whose head was unemployed. For every age group, members of poor households were less likely to be in the labor force than members of nonpoor families.[14]

Retraining programs for recipients of public assistance from the country are especially germane in view of the general trend in current welfare policy toward recognizing and remedying the social roots of unemployment.[15] While it is the intention here neither to deflect attention from the complex configuration of problems that contribute to dependency nor to suggest that work is a panacea for all cases of public assistance, it is important to examine all the facts because of the present policy of wedding eligibility to receive aid with willingness to accept training and to get work. County welfare departments have set up employment units whose functions are to provide vocational counseling, training, and job development services to aid recipients. A vital part of this rehabilitation process is the series of job preparation classes, a group-work approach to the fundamental techniques of job hunting. Intensive study was made of three such classes and a survey made of several more so as to ascertain the characteristics of trainees, teaching techniques, and vocational consequences. Of interest are not only the placement figures but also the outcome as viewed by officials and as seen by the clients themselves.

Among the various categories of aid, which include general home relief, old age security, help for the needy disabled, and medical assistance for the aged, the largest in terms of number of recipients

---

[14] Sar A. Levitan, *Programs in Aid of the Poor,* The W. E. Upjohn Institute for Employment Research (Dec., 1965), p. 3.

[15] Ellen Winston, "Nation's Manpower Revolution," Testimony before the Subcommittee on Employment and Manpower of the Senate Committee on Labor and Public Welfare, 88th Cong., 1st Sess., Part 4 (Aug. 6 and 7 and Sept. 10, 11, and 12, 1963), p. 1289.

is that of aid to families with dependent children.[16] As can be seen
in Figure 3, the past 25 years have shown a marked increase in this
category. The reasons are fairly obvious: (1) the population under
eighteen has increased by about 29 million; (2) the number and the
proportion of broken homes has grown. This being the group to
which retraining efforts are primarily directed, it is important to
review some pertinent history and statistics. Until 1961, the social
work philosophy throughout the United States was that help should

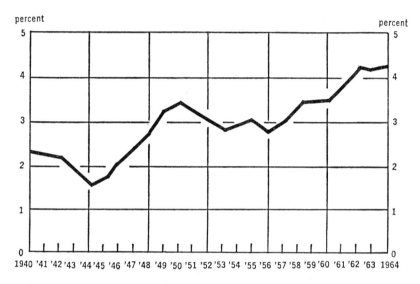

Fig. 3. Percentage of all children below age 18 in population receiving
AFDC, 1940–1964. (Source: U. S. Department of Health, Education, and
Welfare.)

be given to the mother of dependent children since home responsibilities would prevent her from earning a living. The unanticipated
and undesirable consequences of this emphasis was a disruption of
family. It became virtually impossible for a family to receive public
assistance if an able-bodied father was in the house. "The unemployed,
and hopeless, father many times sought to insure aid for his family
by deserting or pretending to desert his wife and children. In practice,
society coerced him into an immoral act, or at least put a premium on
immorality, and then blamed him for his sin." [17] Effective February
1, 1964, the Burton–Miller Act extended welfare aid in California to
unemployed parents. Families became eligible under the following

---

[16] California Department of Social Welfare, *Director's Newsletter* (Sacramento:
Feb., 1964).

[17] Juanita Miller, *The Problems of Dependency*, California Department of
Social Welfare Selective Reading Series No. II (Sacramento: Feb., 1964), p. 7.

conditions: (1) they had one or more children under 18, (2) parents could not find work or were employed only part time and had too little income to meet family needs, (3) they did not own real property over $5,000 assessed value, (4) they did not have personal property valued at more that $600, and (5) they had lived in California at least one year. Certain obligations had to be met in order to receive this aid: (1) the parents must keep looking for work, (2) the parents must accept a job if it is available, regardless of whether it is in their usual trade or line of work, and (3) until a regular job is found, the parents must be willing to attend training classes or participate in a work project, or both, in their community—such as clerical office work; park, street, or building maintenance; hospital aid; child care; educational classes; or rehabilitation counseling.[18] The rationale for the state's having adopted this federal program was set forth as follows.

California is adopting this new program so that families hit by unemployment will not have to choose between destitute living or desertion by the father to qualify the mother and children for aid. Without this program, the unemployed family could get an average $60 per month in county relief, mainly food orders. By abandoning his family, a father could assure his wife and children of possibly $160 per month plus medical care.[19]

Under the new program, the 58 county welfare departments of California became officially involved in work and training activities.

The Burton–Miller Act strengthened a trend already present in the San Francisco Bay area county welfare departments, namely, the development of intensive service programs to help clients achieve self-sufficiency.[20] Trained personnel were assigned to screen the case loads so as to identify individuals whose records showed that they would benefit by specialized direction back to employment. With the cooperation of the Vocational Rehabilitation Service and the State Department of Employment, the welfare agency provided psychological tests, vocational counseling, and referral to schools and classes, work-stations within the county organization, and even outside jobs.

SANTA CLARA COUNTY REEMPLOYMENT AND RETRAINING PROGRAM

In Santa Clara County, where 40 percent of the recipients are Mexican-Americans, the welfare population was found to be typically

---

[18] California Department of Social Welfare, *Aid for Unemployed Families*, Burton–Miller Act (Sacramento: Feb., 1964).

[19] California Department of Social Welfare, *Questions and Answers* (Sacramento: Dec., 1963), p. 5.

[20] Margaret Greenfield, *Social Dependency in the San Francisco Bay Area: Today and Tomorrow* (University of California, Berkeley: Institute of Governmental Studies, 1963), pp. 34–35.

deficient in skills and education and handicapped as to language as well.[21] The 1962–1963 annual report for the Santa Clara Reemployment and Retraining Program sounded an optimistic note, however, for it could show tangible results.

For employment purposes we are dealing to a great extent with a "poor risk" group of people. Generally undereducated and undertrained, often with mental and physical disabilities, and usually starting with few assets for employment, these people are helped by our social workers and reemployment staff to find a place for themselves in the community where they can be self-supporting and have the pride and satisfaction of caring for themselves and their families. Since most of the people helped are family heads, the change from dependency to self-support usually has great meaning, too, for the future of their children.[22]

The report of 1964–1965 indicates that during that year the Reemployment Bureau conducted 6,917 interviews with applicants and recipients and was consulted in 7,140 cases where training and employment were involved.[23] A total of 2,859 persons were assigned to job-related activities. On-the-job training accounted for 567, work assignments for skill development and as credit against aid payments covered 1,267, and 1,025 were enrolled in various classes. MDTA programs have 97 of these students, while LARK (Literacy for Adults and Related Knowledge) included 96 students. The records show that the welfare department discontinued aid to 2,046 cases of families with dependent children because recipients, or members of their households, obtained employment. In a number of instances, reductions in the amount of monthly payments became possible through income from part-time work. During the period of one year, the Bureau referred 2,716 persons and placed 1,134 in permanent and 369 in temporary jobs. An estimated total annual savings of $2,153,633 from discontinuance of aid payments resulted from the employment; of this, Bureau activities helped save $1,027,596 through the placement service.

With the Burton–Miller Act implementing the concept of family unity, many more men are now being referred to the Santa Clara Reemployment Bureau for service. New types of vocational programs have had to be arranged to meet the needs of unemployed fathers. Evidence of this kind of activity is to be found in the course teaching farm laborers how to prune trees in fruit orchards. A high proportion of the enrollees is reported to have finished the training and been placed. Because of added skills, these men qualified for more working

21 *Ibid.*, p. 43.
22 Santa Clara County, Welfare Department, *Report of Re-employment Program,* Fiscal Year 1962–1963 (San Jose), p. i.
23 Santa Clara County, Welfare Department, *Report of Re-employment Program,* Fiscal Year 1964–1965 (San Jose), p. 2.

days per season. The MDTA is running similar programs, for the demand is in the direction of more versatile farm labor. With cessation of *braceros* from Mexico, growers must find competent domestic help. With increasing mechanization of work in orchards, from planting to harvesting, a somewhat higher order of skills associated with equipment operation and superficial repair or adjustment is called for.

For women on relief, the greatest barrier to achieving financial independence is the dearth of child-care facilities. On this matter, the Welfare Department's official position is that it is "as concerned about the proper care of children as it is about encouraging self-support." [24]

ALAMEDA COUNTY EMPLOYMENT UNIT

With more than 6,000 of its cases receiving Aid to Needy Children at the time, the Alameda County Welfare Department and the Council of Social Planning in 1962 jointly sponsored a research and evaluation project of intensive services. Some of the findings included in their report serve as a backdrop for the present substantive data on this county's preemployment activities. It may be well to note that focus continues on the Aid to Needy Children group, but this is now handled under the new concept of Aid to the Families of Dependent Children.

The task of making ANC mothers self-supporting was judged to be more difficult in Alameda County than in California as a whole, mainly because the percentage of Negroes is twice as high and the proportion with recent work experience lower.[25] Other deterrents to successful vocational readjustment were seen in the low levels of education, difficulty and expense of arranging child care, and employers' resistance to hiring (1) Aid to Needy Children mothers, (2) Negroes, (3) women with children, and (4) unmarried mothers.[26] Although the project's success in helping ANC mothers achieve some measure of self-support was greater in the group selected for its potential capacity for rehabilitation than in the sample representing the general case load, it was considered that by and large intensive service had no significant effect toward removing families from the relief rolls. There was evidence, however, that while almost insurmountable obstacles stood in the way of some women's path to employment, for some, the concentrated effort in vocational guidance, training, and job hunting offered promise. Even though a year of

---

[24] *Ibid*, p. 2.

[25] Alameda County, Council of Social Planning, *Aid to Needy Children—Intensive Service Unit Research Project,* Report No. 6 (Oakland, Calif: March 1, 1962).

[26] *Ibid*.

continuing casework was estimated to be necessary for ANC mothers likely to benefit, the costly investment seemed worthwhile if even partial self-support were to result. Three ANC cases off the relief rolls would pay the salary of one caseworker.[27] However, the net gains in nonmonetary, human values were generally regarded as impressive.[28]

The findings of the Council of Social Planning study provided impetus for the activities of the Alameda County Employment Unit to be intensified. Coordination of the services of the social workers and the employment counselors means those welfare applicants and recipients who have no health problem and for whom child care is available are immediately involved in the process of vocational re-habilitation, which may consist of referral to literacy classes, job preparation classes, trade courses, county work projects, or outside job openings. Which of these approaches to the ultimate goal of financial independence is chosen depends on analysis of the re- cipient's three-page self-appraisal, evaluation of his aptitude test scores from the State Employment Service, and the outcome of the personal interview.

"Operation Self-Support," the Alameda County Welfare Rehabilita- tion Section, showed in its report for 1965 that 800 welfare clients had been involved in group instruction projects. These included job preparation, prevocational, preclerical, preclerical-medical, literacy, nurse aide, custodian, landscape gardener, motel maid, home health aide, hospital housekeeper, and hospital dietitian-helper classes. Of the 800 thus trained, 113 were known to be employed, and aid was dis- continued. In addition, 445 clients had been assigned to city, county, state, and federal offices to improve existing skills or develop and main- tain work habits and attitudes. Often they attended appropriate classes concurrently. During this on-the-job training they received welfare grants plus additional allowances for transportation, clothing, child care, and other needs. The County Welfare Office lists 134 of these persons as known employed, with their cases discontinued. It is estimated that with an average grant of $200 per month, if the 247 persons remain employed one month, the total saving is $49,400; or $552,000, if they remain independent for a year.

The officials of the Welfare Department recognize the occupational handicaps of their clientele. Lack of education, skill, and experience are factors in their disfavor. Physical and emotional problems are seen to have interfered with the work life of some. For mothers with young dependents, the cost of child care (reported nationally to average

[27] Ibid., p. 17.
[28] Greenfield, Social Dependency in the San Francisco Area, p. 51.

more than $20 per five-day week per child)[29] frequently makes job-holding uneconomic and impossible. Even with the father now accepted as a responsible member of the household, there are still many families where only the mother is present. The matriarchal pattern established during more than two hundred years and institutionalized by ANC regulations will not change quickly. Consequently, there will continue to be relatively large numbers of women of employable age seeking public assistance. They will also be represented disproportionately among the trainees because of the nature of the job market for the inexperienced and the unskilled. Both training and job opportunities at the lower occupational levels seem to be in relatively greater supply for females than for males. Domestic, service, clerical, and over-the-counter sales jobs are usually to be found. In general, technology seems likely to favor women over the menfolk; in warehouses automated systems do the heavy work and have left only certain clerical procedures to be carried on. Despite legislation calling for equalization of pay scales for men and women, wage differentials are often masked by use of a myriad of occupational titles so that women can be hired to do certain jobs for less money than men.

Because of the heightened emphasis on reduction of relief rolls through job and literacy classes, both locally and throughout the country, this part of the study of retraining examines the policy, procedures, and programs set by the Alameda County Welfare Department, for in most important aspects they are typical of efforts to reduce relief rolls by retraining and reemployment throughout the nation. Fifty-nine clients were followed from their self-appraisal questionnaire, preemployment interview, through their participation in job preparation classes, and into work assignment, or whatever subsequent course of action they pursued. Evaluation of the program comes from the official appraisal, from individual clients' reactions, and from an overall assessment of the place of such an endeavor within the total spectrum of local employment prospects.

The data were derived from three Job Preparation classes, begun February 18, 1964, for 36 women and 23 men. Conducted in cooperation with the city adult education system, the program lasts for a six weeks' period and involves an evening session of two and one-half hours per week. The curriculum includes discussion, demonstration, instruction, and group guidance on all facets of job-hunting. Attention is given to practice in filling out application forms, role-playing in the interview situation, and methods of obtaining such required documents as birth certificates, social security numbers, and

---

[29] California Department of Social Welfare, *Aid for Unemployed Families*, p. 2.

transcripts of school records. Persons from industry and employment offices are brought in as guest consultants to provide factual information on what personnel officers expect from job applicants. For the women's classes, it has been customary to invite a fashion expert from a local department store to talk on proper dress and grooming.

Of the 36 women in the two classes, 25 were Negro and 4 white; the ethnic origin of the rest was unknown. Eight were single; all the others were divorced or separated. With the exception of one unmarried girl of nineteen, all had dependents, ranging in number from one to nine. The average age was 31, the median 30, with a span from 19 to 54. With respect to education, 24 had completed high school and six had taken further schooling for one or two years. The rest were dropouts, one at the eighth grade, one at the tenth, and four at the eleventh grade levels. The class of 23 men listed 17 as Negro, three as white, and three were unknown. As to marital status, 17 were married, two were single, two were widowed, and two were unknown. For all but one trainee, there were known dependents, the average being 4.5. As to age, the distribution was from 19 to 61 with the mean 38.5 and the median 37. There were six high school graduates, one having completed a year of college. Among the others, six had finished the eleventh grade, and nine had left at grades six through ten. One had had only four years of schooling. Although it is of interest to note length of time on welfare in individual instances, totals and averages provide no definitive information. Some cases were new, others recurrent, and others of long duration.

The men's records indicated somewhat more work history than the women's, whose pregnancies and child-care problems were frequently cited as reasons for joblessness. Unskilled laborer was the characteristic occupation of the men, while domestic and factory work accounted for the previous experience of about 20 of the women and clerical jobs for eight others. Police records were listed for ten of the men and ranged in seriousness from traffic violations to armed robbery. Two of the women had prison records.

Study of the case records of each of the persons included in the Job Preparation classes causes one to raise questions about a number of generally held assumptions about schooling and employment. Just because a large proportion of the present chronic hard-core unemployed have had little formal education and are deficient in literacy, we are prone to regard remedial classes as a sure way to employability. And, conversely, there is the facile presupposition that people are unemployed because they lack basic schooling. There is even the hope that prolonged school attendance will have therapeutic value in reducing antisocial behavior; implict in our exhortations to the potential dropout to stay in school is the idea that such a path will lead him toward employment and self-sufficiency and away from delinquency, unemployment, and dependency. Several interesting facts became evident from scrutiny of the case records of the 59 persons selected by professional staff members for intensive vocational service.

1. There are great variations in the level of education carrying the label of the high school diploma.

2. This wide range in quality has little to do with local origin. Persons who have completed 12th grade in California do not necessarily display greater competency with respect to spelling and writing than do the men and women who attained similar grade levels in southern schools.

3. The absence of educational handicaps per se does not guarantee employability or employment. Many personal and social factors, quite aside from schooling, enter into both.

Under almost all circumstances, the state of the job market has very significant bearing on the individual's status as a wage earner. During the 1930's, for example, the well-educated and highly trained swelled the ranks of the jobless; during the Second World War, the payrolls included almost any able-bodied man or woman who wanted to work. In mid-1966, despite much wishful thinking to the contrary, literacy and possession of a high school diploma, while prime requisites for nearly all jobs, are not guarantors of employment. The state of the market is also a major factor, and Oakland's Negro population is at a serious disadvantage in this respect.

To improve the effectiveness of programs aimed at poverty reduction and prevention, the State of California is considering establishment during fiscal year 1966–1967 of twelve multiservice centers, at a total cost of $15,660,000, of which $9,437,000 would be paid by federal funds and the rest by the state. Located close to the people who need assistance, these centers are intended to coordinate activities of various state agencies as they affect individuals and families. Primarily, they are supposed to operate on a "one-door" basis that will put an end to the numerous referrals, fragmentation of services, and scattered facilities that have confused and disheartened clients. The Governor's message on this point read: "Even if government offices are located reasonably near the areas of need, they can present an array of state, local, and federal bureaus, divisions, departments, agencies, sections, and subsections which are enough to bewilder a well-informed citizen, let alone a victim of poverty with limited reading skill. A single center with a single 'intake' process can help him find his way".[30] Viewed as especially necessary and important

---

[30] Edmund G. Brown, *Message to the California Legislature on State Poverty Programs* (March 14, 1966), p. 7.

is the cluster of services related to employment. Here, the specific needs of the illiterate, the unskilled, and other persons handicapped vocationally are addressed. Proposed sites for the centers are the following "high tension areas": South Central Los Angeles, East Los Angeles, Oakland, San Francisco, South San Diego, Venice-La Playa, Bakersfield, San Bernardino-Riverside, Long Beach, Fresno, Vallejo, and Stockton.

How the California State Legislature receives this proposal will determine whether these centers come into being. After the enactment, however, there is still the matter of implementation, a process that may be hampered by the very bureaucratic and jurisdictional barriers that the measure is supposed to counteract. There is likely to be resistance from the already functioning Economic Opportunity Centers, from community action programs, and from county welfare departments—all of which deal with substantially the same client population and in the ways outlined by the State. For purposes of the present research, it is possible only to mention the concept of the multiservice centers. It is a safe assumption that no matter what form the centers eventually may take, nor what their ultimate sponsorship may be, vocational rehabilitation and preparation will be among the most important services offered. Case materials derived from the current experience of the Employment Unit of the Alameda County Welfare set forth clearly the human factors involved in hard-core unemployment and its solution.

Cases from the Job Preparation Classes
of the Welfare Department

Rachelle King, 28, unmarried, the mother of two children aged nine and five, had completed 12 years in the California school system and indicated in her self-inventory that she could type and operate a tabulating machine, her experience on the latter having come from a temporary eight months' Civil Service job four years ago. The record showed that in 1961 she was convicted of grand theft in connection with welfare fraud. Having stated that she was willing to take almost any kind of work so as to be able to send her son to art school, she added that she had lost her previous jobs "because three was temporary. The last one I lost because my children were illegitimate." In response to the follow-up questionnaire, she replied that she had not found the Job Preparation classes helpful because, "I didn't learn anything I didn't already know," and she asked for "help in finding a job opening that hires women and Negroes."

Carrie Kimball, a forty-year-old Negro divorcée with two children, had been a cashier and manager in supper clubs for 15 years. A graduate of a Louisiana high school, Mrs. Kimball had had a year of college. Her comments on the efficacy of the classes are taken verbatim.

The things taught in My Class I Already new. The preparation class should consist of subject you are not familiar with to be prepared for better Jobs. The Instructor Should Know is Subject. These Classes can be improved if the instructor find out what each indivial is quilified for and put them in a group than prepare them for the type of Job. . . . The only help I need in finding work is like of means for transporation. Car fair you can not spend you money to live off to look for work. This statement applies for a number of people I have talked with.

Paula Davis, a white twenty-seven-year-old graduate from a local high school, had taken the commerical course and qualified by State Employment Service standards as a clerk-typist. She had had only two short-term jobs. Fully employable according to the welfare agency's standards, she indicated that care for her five-year-old child would be provided by a neighbor. The problem as seen by the employment interviewer was that Mrs. Davis, a divorcée, lacked carfare and experience, hated to get up early because of her predilection for watching television shows until late every night, and conducted herself in a truculent manner when applying for jobs. As presented by Mrs. Davis, the situation was as follows: "There just isn't any jobs to be had unless you had at least six months experience on a job. A person needs to have some six months job training." She approved of the classes in that they "made things interesting and help a person how to approach an employer."

Mrs. Arletta Lawson, a thirty-nine-year-old Negro divorcée with seven dependents, had completed high school in Texas and a year of business training at the community college in Oakland. Mrs. Lawson had worked in a dentist's office in Houston for three years and had been a waitress and domestic in California. She has taken Civil Service examinations and has rented a typewriter so as to maintain her speed. The interviewer's evaluative notes tell that Mrs. Lawson is very neat and attractive and highly motivated. Despite her training and interest, however, she failed to pass in the Alameda County Welfare Department's clerical review class, failed two tests for county clerical worker, and lacked qualification for referral to a course set up under the Manpower Development and Training Act for calculating machine operators. Responding to the question about the reasons for her continuing unemployment, Mrs. Lawson replied,

I have more experience in the Dental assisting field than clerical and this is a prejudice field where as the white Dentist prefer an assistant of their race and so does the Negro Dentists. There aren't as many Negro Dentists as white's, and when there is an opening among them the Dental Nurse tells her friends about it fust. I am not working as a clerical worker because I have not been able to pass any tests as yet, although I am still taking them and plan to better qualify myself in this field.

She did not consider the job preparation classes helpful, and her comment was, "It is a helpful course for those who need experience in finding a job, but everything which they taught, I had experienced it already in my long process of job hunting." Asked what kind of help she thought she needed in finding work, Mrs. Lawson replied, "If I knew I would have found a job already, although I think there is a great need for the private firms to stop fibbing and saying there is no opening when you're of minority race and hire you according to your qualifications."

Chester Banks, a thirty-year-old Negro with three dependents, completed his high school education in San Quentin prison, where he served a sentence for armed robbery. There he learned typing and carpentry. His previous discharge from military service had been honorable. A medical report indicates that Mr. Banks has an arrested case of tuberculosis, but he regards his health as good, except for occasional attacks of bronchitis. The eight jobs which he held during 1963 included painting, construction, tile setting, short-order cook, and taxi driving. Mr. Banks neatly printed every reply to the questions and returned the form promptly. He saw his situation as follows: "Of course my reason for not having a better job differ somewhat from that of other's. (1) Parolee (2) Negro (3) Inactive T.B. All three of these are vital. I think that the employer fail to realize that we are human and that we have families. And their failure to employ us could have motivated our action's." He regarded the classes helpful "in the sense that they stimulate the mind and encourage the individual job seeker not to lose faith." The interviewer's evaluation states: "Ex-convict who seems very well motivated and potentially capable; cannot get (or hold) job due to prison record." The October, 1964, file shows that the family case was closed in July—the recipient "out of the home."

John Carter, a thirty-eight-year-old Negro with five dependents, had completed high school and two years of college in Tennessee. Chemistry had been his best subject, and his school record showed 40 units of college chemistry. His discharge from military service was honorable, but, prior to 1961, he had acquired a police record for battery and a bad check. Seasonal work in a cannery, cooking in a hospital, and bus driving were his previous jobs. Mr. Carter attributed his lack of employment to a job shortage and stated that he would welcome any training he could get. In addition to following leads in the newspapers and through the State Employment Service, he made a regular circuit of the stores, hotels, and motels. In May, he found steady work at a local motel, and aid was discontinued. An October, 1964, follow-up showed that he was still employed.

Aged thirty-seven, with six dependents, Jack Graham had graduated from an Arkansas high school and claimed two years of premedical training at the junior college level at a local campus. He took extension courses in quality and supervision from an Ohio institute. His military service had ended with an honorable discharge. Five years as an assembler in a radiator factory and a year as a sheet metalworker at a U.S. Naval Air Station comprised the major part of his employment history. His record showed him to be a member of a sheet metalworkers' union. Mr. Graham felt that two factors weighed against him: (1) the lack of a recommendation from the radiator factory, which he had left because of differences with the foreman, and (2) racial discrimination. The vocational notes appended to his record are pertinent:

Intelligent, trained, conscientious, experienced, and qualified to hold responsible position. College man with technical and academic know-how. Perhaps not as flexible and persevering as unemployed person with his ability and family responsibilities should be. Would accept a job in his field if could be directed immediately to it, but doesn't exhibit strong resourcefulness in plying in other directions.

Question of motivation to work. Man in his age group with his skills appears to have many opportunities to be employed. Appearance always immaculate. Manner sometimes pleasant and often belligerent. Has been referred to a number of jobs by the Department in the past two years for which he was qualified. Failed to report on one and was not hired on the major portion. His attitude indicates a personality problem which may preclude job offers. His two year period of unemployment creates unwillingness for employers to hire who otherwise would be most interested in his eight years of sheet metal experience.

The union dispatcher suggested that Mr. Graham's failure to be placed by that organization was due to his irregularity in reporting, this having caused his membership to lapse. Moreover, an antagonistic attitude during interviews and a tendency to complain about unfair dealings on earlier jobs were seen by that official as major handicaps. From the union's viewpoint, Mr. Graham needed psychiatric help to cope with a persecution complex, "90 percent" of the trouble he had encountered in the past being imagined, they said. They also indicated that he was not "willing to take lower level jobs," but reported that this information had come indirectly from employers who had interviewed him.

The counselor's analysis listed as strengths Mr. Graham's neat and smart appearance, ability to verbalize well, good job skills, and work record. His weaknesses were seen to be his somewhat antagonistic attitude, his having left his last job because of a quarrel, and the fact that he had irritated both the union and the State Employment Service people to some extent. Further checking disclosed that there was no record of his having been enrolled in a local junior college and that he had failed to meet the minimum standard in his supervision and management course.

From Mr. Graham's point of view, the reasons for his unemployment were: "(1) Lack of understanding in the field of Human Relations by employers; (2) Lack of well-trained interviewing personnel with respect to hiring minority people; and (3) Practice of Close Shop Policies by the unions." He found the classes helpful "because of the freedom of speech exercised in case study and the counsel you receive while attending classes." His answer to the question as to the kind of help he thought he needed in attaining employment was: "A market for my skills. An employer who would hire me. A better lead to a possible job. Acceptance on self-appraisal. Employers should be shown the necessity of hiring minority groups rather than the disadvantage if there are any." Follow-up in July, 1964, showed Mr. Graham working as a sheet metalworker at the U.S. Naval Air Station in Alameda; a subsequent note dated October 1, 1964, indicated that he had been referred to the Farm Labor Office for placement in September, 1964, and that aid had been discontinued.

Lawrence Sellers, white 27-year-old stepfather of three, was graduated from a local high school. He had been in the U.S. Coast Guard and had held membership in a local of the Teamsters Union. Seasonally employed in a food processing plant, doing odd jobs as machinist and welder, willing to accept any work, Mr. Sellers answered every promising help-wanted advertisement and filed Civil Service applications whenever possible. According to the interviewer's notes, Mr. Sellers was very enthusiastic, well organized in his job hunting, and sincere in his quest for work and training. Very poor performance on the reading and arithmetic sections of the State Employment Service test battery revealed a basic deficiency not previously recognized. To help overcome the pattern of "bad luck in jobs and no work," which Mr. Sellers had stated to be his problem, the employment worker referred him to local remedial courses given under the Manpower Development and Training Act.

Out of the 59 persons included in the three job preparation classes under study, there is information on 29 based on an October, 1964, follow-up. Fifteen of the cases have been discontinued, nine because of employment. It should be noted that four other persons were reported to be working, a fact which could lead to reduced welfare payments and eventual self-sufficiency. Twelve persons were enrolled in training programs, most of the women in the one for nurses aides and the men in county work stations.

The Employment Rehabilitation officials, in an effort to keep "Operation Self Support" closely attuned to the clients' needs, has continued to follow up the individuals who have participated in subsequent sessions. To this end, a questionnaire is sent out to each with a letter, which reads thus:

We want to keep improving our training projects and classes. Your advice and comments can help us make worthwhile changes which we hope will help others entering similar programs.

We would very much appreciate your comments and suggestions, both good and bad, about the training project you have completed. The attached questionnaire and stamped return envelope are enclosed for your convenience. Your answers to these questions will help us improve our training programs. Thank you for helping us plan future training programs.

Very truly yours,

The recipients are asked to respond, anonymously if they wish, to the questions, (1) What did you like about the training? (2) Was the training helpful in finding work? Why? (3) Has the training helped your family? How? (4) What could we add to the training to make it more helpful? (5) What other kinds of training classes or projects do you think we should have? The selected replies are reproduced verbatim.

The first question elicited mostly favorable responses in which the value of a work experience was stressed by those who had been assigned aide jobs in various government agencies. The reply of a particular clerical trainee is indicative: "I liked the training because it not only gave me the needed experience but also helped me with my own personal schedule which is necessary in any job." Employment counselors agree that the latter point can be crucial in achieving a successful work experience. During the discussion in the job preparation classes, it was observed that many of the recipients lacked the conception of time as a useful commodity or resource. Whether this failure had come about through protracted unemployment or whether these enrollees had never developed an appreciation of time could not be explored. The results were apparent, however. Unable to organize their activities, they ran headlong into what appeared to be a luckless pattern of late buses, unreliable baby sitters, and family and health emergencies. One woman missed an appointment for an interview because in the frenzy of preparing for this all-important occasion, she spilled the coffee down the front of her only appropriate dress. What may have looked like the hand of unkind Fate was frequently the cumulative effect of ineptness and improvidence in the planning and allocation of time.

As to the value of the training, the answers were almost all positive. A client of forty-eight, the mother of three, who had been on relief for a year, typed neatly, "I do believe the training was helpful in finding work, as it has built up my confidence in seeking employment. The taking of the many tests that are required and the going in for interviews, my chief stumbling block being my tendency to sell myself short. I have too little confidence in my capabilities." She replied to the next question by pointing out the value to her family of having her own self-respect and confidence restored. A man whose assignment had been as a stock and mail clerk noted, "It helped my family in that they felt I was working for the money I recieved from the country." For a man enrolled in the remedial education program, the benefit was this: "it help my family to lean that it is import to have training to a job and stick with it." Dignity and independence were the two advantages most frequently mentioned.

The number of persons expressing dislike were few and their questionnaire forms contained little constructive criticism. One respondent, otherwise favorably impressed with his civil service work training, wrote, "It was to pushing, and it was not arranged well enough." Another replied, "I had no particular dislikes except that sometimes one would realize that some people in charge were taking advantage of cheap labor." One man stated succinctly, "Some of the employer."

Recommended changes for improvement ranged from special provisions for child care to expansion of the training period. Another offered the thought, "if the program were extented to better skills needful for this era of technology the welfare rolls could be decreased." The suggestions for future training classes or projects were quite specific, covering everything from key-punch operation to cement masonry.

The respondents were asked to offer any comments that they thought would be helpful. A civil service trainee wrote, "I feel that every able bodied and able minded person on A.N.C. rolls should be pressured more toward earning their on living, for their sake and society's sake too!!" A home health aid commented,

the only falt I have about this Home Health Aide is I diden no u had to go
to school to learn to do Demostic Work thats the most I have been doen and
another thing I dont get enough work to support my famlly I dont have a lots
of bills only I do nead to make anough for liven expenses that the falts
other than that I like it fine I wont to work I like to help my self but if I
dont get steady work and more hours I am temped to just quit and get an
aide right now my rent are behind utilets and hardly any food and I have
a child in school and to fead.

The stock and mail clerk mentioned above covered a full page
with his observations.

Overall, I think the training classes are helpful to those who have no skill.
To those who do have skills in one field it would be great to send them to
another skill that would be acceptable to the labor market. The most important thing is job placement of certain minorities. I'm sure the Job Unit
of the Welfare Agency is interested in getting more people to become self-
sustaining and if this be the case job placement should be an important part
of the Job Unit. When I was recieving assistance I had about 17 applications
in for work and was finally hired at NAS (Naval Air Station) Alameda at
lesser pay than is subtended in my skill but I recieved permenant status. All
this was due mainly to the East Asian conflict. So you see your department
as well as the Dept. of labor need some way of helping minorities other than
War or War Hysteria.

The forty-eight-year-old clerk-typist quoted earlier expressed several
thoughts.

The on the job group discussions proved very helpful to me and I think
the others benefitted also. I am now employed as a clerk-typist at the Naval
Supply Center Oakland and enjoy it very much. My youngest is in Children's
Center (formerly Child Care Woodstock) and she is happy. The two older
youngsters are in school all day, come home four days a week and on their
own for an hour until I get home. Quite satisfactory, so far and I am happy
to see that the house is standing, the youngsters have started their homework,
which Mother can correct later, and all in all everything is working out very
satisfactorily. I do appreciate all that the rehabilitation did for me and my
family, and my best wishes and regards to all who helped me back on the
road.

The use of government agencies as a source of on-the-job training
is definitely on the increase. Executives at federal, state, and local
levels are being urged to find places in their organizations for aides
who can perform meaningful tasks without displacing regular personnel. Implicit here is a contradiction, for within the well-run department, all really necessary functions are included in the classification
system and specifically assigned on the payroll. This means that, in
effect, the trainee will actually become engaged in real or in "busy"
work. The former violates the rule; the latter can be demoralizing and

self-defeating. Because the volunteer, unpaid position is not specified in the budget, there are no provisions for such necessary items as desk, chair, and typewriter. Equipping him properly thus becomes a matter of borrowing and juggling, during which process his status as a not-always-welcome intruder can become aggravated. This is particularly true in the frequent cases where supervisors, harassed by institutional and bureaucratic pressures, resent and resist the burden of a non-productive neophyte. Constant emphasis on economy and the increase of automation in government agencies contribute to a movement to-ward reducing and streamlining functions, while regulations restrict the use of unpaid labor. This poses a dilemma of significant propor-tions, for, as the case materials have indicated, a bona fide work ex-perience is an almost indispensable ingredient of vocational rehabili-tation, and the public service seems to be the most logical place to acquire it.

CONCLUSION

Regarded critically, the employment efforts of the welfare depart-ments might be judged as substituting one kind of substandard status for another. Low-level jobs, such as motel maid and nurse's aide, have been called disguised unemployment because the wages paid are inade-quate for today's living standards. Because of their accumulated prob-lems, many welfare recipients are marginal workers, likely to drop in and out of the labor force periodically. If the sum total of accomplish-ments has to be assessed only in terms of cases discontinued or types of work attained, the profit side of the ledger, despite dollar savings claimed, would be rather weak. To be credited, however, are the human values—intangible but nonetheless important. By virtue of the classes and job assignments many persons were able to develop self-confidence, which could be strengthened through a work experi-ence. Just as prolonged unemployment makes for unemployability so employment at one job enhances one's chance of getting another. For many of the trainees, hospital or hotel work was not demeaning nor seriously below their aspiration or ability level. In evaluating the jobs received, one must not project one's own biases. Improved wage rates in these occupations could in fact elevate them to an acceptable degree of respectability.

For some graduates of the job preparation program, the classes and the on-the-job experience served as an entering wedge into occupa-tions newly opened by some local firms' willingness to hire members of racial minority groups. Some of the jobs found for men were in companies and in occupations where discrimination had previously been rife. To be sure, there were still instances of $1.50 per hour janitorial placements, but there were also some paying $2.50 and more with employers and in jobs that once were unattainable. The training and work experience acquired through the Welfare Department's programs may have been the factors that put these people into a favorable competitive position in the struggle for economic existence. This leads us to the interesting hypothesis that one promising way to achieve self-improvement is to become so badly off as to qualify for public aid. In the game of musical chairs that is the quest for employment, players must be ready to take advantage of every move.

There are other lessons to be learned from this study. To begin with, the data reinforce the notion that the terms "employable" and "unemployable" are variable with the social and economic setting. Certainly, no correlation between unemployability and welfare status is necessary. And many factors that work as obstacles when jobs are scarce are certain to be overlooked by personnel managers when qualified applicants are in short supply.

The present focus on vocational rehabilitation in public welfare should not, of course, divert attention from the thousands of persons on public relief who for a variety of reasons are incapable of getting and keeping jobs. To be sure, employment activity wins favor because of its relief roll-cutting propensities, but it should not be pursued to the neglect of other areas of social service. To do so would be very shortsighted. Even under conditions of full employment, there are bound to be large numbers of people unable to maintain themselves decently without public support. The policy of helping people achieve independence by finding gainful employment becomes somewhat attenuated when applied to such cases as women with young dependents whose earning capacity is at best limited and who must make elaborate child care arrangements. The effect on family life is of prime importance.

There are dangers in attributing too much therapeutic value to this aspect of social work. It must be recognized that the success of such vocational rehabilitation programs, despite reference to the nonmaterial benefits, is likely to be measured in cases closed and relief money saved. Forcing applicants to accept substandard jobs or forfeit welfare payments can hardly be interpreted as a successful road to independence and self-sufficiency. If the criterion by which these county measures are judged is simply the number of placements or the number of cases closed, there is a chance that the welfare office will become a source of cheap—and probably exploited—labor, where menial and undesirable jobs can be filled by people who must take them or go hungry. The departments studied indicate an awareness of these possibilities and claim that they are not likely to deteriorate into the trafficking with misery by substituting one kind of deprivation for another.

On the positive side, the county welfare approach, beyond representing a salvage operation, demonstrates the efficacy of concerted action carried out under the guidance of persons familiar with community resources. As was mentioned above, the relief client does in a way have an advantage over many other sectors of the unemployed population. He is sent to be tested; he is provided with remedial training; he is referred to jobs. Many of the unemployed are unaware of the services available to them, timid about requesting them, or too discouraged and apathetic to use them. In numerous instances where immediate jobs are not available, welfare clients are directed to training programs where they can develop skills. Without impetus and direction, it is safe to assume that such persons might not have found or been included in the classes. With the present MDTA legislation allowing for remedial courses, it is almost certain that relief recipients whose problems stem from illiteracy will continue to be enrolled in substantial numbers. Tantamount in importance to the classroom preparation is the on-the-job training arranged by the welfare department. The records show that in many cases the experience thus attained has led to a paying job outside.

The discussion of skill development by the county welfare agencies is not intended to address even in small part the causes and cures of the unemployment and underemployment of relief clients. What has been seen is that implementation of the concept in social welfare to provide service to the families of dependent children makes vocational orientation central in the rehabilitation process. The future activities of these agencies could provide a fruitful area of research into their causes and evaluation of some of the theories and conceptions about the variables controlling employability. We may not find a clear-cut answer to the question whether the need for public assistance comes about because of personal inadequacy or from the dearth of jobs, but we may be able to arrive at a better understanding of the interplay of psychological, social, and economic factors impinging on a person's work life. What emerges most poignantly from study of welfare retraining efforts is the need to provide this kind of full-fledged vocational service to members of our society before they have exhausted their own resources and had to apply for aid.

$\lceil 7$

Retraining Under the Manpower Development and Training Act of 1962: Institutional Programs

BACKGROUND OF THE BILL AND ITS PROVISIONS

In 1961 the Committee on Education and Labor in the U.S. House of Representatives recommended, with dissension from a minority, that H. R. 8399, later called the Manpower Development and Training Act, be passed without amendment. Public hearings, conducted by the Holland Subcommittee on Unemployment and the Impact of Automation,[1] had brought forth consensus among authorities in various fields that unemployment was the nation's most pressing problem and that hard-core structural unemployment appeared to be on the increase. Recognition of training or retraining as an essential remedy was almost unanimous in the Joint Economic Committee of Congress as well as from the group opposed to this legislative measure. Newspapers and periodicals throughout the country had taken a favorable stand on a national training effort, and a public opinion poll had shown that such a bill was the most favored of all the proposals specified by President Kennedy in his second State of the Union message; the one to train the unemployed was favored by 67 percent of the respondents, more than twice the support shown for

---

[1] U.S. Congress, House of Representatives, Committee on Education and Labor, Subcommittee on Unemployment and the Impact of Automation, 87th Congress, First Session, *Impact of Automation on Employment* (March 8, 10, 20, 21, 22, 27, 28, 29 and April 12, 17, 18, 25, 1961).

195

any other item listed.[2] In recommending H. R. 8399 for approval, the Committee pointed out the desirability of continued technological development but recognized the possible impacts of such advances on workers whose skills might be rendered obsolete.

This bill is designed to provide the means by which those who through no fault of their own have lost their jobs and their hard-won skills, or who early in life have entered the labor force without adequate skills, can acquire skills which will give them the opportunity to become productive members of their communities. We must not expect the workers who are displaced to bear the whole burden of higher productivity. The whole nation which benefits from increased productivity has the responsibility to provide the means by which the employees who are displaced can acquire new skills that are needed and will be useful in the economy.[3]

Passage of the Manpower Development and Training Act in the spring of 1962 represented an important public decision to address the problems of structural maladjustment on a somewhat longer range basis than had been attempted in the temporary extensions of unemployment benefits in 1958 and in 1961.[4] Recession unemployment had not been corrected by subsequent periods of prosperity, and federal measures such as these and the Area Redevelopment Act had proved inadequate to stem the rise of joblessness; the new legislation initiated a "positive approach to the problems of unemployment related to labor market imbalances."[5] The emphasis on the national aspects of this approach to manpower adjustment merits attention in view of the research reported earlier in this book. The report recommending enactment of the legislation stated: "The manpower problems to which this bill is addressed are national problems. While significant accomplishments have been made by industry, labor, and government in dealing with dislocations that have occurred in certain areas the total problem is too great for local capacities alone. Moreover, the labor market is a national market and if its needs are to be met national leadership is required."[6]

Of the three titles comprising the law, two related specifically to

[2] House of Representatives, 87th Congress, First Session, Report No. 879, *Manpower Development and Training Act of 1961* (August 10, 1961), p. 4.

[3] *Loc. cit.*, pp. 4–5.

[4] Ewan Clague, "The Economic Setting of the Manpower Training and Development Program," Address before the First Conference on Manpower Development and Training Act of 1962, New York University, New York (Sept. 12, 1962), p. 1, Proc.

[5] U.S. Department of Labor Office of Manpower, Automation and Training, *Manpower Research and Training*, Report of the Secretary of Labor (March, 1964), p. 1.

[6] U.S. House of Representatives, *Manpower Development and Training Act of 1961*, p. 8.

the training program and were to expire at the end of three years. "Title I" is permanent legislation, however, and makes the Secretary of Labor responsible to the President for an annual manpower report dealing with labor market balances and imbalances, analysis of occupational changes, impact of automation and technology, and the occupational structure of the work force. "Title II" is concerned not only with persons affected by persistent and long term unemployment but also with those who are underemployed. Although provision is made for the training of young people between the ages of 16 and 22, only those from 19 to 22 are eligible for training allowances—first priority for which is given to jobless adult heads of families who have had at least two years of gainful employment. Since one of the basic criteria for establishment of training programs is the condition of the local labor market, skill surveys and analyses of supply and demand are an intrinsic part of this nationwide activity. In "Title III," the Secretary of Labor is required to report to the Congress on the results of training endeavors and to evaluate their effectiveness in terms of numbers and characteristics of individuals included, occupations prepared for, and placements made. A subsection calls for development of on-the-job training arrangements. "The Secretary shall, to the maximum extent possible, secure the adoption by the States and by private and public agencies, employers, trade associations, labor organizations, and other industrial and community groups which he determines are qualified to conduct effective training programs under this title of such programs as he approves, and for this purpose he is authorized to enter into appropriate agreements with them." [7]

Dynamics of the Training Act

The MDTA has been viewed as the mainspring of a new partnership between two important government agencies, the U.S. Department of Labor and the U.S. Department of Health, Education, and Welfare.[8] The local institutions around which most of the program revolves are the public employment office and the vocational school system. In implementing the program, the duties of the former are: (1) to determine the occupations where there is a need for employees; (2) to select and refer applicants to courses; (3) to pay training and subsistence allowances to trainees as prescribed by law; (4) to provide job development, placement, and follow-up services. The responsibilities of the Department of Education are three-fold: (1)

---

[7] U.S. Congress, 87th Congress, S. 1991, Public Law 87-415, Title III, Section 204a (March 15, 1962).

[8] Training Guide, *Manpower Development and Training Act Appreciation,* State of California Department of Employment (May, 1962), p. 2, Proc.

provision of needed training facilities and instructors; (2) determination of appropriate curricula and methods for the training; (3) evaluation of trainees' progress.

It is important to note the stipulation that courses be established specifically for the purpose of training those persons selected and referred under the MDTA. Under the terms of the Act, trainees cannot be referred to classes and courses already in existence. While facilities used are likely to be in a vocational high school, a junior college or some other public institution, contract arrangements can be made with a private school or an employer under certain conditions. But all programs were to be newly developed, and *not* in the ongoing classes. This, it must be pointed out, was the MDTA's first major departure from previous training ventures. In California, it may be recalled from the discussion in Chapter 1, standard procedure had been to approve an applicant's training plan so long as it was based on the list of schools and courses endorsed by the State Department of Education. In the preliminary stages of implementation of the Manpower Development and Training Act in California, there was a tendency on the part of State Employment Service officials to regard the setting up of new and separate curricula for MDTA trainees as unnecessary and, indeed, severely limiting. It was argued by some that California State Law S.B. 20, an extended unemployment insurance plan, had allowed for more flexibility by permitting "individual referrals to ongoing courses in approved institutions." [9] The rationale for the new procedure, as set forth in a report by the Secretary of Labor, emphasized the superiority of the new approach in that it would take into account the needs of individual trainees such as, for example, problems of adults returning to a formal classroom situation, education and skill level of enrollees, and instruction that was specifically geared to requirements and standards of performance on jobs.[10]

The inclination of state officials to depend on the approved list for schools or courses of study may have been sound in principle, but, as was pointed out in a somewhat different context in Chapter 1, it led to unsatisfactory results. Accreditation became a meaningless stamp of approval when it failed to discriminate between institutions and programs suspected of misrepresentation and those having impeccable standards. Many persons attracted and reassured by the official certification found that they had been victimized by a fly-by-night entrepreneurial venture. Authorization of extended unemployment benefits under the state legislation hinged almost exclusively on the training

---

[9] Training Guide, 54061, p. 7.

[10] U.S. Department of Labor, Office of Manpower, Automation, and Training, *Report of the Secretary of Labor on Research and Training Activities under the Manpower Development and Training Act* (Feb., 1963), p. 41.

course's inclusion on the approved list with no further check on its merits or on its appropriateness for the particular individual. Although the State Department of Education does have some funds for vocational counseling of adults, there is no evidence to indicate that any such service was provided. Occupational adjustment was largely a matter of trial-and-error on the part of persons who desperately needed guidance. If S.B. 20's strengths were its flexibility and its individualized approach to retraining, its weakness was failure to pursue the process past the rubber-stamp stage. With practically no vocational counseling and no help in assessing the merits of the course selected, the applicant suffered, rather than benefited, from freedom.

Differing from previous training endeavors as to the use of facilities was one of MDTA's first breaks with tradition. Another, and by far its most important, was its recognition of the need for income maintenance along with economic and vocational rehabilitation. During the 1930's, manpower policy had included the former but not the latter.[11] The importance of a living allowance as an impetus to participation in retraining will be seen in the context of the analyses of specific programs and their enrollees. For the present, one need only recall the experience reported in Chapter 2 of young men who had to drop out of a tuition-free welding program for lack of money, and the records of vocational nursing trainees who had to make serious personal sacrifices in order to invest a year in schooling. The value of the subsidy provided under the MDTA to properly qualified persons is readily apparent when the case materials are examined in detail.

Different from earlier retraining efforts and also from the institutional programs, developed through schools, are the MDTA-sponsored on-the-job arrangements. Unlike the former, which involved the field staffs of the Departments of Labor and of Health, Education, and Welfare, MDTA arrangements are largely the responsibility of the Bureau of Apprenticeship and Training of the U.S. Department of Labor. Officially stressed has been the value of this aspect of the MDTA for upgrading the underemployed.[12] Included in this group are persons working below skill capacity, or threatened with skill obsolescence, or unable to find full-time work because of skill limitation. At the time the federally financed training program was being developed, its major architects, Senator Joseph S. Clark and Congressman Elmer Holland, anticipated that on-the-job, and not institutional, projects would predominate. With help from the government, it was hoped private employers would upgrade employees through special

[11] Louis Levine, "An Employment Service Equal to the Times," *Employment Security Review*, XXX, 6 (June, 1963), p. 13.

[12] U.S. Department of Labor, Office of Manpower, Automation, and Training, *Training Facts,* Report No. 13 (June, 1964), p. 7.

instruction at the workplace and make room for newcomers. The Manpower Development and Training Act was regarded as providing the incentive through the subsidy.

Despite its potentialities, however, on-the-job training was neglected almost entirely during the early months of MDTA and has made relatively little headway nationally during subsequent years. The inclination to develop school-based training has been attributed to the relative ease of the latter and complexity of on-the-job training. Though varied, vocational facilities were generally accessible and institutional programs were generally simpler to administer. By contrast, on-the-job arrangements require development of unprecedented procedures, standards, and safeguards. Resistance, if not downright opposition, came from vocational educators, private employers, and organized labor. School officials, who were at the outset disposed to side with the opposition to MDTA on the ground that the law extended the jurisdiction of the Secretary of Labor into the educational field, regarded on-the-job training as a further invasion of their bailiwick.[13] Private employers voiced the fear that government involvement with training on their premises might lead to ultimate intervention in their hiring practices. With only a few exceptions, trade unions originally took a counter position, on the contention that the supply of skilled workers was already sufficient and that additions would undermine current wage levels.

Placing responsibility to administer the on-the-job programs in the hands of the U.S. Department of Labor's Bureau of Apprenticeship and Training was intended to gain labor's confidence, since that agency had for many years maintained liaison with the unions. As an extra precaution against on-the-job training arrangements that might antagonize organized labor, the rules called for centralized clearance and approval of all projects in Washington. But inadequate staff at headquarters made this procedure unwieldy, and the attendant red tape discouraged at least several local unions from pursuing requests for funds. Small companies that might have been receptive to a federally financed training arrangement were prevented from participating because of the stipulation that no program with fewer than ten persons would be considered eligible.

NATIONAL AND REGIONAL TRAINING
UNDER MDTA

The cumulative sum allocated for all programs approved since the inception of the Manpower Development and Training Act in

---

[13] U.S. House of Representatives, *Manpower Development and Training Act of 1961*, Report No. 879, p. 28.

August, 1962, was reported at the end of March, 1964 to be $161,865,-353.[14] During the two subsequent years, an additional $5 million was earmarked for approved projects. This raised the total to about $650 million.[15] During 1964 and 1965, more than half the funds went toward training allowances, and the rest was spent on such costs as equipment, rental, supplies, and teachers' salaries. The distribution among states was far from even, with 16 accounting for about 71 percent of the funds. Of these, eight reported respective commitments exceeding $10 million: New York ($32 million), California ($27 million), Illinois ($23 million), Ohio ($18 million), New Jersey ($17 million), Pennsylvania ($15 million), Michigan ($13 million), and Massachusetts ($11 million). By 1966, occupational training had been approved for some 450,000 persons. Of these 387,000 were institutional trainees (school-based) and nearly 62,000 were on-the-job trainees.

By the end of 1965, the occupational spectrum covered by courses had increased to something over 600 specific areas. Almost half of the enrollees were to be found in categories rated as skilled or semiskilled, over one-fifth in the clerical and sales field, and one-seventh in service work. It is important to note that the title of a licensed practical nurse comes under the heading of semiprofessional and technical; nurse aide, orderly, and ward attendant are regarded as service; welder and automobile body repairman are considered skilled. According to the Secretary of Labor's report,

The trainees are being prepared for occupations that offer the most promising prospects in terms of expanding job opportunities and future stability of employment. More than half of the trainees were enrolled for training in high demand occupations, illustrating the responsiveness of the program to labor area developments. These occupations included draftsman, licensed practical nurse, general office clerk, stenographer, clerk-typist, salesperson, welder, metalworking-machine operator, electronics assembler, automobile mechanic, automobile-body-repairman, service-station attendant, and cook.[16]

Evidently, what is officially interpreted as a positive feature—namely, the "responsiveness . . . to labor area developments"—is subject to different evaluation. Such courses as these were adjudged to be "of the ordinary garden variety, reflecting the state of established vocational education curricula." [17] Whatever the accurate appraisal, it is equally

[14] U.S. Department of Labor, Office of Manpower, Automation and Training, *Training Facts*, pp. 3–4.

[15] U.S. Department of Labor, *Report of the Secretary of Labor on Manpower Research and Training under the Manpower Development and Training Act of 1962* (1966), p. 7.

[16] *Loc. cit.*, p. 16.

[17] Sar A. Levitan, *Federal Manpower Policies and Programs to Combat Unemployment*, The W. E. Upjohn Institute for Employment Research (Kalamazoo, Michigan: Feb., 1964), p. 17.

applicable to California. Out of 350 courses on the active list as of April 28, 1966, about 95 were for clerical work, 46 for licensed practical nurses, and 37 for nurse aide and similar occupations.[18]

It should come as no surprise that placement records follow the same occupational pattern as the training projects. Thus licensed practical nurses, who account for nearly one-third of the individuals completing programs in the semiprofessional and technical group, claim an employment rate of 90 percent for all female graduates. In the service category, just under one-third of those who were involved were to be found in nurse aide, orderly, and ward attendant courses. Their employment rate was 67 percent.[19]

Theoretically, the Manpower Development and Training Act was designed to provide services to segments of the population that had been bypassed by other training institutions. During the first year of operation, however, there was a tendency on the part of Employment Service interviewers to select from the well-stocked files of the jobless those persons who seemed to possess the greatest ascertainable potential. The rationale probably was that Congress and the taxpayers needed a success image in order to support extension and expansion of the program. General public acceptance of the manpower measure and confrontation with more serious deficiencies, as the deeper-lying reservoir of unemployed was analyzed, led to realization of some of the inadequacies of the original legislation. Consequently, amendments in 1963 authorized payment of allowances over a longer training period for individuals who lacked minimal educational skills. As a result, remedial basic instruction in reading, writing, and arithmetic became part of the curriculum. Because of this shift in emphasis, there has been greater attention to the risk groups—those with a constellation of problems. As was evident in the cases of welfare recipients, many of the long-time unemployed have a multiplicity of problems besides those that can be characterized as strictly vocational. Even with a marketable skill, many of this group would probably have difficulty in locating or holding a job without the help they derived from the remedial and supportive aspects of the program.

With the 1965 amendments, the MDTA program was given permanent and fiscal stability. Accepted as a necessary and continuing part of national manpower policy, the Act was continued until at least June 30, 1969. Improved procedural arrangements were devised, and expanded research and demonstration activities authorized. So that adequate remedial education and skill training could be assured the hard-core unemployed, subsidy was extended to 104 weeks.

---

[18] State of California, Department of Employment, Division of Public Employment, Division Notice No. 4471 Q (April 28, 1966).

[19] U.S. Department of Labor, *Report of the Secretary*, pp. 20–21.

The Skill Center

In several large industrial cities such as Detroit, South Bend, and Chicago, a centralized facility, which offers comprehensive vocational services from aptitude testing to skill training, has come to represent the fulcrum of MDTA activity for an area. Here, the unemployed may receive total preparation for work, with remedial studies, social and personality development, occupational exploration, and specific job instruction integrated into a meaningful program. From the point of view of administrative efficiency, the skill center concept improves supervision, provides continuity of operation, and makes for better utilization of teachers, equipment, and space.

With an MDTA grant of two million dollars, the East Bay Skills Center, located in Oakland, California, opened in early April, 1966, with 200 trainees. Another contingent of 200 was enrolled by the end of that month, and it is anticipated that future increments will bring the total to about 1,600. Within one month and with practically no local publicity, a waiting list of hundreds of eager applicants developed but could not be accommodated because further funds would not be forthcoming until the new fiscal year (July) began. Wherever feasible, all MDTA classes in operation in the nearby East Bay communities will be transferred to the new location as rooms become available in the huge industrial plant now being remodeled. Initially, program emphasis is on occupations for men so as to counteract the imbalance that has prevailed in this respect. Accordingly, the first 400 enrollees at the Skill Center are males, and the approved course list includes such trades as office machine repair, automobile and truck mechanics, and welding. An advisory committee composed of representatives of industry, labor, and the community at large reviews prospective programs.

Statistical analysis of the first 400 enrollees shows that they have the characteristics summarized in Table 14. Although scant, the data show an interesting sample of prosperity unemployment as found in the urban setting in mid-1966. Noteworthy is the heavy concentration of men in their prime working years. Also important is the relatively high level of formal education achieved. Further research into this factor may reveal, as it did in the case studies reported earlier, that completion of tenth grade and above bears little relationship to competence in school-related subjects. Even when attained, the diploma is no guarantee of capability in reading, arithmetic, and writing. Moreover, it must be recognized that as more students obtain it, the diploma becomes devalued currency in the job market. The unemployed worker is at a great disadvantage on some occupational levels

TABLE 14

CHARACTERISTICS OF 400 ENROLLEES OF EAST BAY SKILLS CENTER
(Percent)

1. *Sex:*	*Male*	*Female*					
	97.5	2.5					

2. *Age:*

Under 20	*20–25*	*26–30*	*31–40*	*41–50*	*51–60*	*61 and over*
3.25	21	18.75	21.75	21.50	7.25	$\frac{1}{2}$

3. *Head of Household:*   *Yes*   *No*
                               80.5   19.5

4. *Number of Dependents:*   *0–2*   *3–5*
                                   52.75   47.25

5. *Highest School Grade Completed:*

0–4	*5–7*	*8–9*	*10 and over*
6.5	16.5	24.5	52.5

6. *Public Assistance Recipient:*   *Yes*   *No*
                                        27   73

7. *Weeks Unemployed:*

Under 5	*5–14*	*15–26*	*27–52*	*52 and over*
27	23.75	21.5	15.25	12.5

8. *Spanish Primary Language:* 24.5

9. *Unemployment Insurance Request on File:* 25

SOURCE: William E. Rogin, Research and Documentation, East Bay Skills Center, Oakland, California, May 20, 1966.

without it; nonetheless he is not necessarily particularly well off with it. Among this group of 400 men, about 275 of whom were Negro, the tenth grade represented the maximum; but in programs designed especially for the youth, the major proportion of enrollees have completed twelfth grade. Also noteworthy in the data are the items relating to duration of unemployment and eligibility for Unemployment Insurance. Three-fourths of the men had been without jobs for more than five weeks; only one-fourth of them could qualify for the benefits. This means that they had not earned sufficient amounts the previous year. Under these circumstances, the proportion receiving public assistance seems to be very small.

A number of interesting questions suggest themselves. After functional illiteracy has been eradicated by the various remedial measures now in operation, can we assume that unemployment too will vanish? If there is a substantial incidence of joblessness in the ranks of persons who have completed ten or more years of schooling, this may be because their aspirations and qualifications are not realistic. Persons who have completed only six or seven years of formal schooling, on the other hand, are more apt to be reconciled to the car washing and cooks' helper class of jobs; consequently, their chances for employment are good—high turnover making these perennially high demand occupations. But the worker who has obeyed the exhortations to stay in school is likely to seek compensation in the coin of a job with a future, even though the extra years invested really were devoid of educational or vocational value. This new type of unemployed underscores the need for sweeping improvements in public education; it also may augur a shift of emphasis in MDTA from the basic remedial concept to the more skill-oriented training in which specific deficiencies can be identified and corrective measures integrated into the curriculum. This is the area in which the skill center could make its primary contribution in the larger context of manpower development.

MDTA PROGRAMS IN THE SAN FRANCISCO BAY AREA

The MDTA courses selected for special study include both the institutional and the on-the-job types. At the time this research project was being formulated, there were none of the experimental and demonstration variety in operation in this region. Subsequently, the Job Upgraders at Neighborhood House in North Richmond received a grant under that category of the MDTA. The program was treated as an independent enterprise in Chapter 5 primarily because it was a strictly local enterprise when first visited. Federal support has, however, made continuation and expansion of its services possible. The Office of Manpower, Automation, and Training was flexible enough in interpreting its early mandate to underwrite the Job Upgraders because, as was pointed out previously, the techniques used there could provide a worthwhile model for use in other programs for the hardcore unemployed. Representing the institutional courses in this study are programs for (1) chemists' assistants, (2) retail clerks, (3) licensed vocational nurses, and (4) stenographer-typists. On-the-job materials were derived from programs for (1) mill cabinet workers, (2) hospital orderlies, (3) printing pressmen, (4) linofilm operators, (5) operating engineers, and (6) marine cooks and stewards. The overall objective was to examine the implementation of the Manpower Development and Training Act at the operational level against the backdrop of the other training efforts studied so as to ascertain its contributions to society and to the economy.

Chemists' Assistants

This program was selected for special study primarily because it embodies the goals and principles sought by the MDTA. The manager of a local State Employment Office identified, through unfilled job orders, a demand in the industrial community for workers in this occupation. At the same time, the files of the unemployed contained applications of persons who seemed potentially capable of qualifying for the positions if training were available. Moreover, the Chemical Workers' Union and employers in the area were much in favor of a course for chemists' assistants, and the local junior college administrators were receptive to participating in the plan. There is a secondary but nonetheless noteworthy reason for singling out this program. While its form faithfully represented all other institutional MDTA programs, its content was different: it was more professional than most; men were predominant among the enrollees, and it was more imaginative than the major part of the training plans established during the early months of MDTA. It seemed to offer great promise as a bellwether in this national endeavor.[20]

The description of the occupation and training objective is as follows. The assistant performs various routine tests, such as filtration, titration, or precipitation under supervision of any of the various chemists, makes laboratory test reports and furnishes test data, checks analyses with specifications, maintains the supply of chemicals in a laboratory, and keeps the laboratory equipment clean. The training objective is to prepare entry workers for placement in industrial chemical laboratories where a thorough basic knowledge of chemistry, mathematics, and chemical techniques is necessary. The general salary for this occupation starts at $375 per month and goes to $450.

The Richmond office of the California Employment Service estimated, on the basis of expansion and replacement needs as well as current unfilled openings, that there would be opportunities for 60 persons. Set up as criteria for entry into training were satisfactory grades on the general and specific aptitude tests administered by the Employment Service, a high school diploma with at least a B average in one year of chemistry and two years of algebra. The junior college, after consultation with the business representative of the Oil, Chemical, and Atomic Workers Union and several companies, designed a curriculum that concentrated two years of chemistry into 42 weeks. Of the allocated $50,000 for expenses other than subsidies, $32,019 was applied to purchase of new equipment for the school, $15,340 for instructional services, and the rest for fixed charges and incidentals.

When the class started on April 1, 1963, there were 24 students of whom 14 were unemployed heads of families. There were nine women in the group—two of them unemployed family heads. The ages ranged

---

[20] U.S. Department of Labor, Office of Manpower, Automation, and Training, *Manpower and Training*, Manpower Research Bulletin No. 2 (March, 1963), p. 24.

from 19 to 45, with most of the enrollees between 22 and 35. More than half the group had completed over 12 years of school. Nine of the trainees had worked less than three years; 11 had had from three to nine years of experience, and four offered ten years or more. The period of unemployment ranged from under five weeks for nine of the students to over 52, which three indicated. Six had been jobless from 15 to 26 weeks. The ethnic origins were as follows: 13 Caucasian, six Negro, one Mexican-American, one Eurasian, one Indian, one Chinese, one Portuguese.

By mid-June, 1963, six weeks after the training began, seven persons had withdrawn voluntarily. When the course ended, a total of 13 had dropped out. This high rate of attrition was attributed by the authorities to two major factors: (1) inability to keep up with the instruction; (2) need for financial aid. The first point bears particular analysis since it points up a failing common to many MDTA programs. This is the tendency to set up criteria for eligibility that are acceptable to an advisory committee and then to admit persons who do not possess the qualifications. Although a B average in high school chemistry was called for, only ten of the enrollees met the requirement; four had received a C; three had never studied chemistry; and there was no indication on the records of the rest. Although there seems to be some correlation between no grades or poor grades and early withdrawal, it is evident that some of the less well-prepared students did complete the course, while some of the dropouts had qualified in chemistry but should have been excluded for other reasons. One such person was a 35-year-old war veteran with two years of college who had done B work in chemistry. He had been unemployed for more than a year but had, in fact, once held a job as a laboratory assistant. His record showed, however, that he had received psychiatric treatment because of extreme claustrophobia and had been warned that laboratory or factory work might cause a relapse.

Lack of sufficient funds did not, as was thought by the authorities, play a significant part in the dropout rate. There were only two cases in which there was evidence of financial strain; the students were not eligible for MDTA subsidy because they were young and single. Much more important as a deterrent to successful completion was the failure to meet the original entry standards.

The unemployed applicants who had been regarded as likely candidates for jobs as chemists' assistants were not, by and large, the persons for whom MDTA programs were primarily intended. The best trainees were those allowed to participate in the course even though they were neither long-time unemployed heads of families, nor otherwise representative of the group for whom MDTA was devised. The applicants who met not only the explicit criteria of good high school performance in mathematics and chemistry but also the implicit requirement of ability to adjust to a classroom situation, to study systematically, and to carry out homework assignments, were young men and women who had completed their formal education but lacked the specialized skills that would get them into the labor force. Some of them were allowed to take the course, without subsidy, and their performance and subsequent placement in laboratories helped obscure the fact that the course for chemists' assistants had not fully carried out its prescribed function of making jobless heads of families employable through training.

From the point of view of the school, the program's success would have been enhanced by stricter adherence to prerequisites by the Employment Service; this, it was felt, could have been achieved if subsidies were made available to young people. Employment officials were wont to emphasize the change of instructors midway through the course as a disruptive factor contributing to both the dropout rate and the lack of noteworthy accomplishment.

Of the eleven persons who completed the course, seven were found to be employed and four unemployed. The results of the follow-up differ somewhat from the annotations in the official files. For example, the February 14, 1964, entry on the record of Mr. Parker, a thirty-five-year-old exmachinist with no preparation in algebra and chemistry, stated that he was employed full-time in a training-related occupation at $100 per week. His reply to our questionnaire stated that he regarded the course as of no benefit to him, "because I don't feel qualified to be a chem asst." He indicated that his average weekly wages prior to the year of unemployment before the training had been $100 and that he had earned nothing subsequently. Asked whether he was job hunting, Mr. Parker replied, "No. I have decided to start a business of my own." Officially reported as employed in training-related work was a young woman whose questionnaire was returned by the post office as unclaimed. The verbal report was that she had remarried, left no forwarding address, and could not be reached by the Employment Office.

Inquiry into placement as chemists' assistants brought forth the following facts. Of the seven persons thus employed, three were unmarried Caucasian women under 22 who had attended at least several years of college, had no dependents, and received no allowance. The two white males, aged 21 and 27 respectively, were not eligible for subsidy. The other two men, a 34-year-old American Indian and a 40-year-old Negro, did fulfill all the MDTA requirements as to family dependents and the like. It is interesting to note that these graduates, who were from minority groups, were especially easy to place since many of the chemical firms were in the process of what the records refer to as "integrating their work force" and, in fact, have made known their needs for more such employees in line with their observance of fair employment practices.

The second program for chemists' assistants, begun July 1, 1964, had an enrollment of 20; three members had dropped out by October. Continued support came from local industry in the form of participation on advisory committees and promise of jobs. Since in the past companies used to hire untrained and inexperienced young persons for entry positions in the laboratory and then had to provide on-the-job instruction, their receptivity to the MDTA program is understandable. The second course was somewhat longer than the first one, several weeks having been devoted to a review of algebra and chemistry. The selection criteria remained the same. An official of the Employment Department stated that minority groups were represented among the students and that, as before, there were some women included.

Retail Clerks

This program was chosen for special study because it appeared to fit all the criteria set up for an MDTA course. (1) Local businessmen convinced the Employment Service of a shortage of skilled personnel; (2) the Employment Office files had records of unemployed persons who seemed to possess qualifications that, coupled with specific training, would make them eligible; (3) the projected curriculum was unique, with members of the Chamber of Commerce participating as visiting lecturers. Research effort brought forth background information that is germane to an analysis of subsequent development and results. The apparent dearth of Negroes in the downtown stores of Berkeley had given rise to a series of meetings between local businessmen, the NAACP, the Urban League, and interested citizens. The merchants indicated that they had encountered a shortage of qualified Negro sales persons and would gladly hire any who applied. The 53 responses to 300 questionnaires sent out by the State Employment Service strengthened the assumption that a real need existed. With a training program tentatively scheduled for early Spring completion in time for the annual increase in Easter business, the projection of need seemed modest. Organization of the program was accompanied by unprecedented publicity in all the newspapers of the area. The aspects stressed were the earnest desire of business to observe fair employment practices by hiring members of minority groups, the new role of executives as teachers lecturing on such subjects as "Product Information," "Store Services," and "Closing the Sale," and the community spirit shown by this endeavor. In fact, the press releases were written by the Chamber of Commerce and representatives of the State Employment Service. The Berkeley "Equal Opportunity Policy" was printed in full: "We will continue to work diligently with the California Department of Employment and the Berkeley School Board to develop a sales training program specifically for the purpose of qualifying minority race members for detail sales employment." [21]

The course outline developed by the Berkeley Unified School District had three main divisions: (1) Business English and Speech; (2) Basic Arithmetic and Mathematics Review; and (3) Retail Salesmanship and Merchandising. Classes, from 8:30 to 4:30 daily, ran five days a week for six weeks, and were held in the downtown YMCA to facilitate access by the lecturers. In addition to speeches by local shop owners and managers, there was a talk on dress and personal grooming by a model from a well-known agency, and occasional films were shown.

The primary requisites for eligibility were a high school diploma and a grade of 85 or above in the General, Clerical, and Numerical sections of the State Employment Service test battery. During the personal interview, the worker at the State Employment Office tried to assess such factors as interest and motivation. It had been hoped that the class would attract a substantial proportion of men, but only three applied and two enrolled. The third man had two dependents but could not qualify for subsidy because he had less than two years of work experience. His need was for immediate employment and income. It is quite likely that the relatively low entry salary in retail selling may have been responsible in part for the dearth of male candidates. Varying somewhat according to shop, department, merchandise, and skill level, wages in the small, nonunion establishment start at $1.25 per hour and average about $1.40 per hour. The union scale is from $1.50 to $1.82. Parenthetically, it may be of interest to note here that household domestic workers are receiving $1.50 per hour plus carfare. Where commission is paid or specialized product knowledge required, earnings are higher, but this course was geared to the vestibule level and graduates could expect only the minimum.

Due to legal restrictions the State Employment Service could not set up an MDTA program for Negroes. But the way in which the local newspapers and radio stations announced the projected course made the inference fairly clear to the public that Negro applicants would be especially welcome. Although some white persons evidently expressed interest, the entire roster of 35 students accepted for the course was Negro. Their age range was from 17 to 44 with an average

---

[21] Berkeley Chamber of Commerce, Downtown Center Division, "Berkeley Equal Opportunity Policy," Policy 3.

of 27. All but one were at least high school graduates, the exception having completed eleventh grade and then taken a short trade course; seven of the members indicated at least a year of college education. Despite this relatively high level of education, more than half of the enrollees had been jobless over 15 weeks and occupations such as factory worker, baby sitter, and domestic had accounted for the work history of 18. Fourteen of the enrollees were eligible for and received MDTA subsidies; a few indicated that they were also getting some other form of financial assistance, probably public welfare. It should be noted, however, that the class did include seven women who had been unemployed less than seven weeks and that clerical work of one or another kind had been the previous occupation of nine members. Although the record shows only 31 graduating, it would be erroneous to conclude that there were four dropouts. One student who had been accepted decided not to take the course because of inability to support a family without subsidy; another left three weeks early to take a job as a salesclerk. Poor attendance, lack of interest, and emotional difficulties brought about the dismissal of two young women— aged 17 and 20 respectively.

The graduation was accompanied by festivities and publicity quite unparalleled in MDTA history. The local newspaper carried pictures, graduates' names, lists of sponsoring agencies, businessmen who participated in the ceremonies, and excerpts from the speeches. In presenting the certificates of completion, the Chamber of Commerce spokesman referred to that organization's participation in the program as "enlightened self-interest." [22] Elsewhere in that day's issue of the newspaper was a ten by ten and one-half inch advertisement sponsored by that business group, with a large picture of the class. Under it the members' names appeared, so that a prospective employer could make his selection from the photograph. The text read as follows: "The men and women shown above have successfully completed an intensive six-week retail-trainee program, jointly sponsored by the Berkeley Chamber of Commerce, the California State Department of Employment, and the Berkeley Unified School District. Graduates are now available for interviews by employers seeking well qualified applicants for careers in retailing." Noteworthy in all the press releases and advertising was the absence of reference to the MDTA. Although the federal government was the only "sponsor" which had provided funds, it was not mentioned.

The 26 replies to the questionnaires following up the individual trainees revealed a number of interesting facts. Of the 15 persons who were employed as of July 15, 1964, eleven were in training-related

---

[22] "Retail Clerks Class Graduates," *Berkeley Gazette,* Feb. 26, 1964.

occupations, and many of these jobs were temporary and part-time. As far as could be ascertained, no more than six of the graduates were working in companies that had cooperated in the training aspect. Only four of these placements had come through the State Employment Office, the agency that had been encouraged to establish the course because of alleged unfilled jobs in the community. Several competent observers saw a coincidence between the drying up of demand and the lifting of pressure by militant civil rights groups. The glutted condition of the local market became apparent even at the height of the pre-Easter season when this group graduated, and subsequent investigation has shown that many of the local stores are not even accepting applications. For the training-related employees, of whom nine had reported previous occupations as predominantly in the waitress and domestic categories and two had been in the clerical field, the average weekly wage was $55, about five dollars less than most day workers get.

The question, "Do you feel that the course was of benefit to you?" elicited 23 positive and three negative responses. "Did the training help you find employment?" received 15 "yes" and 11 "no" replies. There was no apparent relationship between the two answers, since some persons who received no help were still prone to regard the class as worthwhile. The valedictorian's view was that the value lay in the letter of recommendation she received and the help in recognizing her own strengths and weaknesses—"but no help in finding job." As a suggestion for improvement, she commented, "Excellent course, but give clear understanding that won't get job from it." Rated as the most outstanding student, unreservedly recommended for a job, this twenty-five-year-old former clerk-typist who had completed two years of post-high-school education found her own job as a salesclerk, lost it after one month because she could not handle the work, and was subsequently placed by the Employment Service as a cashier at $50 per week.

Three vignettes from the records illustrate the divergent experiences and reactions that typified this group. Miss Rachel Robinson, twenty years old, had completed one year of junior college and taken a course in key punch machine operation. Unemployed after having worked as a temporary clerk in the Internal Revenue Service and at a production job in a cannery, she was receiving Unemployment Insurance. Her test results were generally better than average, and her class attendance and performance were very good. The teacher rated her outstanding in grooming, selection of clothes, and appearance. When the manager of a local bank visited the program, he offered Miss Robinson a job as teller at $65 per week. She is still employed there.

Karen Hardwick, twenty-six, single, with two dependents, had completed one year of college and had worked as a clerk for six years. She had been unemployed more than one year and received an MDTA subsidy. Her test results were a little higher than average, her attendance record perfect, the teacher's comment favorable. In a telephone follow-up, it was learned that she had derived no benefit from the course and that she wanted no further training ever and would "never take a course like it again." Her main objections stemmed from the fact that this was an all-minority group—"putting a new light on it, promising jobs but didn't come through." Her suggestion for improving the course was, "Discontinue it."

Mrs. Clara Butler, a twenty-seven-year-old mother of two, with husband absent from the home, had been unemployed for 27 to 52 weeks and was eligible for the subsidy. Her previous work was as file clerk at $2.12 per hour. With average test results, she demonstrated that she could learn quickly. Her attendance record was perfect and she received an unreserved commendation. Jobless for three months after the course ended, she was placed by the Employment Service as a $60 per week saleswoman in a small specialty shop. The work turned out to be part-time and temporary. Her answers to our questions indicated that she considered the course of no benefit, her reason being, "I don't really feel it takes six weeks of training to do retail sales. It seems all it takes is good common sense." A follow-up in October, 1964, revealed that she had never liked saleswork and that she had taken a costly course in "I.B.M. machines" at a privately-owned school after having lost the selling job. Still unemployed, she was waiting for the school to place her as they had promised in their advertisements.

Despite the low saturation point of the market, another course for retail sales clerks was set up several weeks after the first one ended. Completed in mid-April with appropriate ceremonies and a reception given by the Retail Trade Bureau and the Chamber of Commerce, the class produced 23 potential salesclerks, all Negroes, and, according to officials associated with the program, less qualified than their predecessors. An October, 1964, report showed nine of the second group to be employed—mostly in establishments other than those represented in the local Chamber of Commerce; eight were listed as unemployed, and the whereabouts of six were unknown.

While successful placements are not the sole criterion by which to judge the efficacy of MDTA programs, they cannot be overlooked in assessing the value of such endeavors. It is quite apparent that in the retail clerks training course, neither the job opportunities nor the long-range good of the students were given sufficient consideration, especially in running the second training class. The business community, threatened by boycott and picketing by militant minority groups, overstated their needs; if continued pressure had been exerted they might have had to do more "showcase" hiring of Negroes. As it turned out, they put very few of the 54 graduates into the jobs that had been purported to exist. While the training may have benefited some of the individuals who found positions for themselves in stores in other communities, there is little in the record to show that the two programs enhanced the employability of a sufficient number to have made this a worthwhile investment of government funds and school and employment personnel's energies.

Licensed Vocational Nurses

There were two reasons for inclusion of the local MDTA programs for licensed vocational nursing in this study. The first was the popularity of this occupation for MDTA classes throughout the country; the second was that the San Francisco Bay area had long offered tuition-free training, such as was described in Chapter 1. We were interested in ascertaining what ends had been attained by this apparent duplication. Widespread indeed is the preparation for this sub-profession as can be seen in the reports of projects approved during the first 18 months of implementation of the MDTA.[23] By 1963 there had been approved under the heading titled "professional and managerial," 315 projects for 9,148 trainees. In this general classification, 59 occupations had an average of about five programs each. Licensed practical nursing alone accounted for 147 projects and 4,777 trainees, or 46 percent of the projects and 52 percent of the persons involved. Mechanical draftsmen came next with 32 projects and 726 trainees, and forester aides third with 20 projects and 437 trainees. For most of the other occupations listed, only one project was listed. Although the number of occupations and the number of entries under each has grown during the current year of MDTA operation, licensed practical (or vocational) nursing has remained among the top few predominating activities in any category.

This is clearly seen in the tabulations for 1964–1965, where licensed practical nurse is found among the top ten training occupations. During that year, 162 projects in the field were approved for 5,917 persons. New York had 20 of them with about 1,200 students; Illinois, California, and Michigan, each with 10 to 27 projects for 600 to 1,000 trainees.[24] As was pointed out in Chapter 1, there are about 40 licensed vocational nursing programs going on as part of the regular public

---

[23] U.S. Department of Labor, *Manpower Research and Training,* Report of the Secretary of Labor (March, 1964), p. 57.

[24] U.S. Department of Labor, *Manpower Research and Training* (March, 1965), p. 27.

adult education system in California. (Description of the work, along with salary and employment outlook, can be found in Chapter 1.)

The instruction planned for the MDTA trainees in Oakland, California, was identical to the ongoing curriculum. The scheduling was different, however. The California State Licensing Board requires a 1,056-hour program, a regulation met by running the classes for three consecutive school semesters with the regular vacations in between. Under MDTA, which allows for a certain maximum subsidy, the classes run steadily, with only weekends and legal holidays off. Students receive six hours of instruction five days a week, with their mornings devoted to clinical work at the hospitals and their afternoons to classroom learning. The MDTA grant of $43,737 for two classes covered the salaries of teachers and a part-time clerk to keep students' records, and it bought a uniform, white shoes, wrist watch with sweep-second hand, and pair of scissors for each trainee. It will be recalled from the report in Chapter 1 of vocational nursing programs in adult education systems that those students buy their own uniforms and supplies.

Slated to start on March 20, 1963, the first of the two classes actually began June 3, 1963: the second began eight weeks later. In establishing criteria for eligibility, there were some differences of opinion between the Employment Service and the school. Under MDTA regulations, the Employment Office was responsible for screening and selecting applicants. The women they referred for training had been subjected to their test battery (B-474), designed to determine aptitude for practical nursing. The minimum age requirement was 17.5 years; no maximum limit was established. All applicants were given a physical fitness questionnaire to be filled out at MDTA expense by their own doctor and a similar form for their dentist. Height, weight, vision, and neurocoordination were the items of importance. In addition, education, work experience, motivation, and need were taken into account. The test battery normally administered by the school for applicants to the established program placed considerable emphasis on verbal and arithmetic ability and seemed to be a more reliable indicator of the student's ultimate performance in classes and in the State Certification Examination. Consequently, the school did not enroll applicants unless they scored in the 25th percentile of a scholastic achievement test used by the school. Out of the first 44 women referred by the Employment Service, six were accepted. In total, more than 60 were sent to the school for the formation of a class of 15. Although this seemed to the Employment Service to be a manifestation of undue selectivity, the school defended its position by arguing that it would be a disservice to the applicants and a waste of public funds to enroll incompetent persons with limited promise of success. With local unions and newspapers taking sides, the matter of selection became a sort of *cause célèbre,* a situation unwarranted when one recalls that the enforcement of criteria reported in Chapter 1 had involved screening of as many as 300 women for a class of 15 or 20, and that even such rigorous maintenance of standards had not prevented dropouts and failures.

To prevent further friction, officials of the Employment Service and the school examined their differences and worked out a compromise for selection of pupils for the second MDTA class. With joint recognition that the B-474 test battery could be applied satisfactorily in identifying aptitude for vocational nursing if a higher cutoff score were established—Michigan having demonstrated this conclusively—the new procedure called for a combination of this plus the reading comprehension and arithmetic measures customarily required by the school.

Fifteen trainees were accepted for each of the two classes. Interestingly, enrollment in the school class remained constant; the first class actually started with only 14 members, one of the applicants having failed to enroll. One termination was made after six weeks, when the student showed that she could not profit from instruction. The discrepancy between her class performance and her original test scores was so great that she was reexamined. The results indicated a strong need for remedial work in reading and arithmetic. Poor attendance record and a lack of dependability were the reasons for dropping another student, suspected of being an alcoholic. The remaining trainees in the two classes ranged in age from 21 to 49, with a mean of 33, a median of 34, and a mode of 35. With respect to age, the enrollees in the MDTA courses for licensed vocational nurses were about the same as the group described in Chapter 1. As for previous occupation, eleven of the MDTA trainees were listed as nurses aides and hospital workers of some kind; twelve had been maids, waitresses, and the like; and the rest had been clerical, sales persons, or telephone operators. Here, as in the public school program reported in Chapter 1, vocational nursing represented more of an upgrading for the Negro group —about 80% of the MDTA classes—than for the white women. The marital status of the MDTA class enrollees was as follows: 12 divorced, eight separated, six married, two single, one widowed. The 20 women who received MDTA subsidy were responsible for 54 dependents. The nine others were self-supporting or depended on their husbands. Almost half of the 60 women studied earlier had relied on husbands, and the rest on parents, welfare, and own savings. Although tenth grade completion was acceptable in school and MDTA programs, almost all of the enrollees of both had a high school diploma. In view of the wide variation in quality of education, this document carried little weight; test performance was far more crucial.

In mid-October, 1964, a conference with school officials responsible for the nurses' training yielded the following information. (1) Because 52 weeks of consecutive class attendance had wrought considerable hardship on mothers with young children, absenteeism had run high. In order to provide the number of hours required by the State Licensing Board, the school had extended the course for about two weeks. By early August, nine trainees from the first class and ten from the second had completed the preparation; 19 took the State Licensing Examination, and 18 passed. Their individual grades were not available, but the report was that the grades were generally satisfactory. There seems to be evidence to suggest that the first group did somewhat better than the second, a matter which deserves further exploration since it could upset the notion that screening procedures had been refined and improved upon in the selection of this group. The school's explanation that the first group was of higher calibre and that the second class was made up of those left over or rejected does not appear to be borne out by the completion record. Whatever the facts of the situation, all the graduates were placed in jobs even before receiving their state certificate.

Judged on the basis of objective criteria for selection, course content, and characteristics of enrollees, there is little apparent difference between MDTA and adult-education-sponsored training classes. The main and very important distinction, of course, is that the former provides a living allowance. This makes a year of specialized preparation available to women who might otherwise become public charges because of lack of earning power. In the early months, officials at the various registries expressed fear that subsidies would have the negative effect of keeping in the programs incompetent persons who would have voluntarily dropped out of the school program. Persons who recognized that they were unsuited to the occupation would, it was felt, be more likely to pursue this career in order to avoid being shelved for a year as the law requires in such cases.

If the effect of financing were an ultimate lowering of hard-fought-for standards, then MDTA programs would be performing a disservice. Nothing in the evidence substantiates this apprehension. In fact, an official of a district nurses' registry who had been outspoken in her skepticism when the program began reported that while she could see duplication when parallel courses were offered in cities, it was the built-in subsidy that made the difference and was of incalculable benefit. As for smaller communities, she found that MDTA was the sole source of training and that hospitals and nursing homes were eager to hire the graduates. She felt that the women entering the courses were of what she described as higher calibre than those enrolled in the cities. She mentioned the recent placement in full-time employment of a widow with four children. The woman had had several years of college, was bright, personable, and willing; but she had no specialized skill and was totally unprepared to earn a living for herself and the children when her husband died. An MDTA class for vocational nursing provided an opportunity to acquire a useful vocation, and the subsidy made it possible for her to spend a year on the preparation.

Because of the requirements of the Manpower Development and Training Act, it would not be possible to utilize ongoing programs in licensed vocational nursing and simply provide subsidy where needed. Only by some such arrangement could duplication be avoided. It must be recognized here and in connection with the MDTA-sponsored clerical courses to be discussed next that duplication occurs relatively seldom and only in those cities where there is a well-developed adult education system. Even in California, where the number of adult classes is impressive, smaller communities' needs have not been met. Hospitals and other health services cannot find enough qualified personnel; at the same time, many women remain unemployed for lack of guidance and training. It is in situations like this throughout the country that the Manpower Development and Training Act provides avenues to gainful employment.

With national legislation providing increased medical care for the aged population, new demands are being imposed on the already burdened nursing profession. An acute shortage of registered nurses has caused a serious imbalance between them and the support echelons such as licensed practical nurses and aides. The salary structure aggravates this disproportion. On the hospital staff in California, the registered nurse receives a salary of $440, while the practical nurse gets $393. On private duty, the former has a fixed daily fee of $28; the latter has $20, with an additional two dollars for mental patients. With such a small increment in salary but such a great discrepancy in responsibility, it is small wonder that the profession seems to have lost its appeal, and its ranks are dwindling. The difference is not great enough to warrant the huge investment of time and money. As a result, the vocational nurse licensed to work under the supervision of the registered nurse often finds herself without direction and expected to perform duties for which she lacks preparation. A subject for at least concern in the reputable hospital, this situation goes unchecked in nursing homes with doubtful standards.

There can be no doubt of the continuing need for licensed practical nurses, and it is obviously not the function of the MDTA to police the profession. However, it is of utmost importance that as the graduates go into service they be provided with the kind of direction they must have. A society that values its health enough to legislate in favor of preserving it may soon have to concern itself with implementing the legislation.

Stenographers' Program

Interest in the MDTA programs for clerical workers was inspired by three factors. (1) This is a family of occupations for which public education has been providing training for years, both as part of the secondary school curriculum in junior colleges, and in adult classes. (2) Private institutions, many of which have earned good reputations, offer clerical training in abundance. (3) Under MDTA, clerical courses are almost as prevalent as are those in the nursing occupations. The question was asked whether MDTA involvement in clerical training was duplicatory: where and how did it meet needs not served through conventional channels? To ascertain the answers, which are basic to the raison d'être of public subsidized training programs, the research included the first secretarial course established under MDTA auspices in California. A subsequent class was studied for purposes of comparison with the first, which was understandably characterized by trial-and-error. Slated to last for 26 weeks with 30 hours of instruction weekly, the first class, made up of 31 women, began on January 14, 1963. During the following six months, 12 dropped out and seven others discontinued the stenographic portion of the training. Thus, the ultimate result was 12 stenographers and seven clerk-typists. The second class, scheduled for 28 weeks or 35 hours of instruction began on August 5, 1963, with 32 trainees, of whom 18 graduated.

Attendance records show a high incidence of tardiness and absenteeism in the first class. Further inquiry revealed that two students had severe emotional problems, one lacked the necessary manipulative skills, another had language difficulties, and another a serious illness. Among those who left the first program early, seven withdrew voluntarily—some because they were unable to keep up with the work, others because of physical or emotional problems, one because of financial reasons, and another because she moved away. Five were dropped because of poor attendance or unsatisfactory progress. Although the attrition rate in the second class was equally high, the ratio of dismissals to voluntary withdrawals was close to two to one, an indication of the more vigorous discipline enforced in the latter. The admission requirements were considerably tightened, so the second group of students had to be able to type at a certain speed as well as pass tests in reading, spelling, grammar, and arithmetic. This qualification for entry brought into the program women who had already had some office training and experience and for whom the course would be a refurbishing and upgrading of skills. In the earlier class it had been found that even though the curriculum had been revised and simplified so that basic typing could be brought up to necessary speed levels, many students were unable to keep up with the work, much less progress to such relatively difficult subjects as shorthand. From the sixteenth to the twenty-sixth week of the second class' schedule, instead of the daily two hours of advanced typing, the group had one hour of advanced typing and one of additional shorthand transcription. In selecting and interviewing possible applicants for the second class, the officials exercised great care in identifying physical and emotional problems which might limit performance in class and on the job.

The age distribution of trainees was from 20 through 52 with a mean of 34.71, a median of 32, and a mode of 27. It is interesting to observe that the large incidence of dropouts was among the older members, a group with a spread from 23 to 51, a mean of 35.33, a median of 36.5, and a mode of 41. As regards education, the range was from eight years to more than 16, the mean being 13.45, the median 13, and the mode 12. (To simplify computation, 16 and over was treated as 16 years.) There appears to be no significant difference in the number of years of schooling completed by those who graduated and those who dropped out. With respect to race, 74 percent of the women were white, 23 percent were Negro, and one was of Negro and American Indian descent. The record shows a higher proportion of nonwhite than white members failing to complete the program. In view of the selection criteria, it should come as no surprise that some 70 percent of the enrollees had been formerly employed in office occupations. The revision in entry standards and curriculum put even greater weight on typing ability and some acquaintance with shorthand, a subject that ordinarily cannot be mastered in less than a year. By and large, the trainees who completed the training were not only younger than the group as a whole but also had had fewer years of working experience. This suggests that length of gainful employment is not necessarily a predictor of ability to benefit from retraining. Some of the older women may have been employed longer, but they had developed personality difficulties or blocks to learning that impeded their progress in the course. With the dropouts from the program showing a comparatively longer period of unemployment than the women who graduated, the question arises whether the factors contributing to their failure to obtain and hold jobs might have some relation to their inadequate performance here. Generalizing from this experience one certainly would have to reject the hypothesis that the person unemployed the longest would apply himself most assiduously to the retraining course so as to become eligible for placement as quickly as possible. There was, however, an interesting correlation between course completion and MDTA support—persons receiving allowances being fewer among the early leavers. Related to eligibility for subsidy were such factors as marital status (predominantly divorced and separated) and responsibility for dependent children.

The placement figures as of mid-October, 1964, about 15 months after completion of the second class, are actually those received through the State Employment Service's follow-up of September, 1963. This is because only three persons responded to the 12-month follow-up of September, 1964. Known to be employed were 15 of the 37 women who completed the course. It would be appropriate to note here the experience of the Research and Statistics Division of the State Department of Employment with nonrespondents. Their analysis of earlier survey results has revealed a distinct bias; the persons who do not reply have been found most likely to be jobless and to change location without leaving a forwarding address. Respondents were more apt to be those persons who have found employment.

The human side of the MDTA secretarial course can be best portrayed with several illustrative cases. One of the trainees, a twenty-eight-year-old divorcée with three children, was a high school graduate with no particular vocational preparation. She was of mixed American Indian and Negro lineage. At the time the course began, she had been unemployed for more than a year and was eligible for MDTA subsidy. Although she had done office work in the past, her most recent experience was as a wrapper and relief clerk in a department store. On the qualifying tests administered by the Employment Service, she had failed to meet the lowest standard of typing speed and accuracy and had tested low in general intelligence and perception. Her class work was noteworthy and her performance in shorthand and typing very satisfactory. Shortly after completion of the training, she found an office job paying $80 per week and has remained steadily employed.

Another student, a fifty-two-year-old refugee from East Germany, had lived in West Germany until 1957 and then emigrated to America. Mrs. Schmidt, a widow with two sons in college, had had three years of college training and had taught school in East Germany. Her only work experience in this country was as the housekeeper in a church home. At the time the MDTA program began, she had been unemployed for more than four months and only one of her sons had a part-time job. Probably because of language difficulties, Mrs. Schmidt scored very poorly in typing speed and accuracy, spelling, and intelligence. Her grades in clerical skill and coordination were good, however. Enrolled in the class and receiving a training allowance, Mrs. Schmidt demonstrated ability to learn rapidly. Because of the language problem, she was advised to drop shorthand and concentrate on the typing. She was placed as a general office worker at $70 per week.

Pamela Roberts, a single Negro girl of twenty, had taken the commercial course in high school but had had no work experience. When tested, she failed the typing speed and accuracy and the general intelligence portions, but she passed the perception, clerical skill, and coordination sections of the battery. Miss Roberts was enrolled in the class but soon had to drop shorthand. Her lack of concentration and tendency to make many typing errors were regarded as deterrents in getting and holding a job. She was placed in general office work at $1.50 per hour, but was soon laid off. When retested subsequently while being considered for another job, her speed had dropped, her errors had mounted, and her spelling and grammar were still poor.

With the December, 1963 amendments to the Manpower Development Training Act in effect by mid-June, 1964, it was interesting to observe the setting up of the third class in stenography. Trainees were no longer required to have had three years of experience in order to qualify for allowances; two years was considered adequate. Because the Employment Service had previously included persons who qualified for training even though not for allowances, the new regulation was felt to have little perceptible impact. From numerous interviews with trainees and with officials, it was learned that this liberalization could ultimately achieve real upgrading of relatively unspecialized clerical workers by encouraging and making possible the development of skills in the higher echelons of office occupations. The greater receptivity and perseverance of the younger workers, as seen in the research, may be an indication that this is the sector of the labor force that could derive particular benefit from these changes. The rearrangement of the schedule of payments from a regular $43 per week throughout the entire training period to $43 for the first ten weeks and $53 for the final sixteen weeks may serve as an incentive to graduate.

An amendment that may influence continuation of the already strong portion of courses for women is the one interpreting "head of family" to include the woman of the house for allowance if the husband is unemployed through no fault of his own and is not enrolled in an MDTA program. As was pointed out earlier in this chapter, about 80 percent of the institutional courses reported in California are for women. Nationally, women represented two out of every five of the unemployed and underemployed workers approved for occupational training under the MDTA.[25] There is good reason to believe that the amendment allowing subsidy to wives of the unemployed, along with the other factors outlined at the beginning of this chapter, will increase the number of women trainees and programs for them.

A much-needed provision for attainment of basic education skills appears in the amended Act. If remedial instruction in grammar, spelling, and arithmetic are taught along with the specifically vocation-oriented subject matter, allowances can be extended beyond the usual training period. A program can now run for 104 weeks with learners receiving subsidy the whole time. The value of this amendment is more apparent when one reviews the records of persons screened or dropped out of programs than when one considers the graduates. Many of the persons who needed training most were excluded from the programs because of inability to meet minimal standards. Recognition of the need for functional literacy to be met by subsidized training is one important step toward helping the hard-core unemployed overcome their handicaps. The amendments allow for application of some of the lessons learned from the Neighborhood House and county welfare experiences, especially that techniques for retraining must take into account the base-line, from which the particular individual starts.

The case materials suggest that economic prosperity has brought into sharper focus the characteristics of the hard-core unemployed. The persons who cannot be absorbed in a period when presumably there are shortages at all skill levels apparently require some kind of extra assistance to make them competitive. The MDTA, by maintaining a policy of flexibility, is responding to present needs by providing remedial instruction, occupational exploration, and specific training. Perhaps as the structure of the unemployed undergoes reconstitution, with more schooling and different aspirations, the MDTA will serve as the vehicle for achieving vocational as well as functional literacy.

---

[25] U.S. Department of Labor, *Report of the Secretary of Labor on Manpower Research and Training under the Manpower Development and Training Act of 1962* (1966), *op. cit.*, p. 9.

[8

Retraining Under the Manpower Development and Training Act of 1962: On-the-job Programs

As was indicated in the foregoing chapter, on-the-job programs have been exceeded by the school-based, institutional type. It was the intent of Congress, we may recall, in fashioning this legislation to encourage industry to train its employees and to get a process of moving up the ladder going. The ultimate purpose was to make room at the bottom of the ladder for the new entrants and the less skilled workers. In this research, which covered all the on-the-job projects in the San Francisco Bay area at that time, it was found that in the initial stages of MDTA the unions and not the employers took advantage of the federal grants. Moreover, the union members trained were not the seriously underemployed, by and large, but more likely either the élite who recognized the personal benefit to be gained or the persons chosen because they were known to be industrious and liable to reflect credit on the program.

During subsequent years, the on-the-job training programs under MDTA increased momentum and developed broader sponsorship. The report for 1965 showed double the number recorded in 1964, with a total of 69,000 workers involved and $35.7 million spent. With training projects covering some 700 occupations, about 6,000 employers participated. Health care and automotive occupations accounted for 8,000 and 7,525 workers respectively, most of them at what is termed the apprentice-entry level.[1] Closer review of some of these job-site

---

[1] U.S. Department of Labor, *Report of the Secretary of Labor on Manpower Research and Training under the MDTA* (March, 1966), pp. 23–24.

activities indicates that here, as in the county welfare rehabilitation programs, there may be danger of subsidizing substandard employment under the guise of training. For example, the preparation of entrants into medical fields demands extremely rigorous control at every stage from selection through instruction and even after placement. How this can be achieved in nursing homes and old-age homes, notoriously understaffed and more often than not lamentably devoid of supervision, is a subject of necessary concern. Moreover, analysis of on-the-job records from the file of Neighborhood House raises some doubt as to the value of the training to be derived in many of the situations. Perhaps without the MDTA subsidy, some of the employers would simply have had to hire help at the prevailing wage and teach them the ways of the particular business in traditional fashion. Such, for example, could well be the case of the liquor store owner, paid $27.50 a week to train a clerk, the manufacturer reimbursed $30 per week for a routeman, the grocer paid $30 weekly to train a clerk, and the nursing home with three trainees at $30 each per week.

Considerably more in keeping with the intent of the on-the-job program are the contracts approved for California in the early months of 1966. The most recent of these cover ten large firms and provide training for 1,572 men in such diverse occupations as aircraft assemblers (Douglas Aircraft, Santa Monica, 150 trainees and Rohr Corporation, Chula Vista, 250), welders (Kaiser Steel, Napa, 350), and electronics technicians (Hughes Aircraft, Culver City, 95). With one-half of all MDTA training slated to fall into the on-the-job category, it is interesting to examine the initial implementation phases as a background against which to assess future developments.

CASES OF ON-THE-JOB TRAINING
SUPPORTED BY MDTA

The following cases represent the sum total of on-the-job MDTA programs in operation when this research was undertaken in 1963. With one exception, they were set up on the initiative of unions.

Millmen and Cabinet Workers Layout

This program in layout instruction for millmen and cabinet workers was among the first few on-the-job programs financed under the Manpower Development and Training Act in the San Francisco Bay area. A cooperative effort between Local 550 of the Millmen and Cabinet Workers Union and the Bureau of Apprenticeship and Training of the U.S. Department of Labor, the program was designed to upgrade journeymen who needed instruction and supervision in layout work in order to qualify formally for that rating, the pay scale of which corresponds to that of foreman. The regular journeyman's hourly wage is $3.65; the foreman and layout man receive $3.90. This local has a membership of about 1,300 distributed in three general categories: 80 apprentices, 300 production workers, and the remainder journeymen. Entry into the production classification is possible without going through formal apprenticeship; progressing out of it into journeyman status is, however, exceedingly difficult.

Layout work is regarded as an élite specialty within the trade, for it entails considerable responsibility. The worker must be capable not only of marking patterns on stock lumber, but of arranging the jobs as specified in drawings and setting up material lists. The skill involved is in obtaining the maximum number of pieces with most effective utilization of wood grain. The criteria for eligibility in the MDTA program were graduation from formal apprenticeship, at least three years of journeyman status, and sincere interest in self-improvement. Announcements were made through the trade paper, and there were about 25 applicants, from whom 15 were selected by the business manager, who knows the membership well. The class was made up of three Negroes, four Spanish-Americans, one Japanese, and the rest white journeymen. All these men were working at the time, the union having practically no unemployed members. No training allowances were being paid, so cost of the program was relatively low.

It may be noted that the union has opposed courses in layout in the public vocational educational curriculum for two reasons. First, it is averred that the men trained in school want to enter the trade from the top but that they lack the basic experience required. "A fellow can put a company out of business with one mistake," a union spokesman maintained. Second, there is the contention that the schools hire teachers who have met the teaching credential requirements but who are not sufficiently well-versed in the trade. The apprentices enrolled in a local vocational school, it is reported, are being taught by a man who has never been a millman and who, in fact, asked to be allowed to attend the MDTA layout course so that he could teach it in the evening trade class. Even though this instructor is a member, he was not recommended as a teacher by the union because he was not considered qualified. The three men whom they regarded as competent were bypassed by the school because they evidently lacked the proper certification.

The MDTA program was a combination of theoretical and on-the-job training, called a "coupled program." One three-hour evening class per week at school and layout at the work place supervised by a roving coordinator comprised the 12-week program; at its termination about half of the men entered the full-fledged layout classification.

Similar promotion is expected for the others, since openings are being created through retirement or death of older members. For the institutional portion of the training, the MDTA allocation was $1,095, and for the job-site supervision, $2,688. After two early dropouts for unavoidable reasons, enrollment remained stable. No absences were allowed; no second chance given. The trainees were generally pleased but felt that they could have profited by a longer course, running perhaps 24 to 30 weeks. Just how any such prolongation will appeal to employers one cannot say. There seems to have been some objection on their part to having journeymen learn while at work; their one concern was to get the job at hand done. Perhaps resistance from the employers' association stemmed from their allegation that they were not consulted sufficiently, and that the union's role in the training program had been too prominent.

The frictional strains and stresses that accompanied the first program for journeyman millmen have not discouraged the union's continued interest in retraining. Shown in a recent regional study to be especially alert to the problems of changing technology, the union once set up a survey course in plastics at a local trade school and is considering one in the use of new materials such as fiber glass and imitation marble mixed with glue. Because it has been dissatisfied with its experience with public education officials and "hampered by the restrictions and red-tape" of the MDTA, the union is investigating the possibility of financing its own future programs. There is some doubt on how such a proposal will appeal to the rank-and-file membership. Heavy competition from other regions of the country as well as from Japan and Germany has posed certain threats, and new materials and processes are beginning to make their impact felt. Awareness of these developments was reflected in the millmen's responses to the questionnaire used in the above-mentioned county-wide survey. But so long as most of the members have steady employment, they do not seem to recognize the need for retraining to be serious enough to warrant expenditure of their own funds.

Hospital Orderlies

Training for the occupation of hospital orderly has been going on for years, but the establishment of programs in many cities has recently gained momentum from financial assistance under the Manpower Development and Training Act. As with licensed vocational nurses, instruction for hospital orderlies is generally administered by the school department and rather classroom-oriented, though certain portions of the curriculum are carried out in hospitals. By contrast, the Oakland, California, project came under the on-the-job classification and was set up through the Bureau of Apprenticeship and Training at the Kaiser Foundation Hospital. This occupation is open to men only and is one for which persistent demand exists. The duties of the orderly are set forth as follows:

Orderly, or hospital attendant. Assists professional nursing staff in hospitals by performing various heavy duties in a hospital. Lifts patients to and from bed. Wheels patients to and from operating room. Carries meal trays. Does cleaning and odd jobs. Bathes, shaves, and dresses patients. Answers call bells. Makes beds. Gives alcohol rubs. Female title: Nurse Aide.

Surgical Orderly (Medical service). Prepares operating room, surgical equipment, and patients for operations. Ascertains kind and time of operation, patient's ward, and attending physician from notices. Positions instrument, surgical supply, and other tables in operating room. Sets up oxygen, carbon dioxide, and anesthetic tanks by standard procedure. Prepares patients by washing, shaving, and sterilizing region of operation and dresses patients in regulation garments for operation. Arranges patients on operating table in prescribed position and drapes special sheets over them. Straps patients to operating table or holds patients receiving anesthetic until they are completely relaxed. Disinfects rubber pads used in operating room, and performs other cleaning duties. Packs soiled linens into bags identified by tags and sends them to laundry. Sterilizes surgical instruments for operating room and wards.[2]

At the Kaiser Hospital where the program was carried on, wages begin at $335 per month and increase to $348 at the end of one year. There is a 12½ cent per hour premium paid for evening and night work. In addition, complete health coverage for the employee and his family, life insurance, and retirement benefits are provided by the hospital. Far from being dead end, this occupation can serve as the starting point for a career in hospital work. As was seen in the foregoing job description, the surgical orderly's functions are quite specialized, as are operating technicians, and the Kaiser Foundation Hospital will provide on-the-job training in this work at full salary for four of the men who have completed the MDTA hospital orderly program.

The State Employment Service screened 50 or 60 persons before referring 13 to the hospital authorities, who made the final choice. Of the 12 men enrolled, 11 were Negro. The educational requirement was officially for eighth grade completion, but most of the students had completed high school and several had gone to college. Men from eighteen years of age and up were eligible; they had to be in good physical condition. After testing the men for specific aptitude in hospital work, the Employment Office conducted interviews to ascertain each applicant's reasons for wanting to take the training, there having been perceived a tendency on the part of some persons to seek entry

---

[2] U.S. Department of Labor, *Occupational Guide,* 2–42.10.

into any ongoing program irrespective of interest. Great care was exercised to choose men who had no police record, since orderlies must be bondable. Morals charges are regarded as an especially serious consideration in this type of occupation. It is interesting to note that several of the enrollees, all of whom were unemployed, had come from higher-paying jobs but had requested training because they wanted to get into something "where automation won't take over"; others had received higher pay but so irregularly that it did not constitute a living wage. One of the men, a professional football player who had attended college, was deferred from his military service in order to complete this course.

During the six weeks' curriculum the class received a great deal of instruction and supervision in all phases of their duties. Kaiser Hospital furnished the seven instructors and was reimbursed for their salaries, supplies, clerical work, and bonding. The budget for expenses came to $1,717, with total training allowances to the students adding up to another $3,096. Stressed along with educational subjects was the importance of professional conduct while on duty, personal appearance, and grooming.

Judged by the personnel supervisor to be of a "higher type" than most men attracted to this occupation, this group lost only two of its original members—the reason being that they were unable to keep up with the work. It was felt that the training stipend had attracted older and better qualified young men than was the usual case. With the exception of the draftee, who had to go into the armed forces, the graduates were hired by Kaiser Hospital. Two were soon terminated, however, because they failed to come to work on time. Since the schedules of hospital workers must dovetail so that no post is left unattended, promptness is a sine qua non. Despite the fact that this was stressed in the preparation, two of the graduates had to be dismissed for unreliability. According to the supervisor at the hospital, five of the hospital orderlies who came from this program are excellent. Now permanent members of the staff, four of them will receive training as operating technicians. One of the men has been assigned to central supply duty and is regarded as the most capable ever to hold that job. Much pleased with the outcome of this project, the hospital will probably request another MDTA contract to run in the near future.

Printing Pressmen

The official job description sets forth the following duties for the cylinder-pressman, who is also called a printing pressman.

Makes ready (sets up), tends, supervises the operation of a cylinder-type print-ing press. Loosens inking rollers with a wrench, removes them from press, thoroughly cleans them with waste, and replaces them in press. Lubricates moving parts of press. Locks form (type set-up or plate) in position on bed of press. Packs impression chamber. Marks out sheet and fills in with tissue or folio. Starts press and runs off a proof sheet. Examines proof sheet to ascertain that ink is being distributed evenly and in proper quantities. Makes an overlay of proof sheet if ink impression is not uniform by cutting out por-tions of dark impressions and pasting onionskin paper over portions of light impressions. Places overlay in impression chamber in exact position on the cylinder that it was originally printed. Instructs cylinder-press feeder to feed sheets into press if press is hand fed. Tends press while it is in operation, making adjustments in inking mechanism as necessary to produce properly printed sheets. Sets and adjusts automatic feeders. Registers forms and mixes colors.[3]

The wage scale in this area is $4.61 per hour or $161.30 per week minimum to $200.

The International Printing Pressman and Assistants' Union, char-tered by the American Federation of Labor in 1895, has a total membership of more than 115,000, which makes it the largest in the industry. Long aware of the effect of automation on employment and the conjunctive problem of retraining members whose skills and en-ergy are replaced by machines, the union, according to its spokesmen, was "almost prophetic" in establishing needed institutions, programs, and agreements "long before the printing industry or the government took decisive action." [4] Claiming credit for being pioneers in craft training, in 1911 they instituted a program at Pressmen's Home, Tennessee. The Technical Trade School of the International Printing Pressmen and Assistants' Union of North America now "houses in excess of three-quarters of a million dollars' worth of printing equip-ment of all kinds [and] is the seat of this union's vast educational program, which has as its basis the furthering of members' technical skill in the art of printing." [5] Besides the original classes in offset work, the curriculum now includes camera, stripping, platemaking, and color separation. Well-developed correspondence courses are also available to members. Local 125, upon whom present interest cen-ters, rotates about three men at the school all the time. Depending on their course of study, their stay can last six weeks to nine months, but the former is more typical. Since the overall program at the Trade

---

[3] U.S. Department of Labor, *Occupational Guide*, 4–48.010.

[4] Fred Roblin, "Arbitration, Automation, Retraining Embraced Years Ago by International Printing, Pressmen and Assistants' Union," Supplement to Western Edition (Advertisement), *The New York Times* (Nov. 18, 1963), p. 36.

[5] International Printing Pressmen and Assistants' Union of North America, *Technical Service and Trade Educational Program*.

School is financed through dues, there is no tuition fee. Students must, however, pay the $25 per week charge for room and board.

A marked shift has taken place from letterpress work to offset printing, which involves camera, platemaking, and stripping operations, so employers need skilled operators in order (1) to turn out the kind of work expected by their customers and (2) to meet the threat from foreign competition. The trend has gone from simple black-and-white advertising to brochures illustrated in color. For example, travel agents, steamship lines, car dealers, hotel owners, airlines, and almost every kind of commercial enterprise publicizes its wares and services in this way. A local department store recently distributed a sale circular that once would have required the services of an artist at every stage; it was turned out mechanically at the rate of 35,000 per hour. With the present practice of accepting international bids, the industry now sends books to be set up in Italy and bound in Germany. Switzerland is an important contender for the printing jobs, and some of the finest work in colored reproductions is being done in Japan.

Spokesmen for the local union are concerned somewhat less with the threat of invasion from foreign competition than with the immigration of workers from other parts of the country likely to secure the new jobs if their own members are not skilled and ready to defend their bailiwick. The fear was expressed that people will be brought in from "back East." Paradoxically counterbalancing but at the same time supporting this negativistic recognition of the need for training was the positive possibility of attracting large publishers to this area because of the existence of a reservoir of competent operators. These may have been contributory reasons for the request for an MDTA project. More basic, however, are the facts that the industry is growing and processes are changing. At least 75 percent of the local membership of 550 are regarded by their business manager as vulnerable, and when it was polled, some 250 indicated an interest in self-improvement.

The MDTA project was set up under the supervision of a joint training committee, two members representing the Associated Printing Industries' Employers' Association, Inc. and two from the Oakland Printing Pressmen and Assistants' Local Union 125. Its purpose was "for upgrading employees in this industry who are subject to being laid off due to technological changes coming about in the industry and the installation of automated equipment. These employees who will enter this training project are considered as 'underemployed'." [6] Because the workers recognized the need for learning

---

[6] U.S. Department of Labor Form OJT-3 Attachment B, "Justification and Explanation of Expenditure and Operating Procedure."

the new processes in order to upgrade their skills and protect their job security, they were willing to take the instruction on their own time.

Equipment and space were rented at a private printing plant for four nights per week, three hours each night. Two classes of about 20 came on Monday and Wednesday evenings, and two on Tuesdays and Thursdays. The course ran for 20 weeks, after which a new group of 40 was enrolled. Since some group supervision had been deemed the optimum teaching arrangement, the men worked in units of six or seven with three job instructors moving from one to another. The teaching staff was made up mostly of foremen chosen right from the industry, and it was considered by the union to be exceptionally able. To cover the expense of rental, supplies, teachers, and clerical help, a budget of $3,631.40 per month was appropriated. The total cost of the program, through which 120 pressmen progressed, was $86,500.

Selection of trainees was, according to the formal proposal, to have been handled by the Joint Training Committee.[7] The official qualifications were a minimum of five years of employment in the industry and the Committee's reasonable certainty that "the employee is 'underemployed' or his employment will be in jeopardy due to installation of automated equipment." [8] According to the business manager of the union, who in fact did the actual referring of students, the first two classes of 20 each were chosen on the basis of necessity in the plants. The response from the membership having been enthusiastic, there was apparently a substantial number to draw from. The age span of the enrollees was from 26 to 55, since pressure for training had come from some of the members aged 40 or so. Some of the union members were reported to be underemployed—likely to work only about nine months of the year; the kinds of job that they could handle were becoming scarcer. But men of this type did not seem to be included in the program, and the rationale was given that they had not sufficient interest and, perhaps, lacked the capacity for learning. A union representative offered the opinion that unemployed pressmen could be placed in jobs "if they got out of the rut," but apparently they were not invited into this program.

The attendance and completion record of the classes for printing pressmen attest to the interest of the men who were selected. There were no dropouts and practically no absences. Although all the men were employed in full-time jobs and participated in parent-teacher organizations, bowling leagues, and the like, they missed few sessions.

---

[7] *Ibid.*
[8] *Ibid.*

By mid-June, 1964, 120 employed printing pressmen had completed the course. The Bureau of Apprenticeship and Training and the union then drafted a proposal for a new program in multicolor offset printing for some 175 members.

With local vocational schools offering trade-related classes in these and similar processes, it was interesting to get the educators' and the union's point of view on the need for and the accomplishments of a separate MDTA program. The Department of Vocational Education's resistance to the project was made known in the early stages. The schools' stand vis-à-vis this training was that they have the equipment and competent personnel and that their efforts were being duplicated unnecessarily. The union claimed that the specialized skills could be taught far better in a modern shop than in a classroom, and, in fact, the city college administrator stated officially that his school did not have the proper apparatus for this particular work. In the regular evening classes for apprentice and journeyman pressmen, the school follows the hard and fast rule of admitting only those persons who are employed in this occupation and who are thereby members of this union. But according to some union spokesmen this is too lax an intake policy, imposing only minimum standards. As a consequence, most of the enrollees have "reached the limit of their capacity. When the bucket is full, it's just full. Some of these men go to school just for the sake of going to school." While regarding any training as having potential value, these spokesmen maintain that many workers cannot benefit from further instruction and that expenditure of effort in that direction is futile for everyone concerned. By contrast, the union claimed that under the MDTA arrangement it could select so judiciously that all trainees stood to achieve maximum results. In fact, it was pointed out, all members who could realize self-improvement had passed through the MDTA course. That there is much satisfaction with this arrangement became very apparent in a union spokesman's statement that the MDTA program had done the organization "much good," that unions are always subject to a great deal of public criticism, and that so constructive an enterprise helped create a favorable image.

Linofilm Operators and Teletype Machinists

Since both these programs were organized by International Typographical Union Local 36 to help its members prepare for the changes taking place in the industry, they are reported under one heading. In setting up the local arrangements, the union carried into operation a statement put forward by its national, to the effect that, "We claim jurisdiction over any and all processes which are substituted for work we have traditionally performed; our people need training to do the new jobs." [9] Although the parent organization maintains a multimillion dollar educational facility at its Colorado Springs headquarters, the only specific assessment at the local level is for the apprenticeship program. Any member may go to the Colorado center, but he has to pay his own way plus room and board. With the latest equipment and even a computer supplied by manufacturers, this program covers every phase of printing and is at present concentrating on the electronic technology usurping the linotype. Dramatized by the New York newspaper strike of 1962–1963, the introduction of the linofilm process is now making an impact on the West Coast. Almost all persons in the trade are faced with the new machines and must either acquire the skill needed to run them or find jobs in small shops that do not have them.

Convinced that journeymen would either have to learn to man the new equipment or lose the jurisdiction to someone else, the local worked out two programs with the Bureau of Apprenticeship Standards and Training under the MDTA. One was to teach employed linotype operators to use the linofilm keyboard; the other was to teach machinists in the trade to repair and maintain the teletype-setting equipment. All these workers were employed full time—those in newspaper plants earning a minimum $143 weekly and those in commercial shops on the same scale, which starts at four dollars per hour. The typographers having established the equal-pay-for-equal-work rule long before this was enforced by law, many women are found to be among the membership at large and among the trainees in the MDTA program in particular.

In conjunction with the six-year apprenticeship in typography, the local community college runs a fully-devoloped curriculum. Besides teaching the principles of the linotype method to apprentices, the school offers a course in paste-up, for handling reproduction proof for offset work. Here the students learn how to handle the product of the machines but not the machines themselves. The two instructors, who were selected from about 30 applicants who were union members, attended specialized sessions at Colorado Springs. This kind of training, though valuable in many respects, did not help the printers learn to work on the new electronics equipment.

Linofilm operation, which is not yet included in the Department of Labor's *Occupational Guide*, requires above all else a fair amount of typing ability, 45 words or more per minute. So important is this skill that typing has now become a standard requirement for entry

---

[9] As quoted in, "Democracy's Way at the ITU," *Business Week* (June 6, 1964), p. 80.

into an apprenticeship, and it may be the prime requirement, in fact. Reports from other countries indicate that girls just out of high school are employed as linofilm operators. The keyboard of the lino-film machine is like that of an electric typewriter and quite different from the linotype's. Consequently, the operators had to forget the 90-key mechanism, with separate lower case, upper case, figures, and capitals, and develop a new manual pattern. The MDTA program that was organized to help them make this adjustment cost $7,925. It was set up in rented space at the Oakland Labor Temple, a building open and maintained almost all the time. The regular rent of $92 per month was reduced to $72 for this course. A fee of $375 per month was paid to the Merganthaler Company for rental of a keyboard, whose purchase price would have been $17,000. A teacher from that company brought pertinent films and slides to illustrate his lectures, which formed part of the training. Practice on ten rented electric typewriters was under the supervision of a retired typing teacher who at one time had been employed by a local news-paper to train its own personnel. When a worker had demonstrated his ability to use the typewriter, he was given the opportunity to operate the linofilm keyboard.

Starting on June 17, 1963, four different classes with about ten men in each were conducted weekly. The sessions were four hours long and scheduled to suit the needs of the workers. One was conducted at ten in the morning, another in mid-afternoon. The length of train-ing varied considerably among enrollees, some attending as many as 20 to 25 weeks and some for only two or three meetings. Others came in for just one session to show the instructor that they could work on the linofilm machine, and thus they received official endorsement in the eyes of their employer of a skill that they already had. It is not clear from the records how many of the 37 linotypers were such dropins. Because there was ample practice equipment, the union accepted all apprentices and journeymen who applied and allowed them to remain as long as they wished. Each student was required to put down a $20 deposit upon entering the typing course, but this was returned to him upon his satisfactory completion. Without this financial involvement, linotype operators' interest in earlier typing classes had rapidly dwindled. The linofilm course ran until March, 1964, by which time all members who could have derived benefit from it had been included. The union makes the assumption that the 37 graduates received further training at their work place as their companies introduced new processes.

The second typographers' program, for teletype maintenance, began on May 1, 1963, and ended in July, 1964. These workers repair and maintain the keyboard and the line-casting units of the teletype setter, a machine which has been in use about twelve years. Since electronic units are now part of the equipment, the maintenance men required instruction that could not be gleaned from the manuals put out by the various manufacturers and vendors. Written in engineering rather than in printing terms, these manuals had always posed difficulties but never any so great as those generated by electronics. Training had to be directly on linotype machines, but few of these were available for teaching purposes until a local newspaper offered the use of its plant at no cost for four hours on Sunday afternoons. The only important expense, therefore, was the salary of the two instructors, who met with their respective classes on alternate Sundays—each for 30 weeks. Total budget for this program was $2,416. By running parallel classes on alternating weeks none of these workers had to sacrifice all his Sundays; in case of a lost lesson, make-up was facilitated.

To publicize the program, notices were sent to the Bay Area Type setting Machinists' Society, a group that meets monthly to discuss new techniques and equipment. Some of the men were already attending classes in electronics on their own or had been sent by their employers to the linofilm manufacturers for training. All machinists in the trade were invited to apply for the MDTA class, and the response was so great that selection of the 12 men for the two classes had to be confined to those in plants where the new devices were in operation. No change in status, upgrading, or extension of employment was involved. There was, however, the likelihood of job insurance because plants introducing the new apparatus paid a premium to the machinist who could work on telefilm. Workers not updated had to find companies still using the obsolescent hot-lead process.

Linotype machinists came to the classes from all parts of the San Francisco Bay area, some traveling as much as 50 miles each way. Although only 12 men could be trained at a time in the two classes, some 30 journeymen came in to observe. Ultimately, 27 were enrolled and given instruction. Students ranged in age from 25 to 64; there were no dropouts. Since many of the printing establishments are small, staffed by from five to 25 men, this practical training was regarded with much favor by employers. In fact it was reported by a union spokesman that both MDTA programs had generated a good deal of interest in training among the owners of newspaper and printing plants. Although mechanization and automation in this industry are seen as creating a serious labor displacement problem, there is also recognition that there will be a need for technicians who can maintain and repair the computerized systems. Firmly convinced that training for such occupations can be conducted by the trade and on the job instead of by a school in a classroom, the union is contemplating the possibility of applying for another project under the Manpower Development and Training Act.

Operating Engineers

Members of the International Union of Operating Engineers are the workers who maintain and run pieces of construction equipment rather than design them, as might be inferred from their occupational title. The official job description is, "a worker who is skilled in the maintenance and operation of all power construction equipment ranging from air compressors to steam shovels. Worker usually serves an apprenticeship of several years during which he is gradually instructed in the care and operation of increasingly complex machines." [10] Numbering 290,000, the International has an $18 million dollar treasury and relatively effective control of at least its construction jurisdiction.[11] Although the use of closed-circuit television under the remote control of a computer may ultimately replace the tractor operator and helicopters may usurp the work of the crane, the indications for technological change in the near future seem to be mainly in the direction of larger, more powerful equipment. Already, there are machines that can pick up 110 tons in one scoop; another, weighing 2,400 tons and operated by one man, picks up 55 cubic yards of earth at a single bite. Since its inception, the operating engineers' union has demonstrated, in addition to its achievements as an agent bargaining for better wages and working conditions, an ability and pride in adapting its membership to the new demands of the trade. Because construction work is extremely intermittent and likely to be spread over great distances, employers maintain only skeleton crews but look to the local union to supply them with as many as several thousand operators at short notice. In its role as manpower agency, the IUOE discharges the functions of labor recruitment, training, allocation, assignment, and even discipline.[12]

The job classifications of operating engineers are among the highest paid in the construction industry. Annual take-home pay is, however, generally derived from work during only certain months. The winter's snows in the East and both snow and rain in the West limit activity to such an extent that the San Francisco local of the union estimates that most of its members work only slightly more than half of the

---

[10] U.S. Department of Labor, *Occupational Guide* (Construction), 5.23.910.

[11] Garth L. Mangum, *The Operating Engineers* (Cambridge, Mass., Harvard University Press), p. 58.

[12] Mangum, *The Operating Engineers,* p. 271.

year. Regarded as an effective antidote to scanty and irregular assignments is a worker's versatility. The man with a wide variety of skills is considered likely to have most earning power.

Because tight production schedules prevent learning at the job-site, the journeyman has had until recently little opportunity to learn to run the machines. A retraining program in New York State and the one studied in California may foreshadow a change in the pattern of skill development for operating engineers. Local 137 in Westchester, Putnam, and Dutchess Counties in New York worked out a training arrangement for its membership with funds from a Joint Management Fund, established as part of the collective bargaining agreement with employers' associations. With seven bulldozers, four motor graders, four front-end loaders, and three hydraulic backhoes, rented at off-season prices from local contractors, the Westchester experiment has completed two years of successful operation. In 1963, about 80 members of the union participated in the program, where it is reported that $184,000 worth of equipment was involved and 3,837 gallons of fuel used. The claim is made that students taking the training in the winter of 1962–1963 increased their earnings by 50 percent over a similar period in 1962.[13]

The International Union of Operating Engineers Local 3 in San Francisco has a membership of about 22,000 in Northern California and some 6,000 to 8,000 in Utah. Its jurisdiction, however, extends over Northern California, Northern Nevada, Utah, and Hawaii. Local 12 in Los Angeles represents 20,000 in Southern California and Nevada. IUOE spokesmen estimated that half of the members were underemployed, perhaps to the extent of working for only eight or nine months per year, because of limited skills. Local training money at one cent an hour for every hour worked goes into the fund for teaching apprentices; a formal program of this type is now of three years' standing. There has been no formal program for journeymen. The wage scale for oilers is $155 per week; operating engineers, $180 per week, and foremen $200 per week; but these rates are the minimum and may be increased. Depending on the contract, there is likely to be considerable overtime on jobs where schedules are tight.

Local 3 of the IUOE applied to the Office of Manpower, Automation and Training for a grant under which to set up two consecutive sessions during the off-season for upgrading their underemployed members. The proposal, processed through the Bureau of Apprenticeship and Training, was approved with an allocation of $240,000. The

---

[13] New York State Department of Labor, *Industrial Bulletin*, XLIII, 5 (May, 1964), pp. 18–19.

program was designed for men in the union who, because they were familiar with limited operations, did not have enough skill to remain working even though they knew something about earth-moving. Because large pieces of equipment had to be used under simulated work conditions, selection of a site was very important. There had also to be some way of housing and feeding the 150 men planned for each session. Forestry camps, generally tenantless during the winter, were disqualified because the terrain around them was usually at high elevations and, consequently, totally unlike the ground conditions the men would encounter. The U.S. Department of the Interior would have cooperated by allowing use of property under Land Management jurisdiction, but the pieces were isolated and scattered. Arrangements were finally made with authorities of the U.S. Army for use of Camp Roberts, a base active during the summer in the training of reserves. Situated in Paso Robles, about 200 miles south of San Francisco, the camp could provide adequate housing in empty bachelor officer quarters and there were plenty of practice areas, such as an old county road and runways that the military was glad to have rebuilt as work projects. Estimating the cost of training each man to be $804 for the six-week session, the union sought some way to feed the group within the allotted living expense budget of five dollars per diem, of which one dollar was already being paid to the Army for lodging.

Finding that caterers in the nearby small towns and cities were beyond the project's means, an interesting symbiotic arrangement was set up with the Marine Cooks and Stewards School, located in Santa Rosa and discussed in Chapter 4. With the Camp Roberts mess hall as a job site and the operating engineers as their "passengers," 32 trainees underwent the kind of instruction they would have had at the aforementioned school. Among those reported to be enrolled in the program were nine Negroes, two Mexican-Americans, two Orientals, and one Samoan. This time, however, a separate MDTA grant paid allowances, teachers' salaries, and other related expenses. Under the supervision of the chief cook from one of the luxury liners, the subprogram supplied Local 3 with meals having two entrées for two dollars per day per man. Dormitory facilities at the camp were provided for the marine cook and steward trainees, who were enrolled for 12 weeks in groups of about ten each. Two MDTA grants to the Marine Cooks and Stewards Union for this on-the-job training program totalled $50,000.

Equipment, leased from cooperating general contractors in the area of Salinas, California, at rates paid by the State Highway Construction Division, maintenance fees, and incidental expenses such as toll calls and two telephone lines to Camp Roberts came to

$132,990. The instructors were described by officials as highly competent because they generally worked as job superintendents doing hiring and firing for contractors. Not including subsistence allowance for trainees, "Item 14" of the contract with the Office of Manpower, Automation, and Training called for $68,140. This was explained in "Exhibit A" of the union's proposal as follows:

Training Personnel Services for Operating Engineers[a]

1	Camp Manager	@ $275/week	$3,300	
1	Assistant	@ $255/week	3,060	
2	Clerks	@ $190/week	4,564.80	
15	Instructors	@ $235/week	42,300	
1	Maintenance Man	@ $235/week	2,820	
1	First Aid Man	@ $190/week	2,282	
		Total	$58,327	$58,327

Social Security and Disability Insurance @ 5 percent	2,916
Workman's Compensation (except clerks) @ $3.78 per $100	1,946
Clerks' Workman's Compensation @ $.15 per $100	11

Fringe Benefits: .15 Vacation Fund
                       .15 Pension Fund
                       .01 Retired Pension Fund
                       .01 Apprenticeship Fund
                       .17 Health and Welfare
                       .49 per man hour

21 men x 40 hours per week x 12 weeks = 10,080 hours

@ $.49	4,939
Total	$68,140

[a] Exhibit A, Statement of Contractor's Training Cost, Project number CA: J 41, p. 6.

The trainees all lived at Camp Roberts and received instruction five days a week. Because of the nature of their work, they were used to being away from home for extended periods, many of them accustomed to staying in trailers close to the job-site. The trainees' daily schedule called for about four hours of practice at the job-site. With ten men to the class, this meant that each man got 40 minutes on the machines. The ratio of one piece of equipment for every ten men appeared during the first session to be inadequate and efforts were made to improve it. With fifteen instructors on the staff, there was one for every group. Observation of other operators at work was considered valuable, too, since safety is a factor of utmost importance and good habits could thus be inculcated. Each enrollee was allowed $35 per week subsistence and from a minimum of $43 to a maximum of $55 per week for training, plus transportation allowance from home to Camp Roberts. Each man was charged seven dollars per week for living quarters, the receipts from this being allocated to heat, lights, and water. A weekly assessment of $28 covered meals and housekeeping services.

The program was publicized through newspapers and television in both northern and southern California. Since the winter of 1963–1964 was relatively mild, with only moderate rainfall, unemployment among members was estimated by the union to be somewhere between 4,000 and 5,000, rather low for that season of the year. There were about 1,000 applicants, from which the classes of roughly 150 each were to be chosen. In order to qualify, a trainee had to have been working on heavy construction equipment for a minimum of three years. District managers of the union selected the men according to several criteria. (1) They had to be unemployed; (2) their earnings during the past year should not have exceeded the $7,000 to $8,000 bracket; and (3) they had to be realistic and serious, characteristics which it was felt could be assessed by responsible personnel in the districts. Assignment to the Camp Roberts program was intended to be a prestige item on a man's record, and care was exerted to dispel any illusions about its being a rest-cure or a vacation. In fact, the business manager described a visit during which a trainee criticized the food; the complainer was promptly reminded that the quality and variety far surpassed any he must have been accustomed to when camping near a work location and that further manifestations of malcontent would lead to his dismissal. To quote one official, "The men never had it so good."

The first session, bringing together 154 men, opened on January 26, 1964; the second, opening on March 8, 1964, enrolled 147. The mean age of the group was 39.9 and the median 40. Estimating on the basis of known number of years of school completed, 10.7 was the average and 12 the median. Information regarding the ethnic origin of the enrollees was not forthcoming, although it was indicated that persons from minority groups were practically excluded from the union until the establishment three years ago of an apprenticeship program. Emphasis on the nondiscriminatory practices observed at present leads one to assume that they were not in operation before. Reported earnings for the entrants, as shown on their application forms, ranged from zero to over $9,000. The median annual earnings stood at $5,469, with the interquartile range—or middle 50 percent of the earnings—being from $4,586 to $6,607 for the preceding year.

In mid-July, 1964, a detailed questionnaire that was developed and sent out with the full cooperation of Local 3 of the International Union of Operating Engineers brought a 55 percent response. This was somewhat higher than the returns received by the State Employment-Service to their third follow-up, dated June 1, 1964 for the first class and July 1, 1964 for the second—these being 48 percent and 44 percent respectively. The reasons for the difference are quite apparent. (1) The State Employment Service had already canvassed the groups twice before, and the graduates were probably tired of filling out the same forms, possibly with the same answers, since their employment situation and evaluation of the training program would not have differed much in July from what they were in May. (2) Our questionnaire went out with a letter from the union's business manager bespeaking cooperation in the effort, and replies were directed to his office. These could have been returned unsigned, since a preestablished code would have identified them for use in tabulations. But many members, possibly in the hope of currying favor vis-à-vis placement in jobs by the union officials, identified themselves, especially when indicating satisfaction with the training. Analysis of our results and comparison with those received by the State Employment Service give reassurance that the basic facts about employment status of the trainees, the skills acquired, and the value of the program were not too seriously affected by the union's role. As will be seen later in this chapter, some of the comments, signed and unsigned, reveal very interesting reactions to the training.

The full value of the Camp Roberts experience would not be felt until the off-season, when lack of versatility ordinarily impairs some workers' all-around usefulness; consequently it could not be assessed immediately for the completion came at the time of normally high employment activity. Several criteria were considered valid for assessing the program's worth. (1) Were the graduates, both employed and unemployed, working at this time last year? In other words, was there any indication that the course had improved their earning capacity during the season? In this connection the respondents were asked whether they felt that the training had helped them obtain their specific jobs. (2) Accepting the assumption that extension of the men's capability would lead to a total of more employment per year, the men were asked to list the new skills they had acquired during the training. (3) The men were asked to evaluate the program according to a grading scale. Their suggestions for specific improvements were also requested.

The July, 1964, employment status of respondents is compared with that of July, 1963, in Table 15. The reports on present employment received in answer to the questionnaire were entirely consistent with those received by the State Employment Service in its third follow-up about two weeks earlier. Of the 138 trainees who responded, 108 or 78.3 percent were at work, and 30 or 21.7 percent, idle.

The foregoing figures indicate a slight drop in employment in 1964.

TABLE 15

EMPLOYMENT STATUS OF TRAINEES, JULY, 1963 AND JULY, 1964

(n = 166)

Employed			
1963a		1964	
Number	Percentage	Number	Percentage
146	87.9	136	81.9
Unemployed			
1963		1964	
Number	Percentage	Number	Percentage
18	10.8	30	18

[a] 1963 figures do not add up to the total of 166 nor percentages to 100% because one worker's status was not known.

For this group of workers, the training program seemed to have caused no discernible improvement. It should be recalled, however, that the data are based on the reports of only 55 percent of the graduates. The other 45 percent, who failed to respond to the union's plea for cooperation, might have provided different information. They all might have been away from home and on the job working; they may have remained unemployed and so, too disenchanted to respond. Because of the close correspondence between the reports we received and those tallied by the Salinas office of the California State Employment Service, however, it is probably safe to assume that the pattern would not have been drastically altered if more of the questionnaires had been returned.

From the replies received, it was learned that eleven men who were jobless in the summer of 1963 were working in the summer of 1964, that 22 who were employed during the summer of 1963 were without jobs in the summer of 1964, and that six were without work both years. From the experience to date, it can be inferred that the net benefit derived from the program seems to be marginal. More of these men were at work the previous year without the training than the following year with it. If this is truly typical of the group's employment at the height of the season, there seems to be reason to question the program's effectiveness in getting them off-season assignments.

This inference is supported by the replies of the 132 employed graduates, 29 percent of whom reported that the training had helped get them their jobs; the remaining 71 percent reported specifically that it had not helped. Confronted by these figures, union representatives explained that local dispatch offices were likely to have a surplus of men on some lists while operators in other categories were in demand. As a graduate from Camp Roberts, a worker could get his name on another list, but his place would be at the bottom, and he would have to prove his mettle in order to move upward.

To the extent that acquisition of new skill may be construed as a measure of enhanced employability, it was considered advisable to canvass the members to ascertain what they had learned during the training. The question, "Did you learn new skills during the training?" brought forth an 88 percent affirmative answer. Three categories of work seem to predominate among those reported as learned: (1) operation of rubber-tired equipment, (2) running the bulldozer, (3) grade-setting. In view of the classes' age distribution, which showed a median of 40, the popularity of machines with rubber tires is difficult to understand; most operating engineers by the time they reach 40 avoid rubber in favor of bulldozing, which is less taxing on the physical system of the driver. Even while listing the new skills they acquired and setting forth generally favorable reactions to the program (see Table 16), the men were almost unanimous in their

TABLE 16

Opinion Poll of the Operating Engineers, July 15, 1964

Evaluation*	Number	Percentage	Number	Percentage
1. Useless	1	1.1	—	—
2. Satisfactory	18	21.1	10	12.3
3. Rather Helpful	35	41.1	24	29.6
4. Excellent	27	31.7	40	49.3
5. Satisfactory and Rather Helpful	2	2.3	2	2.4
6. Satisfactory and Rather Helpful and Good	—	—	1	1.2
7. Satisfactory and Excellent	—	—	1	1.2
8. Rather Helpful and Excellent	1	1.1	1	1.2
9. Very Helpful	—	—	1	1.2
No Definite Answer	1	1.1	1	1.2

* Numbers 5, 6, and 7 were the respondents' own combination of the alternative choices.

criticism of the course for having provided too little practice on equipment; there were evidently too few pieces and not enough time allocated to learning to run them. The three aspects of the program that drew complaints were (1) the amount of equipment and allocation of its use, (2) the calibre of the instructors, and (3) the lack of organization in the curriculum.

Asked to grade the program on a rating scale, the graduates responded with a general endorsement.

Illustrative Case Materials

There seems to be little meaningful relationship between the skills acquired and present employment status, or between either of these variables and attitude toward the course. For example, many of the graduates placed the course in the "excellent" category although they were unemployed, working at jobs that did not utilize skills gained during the training, or felt that they obtained their present job quite irrespective of the Camp Roberts program. In addition, some of the most caustic remarks set forth under the "other ideas" heading were accompanied by a "rather helpful" or even more laudatory rating. One respondent, who rated the training as "rather helpful," indicated that he had been acquainted with the rubber roller before, had learned grade setting in the program, was employed the year before at this time, and had had no job since the Camp Roberts experience. Another graduate reported in the State Employment follow-up of June 1 that he was employed as a gradesetter at $4.30 per hour but that he did not like this type of work because it gets "too low a pay compared to operating equipment, would prefer to operate equipment." He further indicated on the questionnaire that the training had not made it possible for him to perform the job adequately. His list of suggestions in the State Employment Service follow-up of March 15, 1964, read as follows.

1. Better organization: the equipment was not run for eight hours as it was paid for, due to poor scheduling or lack of good communications. Also, poor communications kept personnel in the "dark" most of the time.

2. More time on equipment. Could have recieved as many hours in three days as I did in six weeks at Camp Roberts on the job site.

3. Use of equipment that we would most likely get to run in field: Most of equipment was of the newest type, which we see very little of in the field and if we do see it the older and more experienced operator always gets to run it.

4. Better instructions: Much of the time there was no one overseeing the job or observing the operators.

5. Make the training school shorter and more condensed: Most of us depend on the weather for work and making us sign up for a six weeks course (which is much too long of a time to predict weather) causes many of us to miss work if the weather should clear up, as was the case of this last class.

This man did not return our questionnaire; others, just as critical but less articulate, indicated similar dissatisfaction, but they set down a rating of "rather helpful" on the forms they sent back to the union, which were then turned over to us for analysis.

Mr. Ames, whose last year's earnings were listed as between $6,000 and $7,000, was classified as a mechanic and welder. The State's second follow-up, dated April 26, 1964, found him unemployed. His suggestions for improving the program were specific.

1. Servicing of equipment could be improved—2-Cat 12 Blades lost 4 Hrs. each waiting for engine oil. 1-L.W. Blade down 1½ days—broken fan belt.

2. Le Tourneau-Westinghouse Blades spent a lot of time in the shop or broken down in the field. Most of the time there was only 2 blades for 10 men which would give each man a little over 20 min. Blade time a day.

3. This program done me a lot of good and I know it will improve my chances of employment. I am not employed at present but expect a call any day.

Mr. Ames did not respond to the State's subsequent request for information, but he did reply to the one sent to him by the union as part of the research project. On a form postmarked July 16, 1964, he stated that (1) he was employed; (2) the training at Camp Roberts had not helped him get the job; (3) he was working as a mechanic and welder, his trade before entering the program; (4) he had acquired skill as a rough blade operator; (5) his present job did not utilize this skill. He checked "satisfactory" and "rather helpful" as his opinion of the course. Under suggested improvements, he favored "more practice" and "more equipment" and volunteered the information under "other ideas" that "some blades were junk."

A signed response from an oiler who had completed eleventh grade, earned $5,000 to $6,000 for four months' work in 1963, and applied to learn to run the blade indicated that he was now employed, that he considered the training excellent, but that he was not using his new skills. His comments were interesting.

I think it is one of the best ideas that could be put to work that I have ever been a part of. I think that next year it will be a lot better because it is like anything else it takes a little time. I think it would be a big mistake if it were not continued it has not helped me on the job I am on but will in the future. I hope I am working at school time next year but if I am not I would like to go again to learn some more how ever you do need some more equipment for as many trainnes as you have.

The mark of "excellent" was received also from an unemployed mechanic and welder who had earned between $7,000 and $8,000 last year and who had come to Camp Roberts to learn to run a bulldozer. Working last year at this time, he now listed "rubber tired loder and doger" as new skills. The ideas he offered for improvement are reported as written. "I think that the union Should try to place the men that took the training at camp and made passing grades on the job that they were trained for in Stade of Sending them out on Jobs other than What they trained for. I can name Several men that took the training that have bin placed on Different jobs then they took training at Camp Roberts. I for one."

Since it is satisfied that the Camp Roberts experience had achieved its goals of broadening the skills of the members and of helping upgrade them, Local 3 of the International Union of Operating Engineers is now preparing a proposal through the Bureau of Apprenticeship Standards and Training for a project for the early months of 1965. The budget of $600,000 is planned for the training of about 500 men, of whom 350 will come from Local 3 and the rest from Local 12. In an effort to improve the ratio of equipment to men in order to have one piece to every five enrollees, the union is investigating the possibility of getting surplus equipment from the U.S. Army. For their part, the Marine Cooks and Stewards are working up a companion program—this time for 52 trainees. The idea seems to have won the favor of representatives of the ship owners, the union, and the government agencies involved.

CONCLUSIONS ON RETRAINING UNDER THE MANPOWER DEVELOPMENT AND TRAINING ACT

Because there are such vast differences between the institutional and the on-the-job programs under the MDTA, systematic analysis of each type has had to be conducted quite separately. Our evaluations, except where direct comparisons are in order, must also be presented discretely.

In reviewing the data collected on institutional programs, we find that a workable assessment of demand occupations has been lacking and almost impossible to obtain. As was shown in the study of private companies, fluctuations in business conditions hamper prediction. Calls received by the State Employment Service cannot be accepted as an index because (1) only certain firms recruit workers this way, and (2) only certain limited categories of help are likely to be sought through that office. Moreover, a number of instances of strong demand, as in the case of automobile mechanics and power machine operators, turn out to be openings in nonunion shops seeking cheap labor while the union has enough unemployed journeymen to fill available jobs. Demand can be extremely evanescent, and that is another serious problem. The rapid generation of need for Negroes trained in retail selling that grew in response to threatened boycott by militant groups and vanished when they turned their energies elsewhere is but one example. Until present demand and future manpower needs can be properly ascertained, especially in light of forthcoming technological changes, meaningfully projected, there seems to be little hope that the MDTA can embark on any except the pedestrian kinds of programs. The courses for office help and hospital workers are bound to prevail just so long as measures of occupational demand remain inadequate.

The labor market information upon which on-the-job training projects have so far been based, seems just as inadequate and possibly more subject to bias. For example, the need for layout men was expected by the union to become very great if foreign competition and skill obsolescence due to new materials could be stemmed. However, if large contracts continued to go to out-of-state firms, and if prefabricated plastic and metal cabinets and window frames outmode construction with wood, the layout man will vanish precisely as the cutter in the shoe factory is disappearing because synthetic substances are replacing hides. The program may have supplied selected members with some job security for the near future, but it gave little evidence of improving the employment outlook for the membership at large. In the case of the operating engineers, the training program was predicated on the assumption that underemployment would be corrected by increased versatility, that workers had short-term jobs and long interludes between them because they were limited to one piece of equipment. While this hypothesis had to wait until the off-season to be tested fully, it was considered that the value of the training could be assessed to some extent by comparing the graduates' employment status in July, 1964, with that of July, 1963, both being at the height of the season for out-door construction. The findings indicate that, ceteris paribus, the training did not improve chances for employment. Either the course did not achieve its purpose of broadening the enrollees' skills, or the proposition that jobs were waiting for the better trained was erroneous. Until one or the other was firmly disproved, organization of a more ambitious program seemed premature. In the case of both on-the-job and institutional projects, demand must be established objectively and professionally and not on the basis of political expediency. Because better assessment measures are needed, it is important that all sectors of the business community be consulted. It is improper for any one group's view to be regarded as definitive.

On the critical matter of selection of trainees, the State Employment Service has the responsibility in the case of institutional programs. It will be recalled that the men enrolled in the Kaiser Hospital orderly program were screened and referred by that agency. Enrollees in the union-sponsored on-the-job projects were in many cases supposed to have been chosen by joint labor and management committees. Except for the printing industry, where employers wanted certain of their men trained to run the new equipment, the union officials had sole authority in designating the candidates for inclusion. Knowing intimately what the trade requires, and having some personal contact with individual members may be considered positive factors; but these may be offset by the part favoritism plays in awarding training and upgrading opportunity to selected members of the rank and file.

Objectivity and impersonality, as required in selections made by the State Employment Service, were applied rather sporadically and with questionable success in some of the institutional programs. With the delays attendant upon getting a project approved, finding a teacher, arranging for rental of equipment and space, there was always erosion of the list of promising students: the best of them found jobs, and the longer the course was deferred, the more attrition there was among the selectees. The result in the case of the chemists' assistants was that hasty, last-minute referrals were made so as to justify conducting the class at all. Quite irrespective of the requirements pertaining to mathematics and chemistry, persons were enrolled without knowledge of either subject. Failure to meet original entry requirements caused most of the dropping-out. Also, the record of one of the students contained the statement that his mental balance would be endangered by laboratory work. The importance of enforcing rigorous standards for admission was shown in the difference between the two classes in stenography which were studied. The first was characterized by frequent tardiness and absenteeism, and several students were found to be lacking in such fundamental requisites as emotional stability, manipulative skill, or knowledge of English. The second class had just as high a proportion of dropouts, but here those who were forced out outnumbered those who left on their own accord by two to one. This finding seems to suggest that more careful selection procedures screened out the less motivated; the fact that only 56 percent of the class completed the program underscores the need for either (1) curricula which are more realistically organized to correct the deficiencies of the entrants, or (2) more sophisticated tests and measurements to identify the less capable. Which alternative should be sought depends, of course, on the goals set for the MDTA to achieve.

The research points up the not unexpected finding that there was more likelihood of a mismatch between capability and performance in the institutional programs than in on-the-job projects run by unions. This need not be construed, however, as an indictment of the former or an endorsement of the latter. Choosing currently or recently employed workers for upgrading through trade-related instruction involved practically no unknown factors, especially since union managers and agents claimed that they maintained individual contact with members. The State Employment Service, on the other hand, not only had to scan hundreds of application forms and test results but had to identify potentiality that could be developed into a salable *new* skill. The fact that there has been so little variety in occupations for which training is being offered may have been another deterrent to optimum assignment.

By far the greatest obstacle encountered by the State Employment Service in selecting properly qualified candidates for training is the budgetary limitation it must operate within. The local offices are allowed a total of 12 hours for each person chosen and enrolled. When one takes into consideration the fact that two to three hours of this time must be devoted to the periodic follow-up of individual trainees, one realizes that the allocation is inadequate. When data-gathering reaches 30 percent of the funding, other aspects of the program suffer, as was seen in some of the inappropriate assignments.

Critics of the institutional programs have alleged that they are duplicatory of vocational courses already in existence. That there appears to be superficial duplication cannot be gainsaid. Scrutiny of programs in such an urban complex of communities as that included in the San Francisco Bay area shows that courses in licensed vocational nursing, stenography, clerk-typing, and many others likely to be offered under the MDTA are already part of the curriculum of local school systems. Of course, it must be recognized that MDTA funds could not be appropriated for ongoing facilities, but were intended for new programs. To be sure, this regulation has had disadvantages, as was indicated earlier, for the unemployed have to be fitted into those occupations specific classes are offered for. This requirement, in addition to the paucity of categories in which a continuing demand for workers has prevailed, has led perforce to what looked like duplication. But there were differences, and these were crucial.

The most striking divergence from the standard adult education program was that students were subsidized, and so they could devote full time to acquiring the skill that would make them employable. This factor is extremely important, as can be seen from the experiences cited in Chapter 1 of persons who could not afford training. With amendments to the Manpower Development and Training Act now extending benefits to cover fundamentals of basic literacy as part of the vocational rehabilitation process, the whole retraining effort may become more effective. Research into the institutional programs organized prior to enactment of the new laws pointed up the urgent need for monetary allowances so that the unemployed head of a family could take time out to acquire a salable skill rather than wasting energy in search of a type of job that is on the wane. Another contrast was the work-oriented structure of MDTA programs. Unlike the standard "cafeteria-approach" discernible in most adult schools, the MDTA curricula were geared to current job requirements. A case in point would be the stenography course, where students were given a full schedule of shorthand, typing, arithmetic, English, business machines, and lectures in grooming and deportment. Concentrated attention to each student's needs by the teacher, the school coordinator, and the worker from State Department of Employment were another departure from the ordinary classroom situation. Personal attention manifested recognition that persons who have lost their jobs or who have never been employed need a special kind of help not only in acquiring manual skills but also in rebuilding a favorable self-image and confidence.

In sum, it appears that in the urban milieu, institutional MDTA programs may possibly duplicate ongoing classes with respect to equipment and subject matter but that there are significant differences in pedagogical approach. Moreover, school administrators have stated that their space, personnel, and facilities were not adequate to accommodate all the unemployed who have been served through MDTA arrangements. Less than sufficient in urban California, adult vocational education is frequently nonexistent in smaller communities. As was pointed out in our earlier discussion of the MDTA program for licensed vocational nurses, cities and towns with no such facilities were suffering from a shortage of trained personnel for hospitals and rest homes and an oversupply of job seekers with no prospects of employment. In assuming the responsibility for setting up programs, selecting trainees, and making subsequent placements, the small offices of the State Employment Service assumed a more active role in the life of the community, far beyond the passive functions of a labor exchange or a disburser of unemployment claims.

The institutional programs appear to be less vulnerable to the criticism of duplication of retraining effort than the on-the-job programs are to the charge of substitution. As was learned in the study of retraining efforts of unions, some of them already have training funds established through collective bargaining; the indications are that there will be more as job security becomes a more urgent issue in contractual agreements. As seen in Chapter 4, involvement in the updating and upgrading of journeymen has been the official policy of some unions for years, and their national headquarters and locals carry on systematic programs without assistance from outside the industry. The Marine Cooks and Stewards is one such organization, and its involvement in an MDTA program stemmed primarily from its willingness to be of service to another union and not from a serious

need for a training facility in addition to the one discussed in Chapter
4. Some of the parties to local on-the-job contracts with the Office of
Manpower, Automation, and Training through the Bureau of Apprenticeship and Training were unions that maintain educational facilities
of their own. From interviews with union spokesmen, it was learned
that some of the programs would have been paid for with union funds
if the MDTA money had not been available and that, in fact, impatience with bureaucratic red tape might influence a decision on the
part of locals to conduct their own retraining programs in the future.

Conversely, but very significantly, the spokesman for one large
union, which had received a substantial federal grant and planned to
request an even larger one, stated unequivocally that he would not
spend union funds on such a project if federal money were not forthcoming. This was the position taken even though (1) training and upgrading had been prominent in his campaign for election to his post,
and (2) he had publicly acclaimed the results achieved by the completed programs. One cannot help but raise the question how the program could have been so satisfactory when provided free of cost, but
not good enough to warrant an investment by the union. Perhaps the
answer lies more in federal policy than in the labor union's practice.
It is clear that the on-the-job aspect of the MDTA has lagged; it is
also apparent that the government agencies responsible for arranging
this type of program encouraged unions to participate quite irrespective of their ongoing training endeavors. That they found some locals
receptive facilitated the establishment of projects and improved everyone's public image. The union demonstrated cooperativeness toward
the government as well as its concern for its membership; the Bureau
of Apprenticeship and Training claimed credit for retraining underemployed journeymen; the long-range prospects for the Manpower
Development and Training Act were enhanced, since organized labor's
original objections and fears regarding the legislation may have been
allayed. The element of making everyone involved look good is apparent in the development and operation of many programs, especially
but not exclusively those of the on-the-job type.

Similarly, the matter of substitution of effort in the on-the-job situation becomes important when appraising the involvement of business and industry. Many employers are receiving double bounty in
that they are being paid to train workers they themselves need and
would have had to instruct at their own expense. So far, there is little
evidence of the creation of entry opportunities in any number by
virtue of mid-career advancement through MDTA, on-the-job arrangements. In the cases studied, some journeymen received benefit, but the
technology affecting their skills was causing apprehension about an
oversupply of workers and union restrictions remained tight. Another

form of substitution could be seen in the use of small entrepreneurial establishments as training sites. One questions the need and value of a subsidized sales experience in a local liquor or grocery store, and one wonders about its quality and transferability as well. As for the nursing and convalescent homes utilized in this fashion, there is the possibility of indirect support to substandard employers.

About placement results, much less is actually known than appears in official reports. There seems to be a tendency to emphasize the successes even though, as was pointed out, the programs may have had hidden value perhaps not reflected in immediate work record. In September, 1964, the Berkeley office of the State Employment Service sent out letters requesting follow-up information from the 37 women who had completed stenographer-typist training one year ago. There were only three replies, a lack of cooperative spirit that has puzzled and distressed the authorities. Lacking recent data, the Employment Service has had to incorporate in the statistical record the placement figures derived from its survey of September, 1963. In other instances, persons were counted among the employed when there was no concrete evidence to the contrary.

In the statistical compilations relating to on-the-job programs, all enrollees who were not classed as unemployed were included in the ranks of the underemployed. Obviously, this category requires much firmer definition, since many trainees—such as millmen, printers, and many of the operating engineers—were receiving good wages or already had the capacity to do so. Although the claims made by persons responsible for the operating engineers' program could not be put to full test, it seems reasonable to assume that the men who completed the course should have had at least as good an overall employment record in the summer, 1964, as they had had in the summer, 1963, prior to the training; but the research findings and those of the State Department of Employment showed that the 1964 unemployment rate was higher.

To overlook the organizational stresses and strains generated by the MDTA would be to ignore a fundamental problem in its implementation at the local level. To investigate them in detail was not the purpose of this research study, however. The competition for power and prestige which is in evidence, and the frictions that are generated among government bureaus are no new phenomena in a democracy. Large scale programs perforce bring about alterations in relationships and authority, and the process of change is neither comfortable nor easy. Just what MDTA's ultimate impacts on organizational structure will be cannot be predicted from the first few years of operation. With respect to functional aspects, several interesting shifts in focus have already occurred. (1) The Bureau of Apprenticeship and Training has considerably broadened its sphere of interest and activity; instead of concern merely for apprenticeships and training in specific, isolated situations, the Bureau has become much more involved in the overall situation of employment and unemployment. (2) The State Department of Employment has been put in a better position to serve as a dynamic manpower center, not just a place to file job-hunters' applications.

[9

Summary: Retraining Trends in Perspective

INTRODUCTION

Retraining stands high on the priority list of approaches to a comprehensive employment and manpower policy in the United States.[1] Nonetheless, despite general acceptance of the idea that retraining will provide a means to more effective labor force participation, there has been only limited substantive research to ascertain what kinds of programs are in operation at present and what sectors of the population can be reasonably expected to benefit from them. Such empirical information is of primary importance in the articulation of needs, in the formulation of realistic policy, and in the institution of appropriate action. This study has been conducted to assess ongoing endeavors under all major types of sponsorship so as to attain an understanding of their dynamics and their strength and limitations. The research included programs under public adult education, the federal Civil Service, private companies, labor unions, social service agencies, and the Manpower Development and Training Act and other pertinent legislation.

Acceptance of retraining as an important vehicle for improved labor force participation carries with it no assumption about effects on overall unemployment rate. Speculations of this kind would be inappropriate in this context and conjectural under almost any circumstances, since we lack the tools to measure definitive variables. So

---

[1] Subcommittee on Employment and Manpower of the Committee on Labor and Public Welfare, U.S. Senate, 88th Congress, Second Session, *Toward Full Employment: Proposals for a Comprehensive Employment and Manpower Policy in the United States* (Washington, D.C.: 1964).

far, there are no adequate predictors of the extent and direction of technological and other changes that will affect production processes, consumer demand, and living patterns. We can neither forecast labor force requirements accurately nor identify future skill obsolescence.

We are nowhere near a measurement of the present impacts of automation, to say nothing of those still to be faced; we cannot assess its job-making or job-displacing potential. Nor do we know whether a better educated or more highly trained work force will necessarily lead to a lowered rate of unemployment.

Conflicting theories about economic causes and cures of unemployment abound. What percentage rate is tolerable and even desirable, the extent that tax cuts stimulate business activity and increase hiring, whether structural adjustments will bridge the gap between people and jobs—all these ideas have been aired and argued. The economic aspects of unemployment may be unclear, but it is apparent that serious social problems attending the phenomenon demand solution. We have seen that vocational handicap is a self-perpetuating phenomenon, handed from generation to generation, and we recognize the hard-core unemployed and its ever-growing and crystallizing periphery as the makings of a caste alienated from the world of work. Represented conspicuously among them are men and women whose present unemployment will turn into a permanent state of unemployability. Retraining per se may not provide them with jobs, but it can sometimes break the pattern by serving as leverage for movement into the work force and perhaps upward, too.

Unemployment as we are experiencing it is a distinctly American complex of problems, perhaps generated by them and certainly understood best in light of the particular economic, technological, and social influences of our time. There seems little use, therefore, in seeking guidelines through nostalgic reference to other periods in our own history or by investigation of other countries. Indeed, if one were to rate the industrialized countries of the world on a scale of technological advance going from underdeveloped onward, one could seriously hypothesize that America is overdeveloped, and that the problems of unemployment which we are trying to cope with have yet to be faced by those lower down on the scale. Consequently, to study the apprenticeship system of a foreign land or to emulate its vocational education practices can have only limited value. Labor organization in America and the standard of living that prevails in this country make the former anachronistic; our democratic institution of equal educational opportunity makes of the latter an unsuitable model. Consequently, looking to other times and places for solutions to our problems of persistent unemployment can do little more than provide us with materials for a frame of reference.

Because retraining is a very important way of achieving more equitable distribution of job opportunity, this research has been directed to appraising many programs organized under different auspices for various kinds of workers, but with the implicit or explicit purpose of improving employability. Retraining as a dynamic process is taking on new dimensions as a weapon in the attack on deprivation and poverty: new legislation has expanded its scope; new techniques for promoting it are being applied; new public attitudes toward it are being generated.

ADULT EDUCATION

In Chapter 1, adult vocational classes as a means to acquiring new skills were examined. Study of education at this level and during the earlier years of compulsory school attendance has pointed up the fact that some of the difficulties encountered in retraining the labor force have their roots in the educational system. For example, there are young people emerging from school without a working knowledge of arithmetic or English, persons seeking entry into the labor force with no skills, workers who face obsolescence but who have almost insuperable distaste for the learning process. In a word, the first lesson derived from investigation of retraining is that there is an overwhelming need for *training*. The American education system in general and the vocational aspects of it in particular require extensive overhauling. Lacking a clear-cut educational philosophy, the entire approach to free public schooling is based on the pseudoegalitarian assumption that by making a college-oriented curriculum accessible to all students, we have fulfilled true democratic ideals. The well-known fact that only a relatively small percentage of our high school graduates even enter college,[2] and that the investment of nine to twelve years of their time has brought many of the others little appreciable return has not effected any significant changes in school programming. Within the educational framework in cities where they are offered, vocational courses occupy a unique and unenviable position. Generally, they are enrolled in reluctantly and by default, and the industrial division is poorly equipped and inadequately staffed. Even when these deficiencies have been corrected, pride and prejudice prevent most students from actively seeking entry.

The high attendance records in public adult vocational classes, where they are available, may be an indication of the fact that people eventually recognize and try to remedy their shortcomings, but it

---

[2] Sar A. Levitan, *Vocational Education and Federal Policy*, W. E. Upjohn Institute for Employment Research (Kalamazoo, Mich., May, 1963), p. 1.

would be patently absurd to impute this motive to the greater part of the enrollees. With the potpourri of offerings, students sign up for a myriad of reasons, ranging from whim, as in the case of devotees to a hobby, to pressing urgency, as in the instances discussed in this book. The public vocational system often fulfills a useful function in providing a recreational outlet for adults. This is altogether desirable. If predictions about the increase of leisure in our society come to be realized, this aspect of the adult school could expand as students develop latent interests and seek new modes of self-expression.

The adult education system is promising in its avocational role; however, it is not too convincing as a vocational center. There are few cohesive programs organized to help adults gain entry into occupations. Little attempt is made to provide the guidance services that are much needed. Course offerings have no relationship with the current labor market and, indeed, often run as though oblivious of it. The amount of communication between school and State Employment Offices has been somewhat increased by virtue of implementing the Manpower Development and Training Act, but not enough to avert such poorly conceived efforts as the electronics assembly class described above, for example. Perhaps there should be some reevaluation of the criteria for setting up programs, for the present requirement is simply that a specified number of persons should manifest enough interest to sign up. While one would not advocate prohibitive selection, one cannot help but wonder also whether the almost unlimited access to some programs does not constitute raising false hope and wasting public funds. From the school's part, the lure of reimbursement for daily attendance may outweigh other considerations that should be taken into account in curriculum building.

As a desideratum for operating scores of classes exclusively for apprentices and members of certain trade unions, this compensatory funding has an effect that seems to violate the principles of free public instruction. And yet the schools make great efforts to attract these programs and to rationalize entrance restrictions on the ground that the union has filled the registration to capacity. What emerges as a paradox is that, despite educational administrators' loyal defense of these practices, many union spokesmen have expressed dissatisfaction with the schools; they claim that instructors lack trade competence, that much of the course content is a useless exercise based on outmoded textbooks, and that educational institutions—especially the community colleges—overemphasize the generalized, academic aspects to the detriment of those that are specific and trade-directed. Unions that can afford training programs of their own often set up independent facilities; others may continue to use the schools but criticize teachers, curriculum, equipment, and methods. The advent of on-the-job programs under the Manpower Development and Training Act has given some of these unions a welcome alternative as well as an opportunity to voice many of their objections to institutionalized instruction, of which they have been the beneficiaries.

Although they make few public claims to having themselves provided occupational instruction of a coordinated kind that can lead to employment, vocational educators have as a group been hostile to the Manpower Development and Training Act. Resentful of the invasion of their traditional preserves and suspicious of innovation, many school personnel have expressed opposition on the ground that standards will be lowered and any hard-won recognition by the public forfeited if the unemployed are enticed into accepting retraining through specially arranged courses and monetary allowances. While apt to regard the MDTA efforts as duplicatory of their own, school people have provided little conclusive evidence to substantiate this position. As was learned from investigation of MDTA programs, ongoing courses in the regular adult education system could not have accommodated the number of persons found to be eligible for it and interested in retraining, nor were the conventional courses geared to repair the particular deficiencies of the vocationally handicapped. Inquiry into the means of support of students enrolled in the courses for welders, vocational nurses, and electronics assemblers discussed in Chapter 1 pointed up the fact that in many cases, there was urgent need for financial help. By provisions for subsidy to trainees, MDTA programs have served a sector of the community for which retraining was otherwise a serious burden and a drain on limited resources.

Recent comprehensive and evaluative studies of vocational education in America, interesting developments in trade and technical programs at the high school and junior college level, and legislation providing funds for research into and improvement of the total educational system may presage noteworthy changes, which, even though initiated in the earlier school grades, may ultimately be reflected in the adult programs. Once we have overcome the archaic notions that learning must be an unpleasant ordeal, that education is pure only when divorced from reality, and that preparation for college is the prime purpose of the system, we may begin to bridge the gulf between school and reality. When this occurs, adult vocational education can assume the necessary function of realistic retraining and continuing self-renewal through learning.

FEDERAL GOVERNMENT

The federal government, in its role as a large-scale employer, conducts a variety of retraining programs. The results of the study

of the ways civilian personnel are protected against skill obsolescence and prepared for new assignment can be interpreted more
meaningfully after several popularly-held misconceptions are dispelled. To begin with, government agencies cannot, any more than
private enterprises, ignore cost considerations. Budgetary restrictions from the top echelons, international and domestic political
pressures, and Congressional temper exert constant control. Always
subject to orders that can peremptorily call for a change of product
development or cut the size of the work force, the federal organization enjoys little autonomy. Many bureaus must maintain operations at a level that is competitive among themselves as well as
with the outside economy. A case in point would be the various
United States-owned shipyards, which bid against each other on construction and repair jobs and have to justify their continued existence
by matching the efficiency of the private companies. The second
matter that requires clarification has to do with the civil service
worker's job security. Quite contrary to the notion that he has life
tenure, the fact is that he is extremely vulnerable to reductions in
force and shifting personnel requirements. Consequently, when technological advances and alterations call for a reconstitution of product
and process, the job structure changes and so must the employee's
skills.

The case study of aircraft instrument technicians provides a model
for on-the-job training which is closely attuned to the demands of new
equipment and techniques. Identified were such vital ingredients as
(1) precise selection criteria, (2) orderly progression through shop
stations, where production planning made learning and teaching
possible, (3) carefully defined goals, an understanding of which was
in evidence at every stage of the process, and (4) the emergence of
versatile craftsmen, for whom technological change spelled opportunity and advancement. The case at the Alameda Naval Air Station,
with an elite group of trainees and optimal scheduling, with allowances made in the respective shops for the handicap of in-service
instruction, highlights the essentials of successful in-service retraining.
The McClellan Air Force Base experience is an example of a large-
scale redeployment of industrial personnel, with obvious ramifications
from the point of view of human relations as well as from the practical
side.

The Internal Revenue Service's retraining activities associated with
the introduction of electronic data-processing gave reality to a phenomenon often claimed but rarely seen: when the computer takes
over, new and upgraded jobs result. In the case of this government
agency, faster processing of returns and better checking techniques
have created the need for more workers capable of assisting in the

preparation of tax forms, and a large staff is also required for enforcement work. The philosophy of redeployment by skill development underlying the personnel policies of the Internal Revenue Service's nationwide conversion to an automated system provides a blueprint for effecting viable transition with a minimum of displacement and career disruption.

The study of these programs for the retraining of civil service workers explored the government's employment policies in operation. Since channels through many layers of administration and authority must be traversed in the course of implementing any program, no claim is being made by a responsible official for universal success. A definition of the federal establishment's commitment to workers facing technological displacement is still in its formative stages. It is, however, the subject of serious consideration in all branches of the government, and, as shown in the case materials, progress is evident.

PRIVATE INDUSTRY

The responsibility accepted by private companies in the retraining of their employees was investigated by inquiry into all of the programs going on in the San Francisco Bay area at the time this research study was begun. The fact that such comprehensive coverage could have been achieved indicates a paucity that is characteristic not only of Northern California, where large manufacturing enterprises are scarce, but of the country as a whole. The findings provide possible clues to when, how, and to what extent industry utilizes retraining as a means of coping with changes in personnel requirements.

Quite contrary to the rather prevalent idea that retraining is to be found only in the large corporation, evidence shows that company size is not the single deciding factor. It was found that the small firm can act in an effective manner to protect its work force against skill obsolescence and, in fact, might even have the advantage of being able to identify the exact spot in the organization where updating is needed. Such was the case of the local die-casting manufacturer presented in Chapter 3. The quality control class discussed in that context need not have been the sole example of its type, for it is a safe assumption that this company's problem was not unique. In every case of industry-sponsored retraining, the desideratum was a shortage of workers in a particular category. Conversely, when there was no clear-cut need for workers displaced for one or another reason, no systematic attention was paid to salvage possibilities, nor were humanitarian considerations involved to any appreciable extent.

The main obstacle to retraining by private industry seems to be the inability or unwillingness of management to forecast product and process changes and, consequently, alterations in number and skills of workers. According to some research, large business concerns have been known to repress information about anticipated changes lest competitors benefit from it. Only one of the cases involved a company so obviously restricted; several of the other cases illustrated the difficulty of predicting personnel requirements because of completion or cancellation of contracts. Fluctuation in work flow, rather than technological change, rendered prognostication impossible. Another obstacle, encountered in almost every retraining effort observed, was that of worker apathy or resistance. Inclusion of this pervasive factor in the context of industry-sponsored efforts is appropriate because it seems to have most potency here. Few companies try to overcome this barrier unless there is a serious shortage of help. In the study of tracer lathe operators, for example, it was observed that failure to evoke a favorable response from present employees virtually forced a company to recruit from outside.

Several interesting clues to the question of worker motivation emerge from the research into private companies' efforts. The positive factors of job security and upgrading seem to outweigh the negative one of displacement. Retraining that has only nebulous value is the least attractive; few workers are willing to invest their time and energy unless they perceive a definite goal. True involvement, with instruction on company time, geared to clear promotional opportunities, seems to have the appeal. Some companies reported that in-service retraining for blue-collar workers had proven unsatisfactory because selection was regulated by seniority rules; this meant that oldsters had to be given first preference quite irrespective of their learning capacity. Company practices such as leap-frogging younger men whom they considered more promising or introducing aptitude tests as a screening device were discouraged by the union. The research suggests that the solution lies in the kind of cooperative action between labor and management seen in the case of the American Can Company and the United Steelworkers' Union.

Unless private companies have large blocks of unfilled jobs accessible to their present employees, it is unlikely that the pace of their retraining efforts below the managerial level will undergo much change. All other things being equal, industry accepts little responsibility for insuring workers' job security through in-service training. In the cases reported, definite need for a new classification or better calibre of personnel inspired the retraining effort. And continuation or repetition of such endeavors depends almost entirely on the firm's requirements in the near future. If the introduction of labor-saving equipment seems a sufficient threat to warrant action, unions will probably become more aggressive in their demands to safeguard job security. Whether these demands result in the development of more retraining programs or in such ameliorative measures as shorter hours, sabbatical leaves, or automation funds, no one can foretell. Extrapolating from experience to date, it is safe to assume that the role of firms vis-à-vis retraining will not undergo significant alteration unless special incentives in the form of tax reductions or other inducements are forthcoming. Private industry can, however, cooperate in the national effort to achieve optimal manpower utilization while taking full advantage of all scientific advances. Without divulging trade secrets, industrial leaders could apply some of the highly developed forecasting techniques already used in production, inventory, and marketing to their personnel needs. It is because this kind of information is not available that so much retraining is of an ad hoc nature.

LABOR UNIONS

In the sphere of union sponsorship of retraining, more interest was generally found on the part of locals whose parent organizations had a well-defined program upon which to draw. This likelihood was bolstered when funds, set up through collective bargaining, were available for the upgrading and updating of the members. In addition to these two obvious conditions, the most clearly apparent reason for union sponsorship was the official desire to establish and maintain jurisdiction over all present and future facets of the trade. Recognition of possible encroachment from outside and fear of skill obsolescence did not come from the rank and file. Union spokesmen were unanimous in reporting that even when seriously threatened by changes in their craft, men were disinclined to enroll in training courses. Vigorous and aggressive educational campaigns were required in many of the cases, and plans for classes were frequently abandoned for lack of students. The fact that younger men appeared to be most responsive seems to be an argument against undue emphasis on seniority as a criterion for eligibility for retraining.

Union size or affluence had little apparent relationship to retraining interest. Some of the largest labor organizations had no training fund except the sum allocated to the apprenticeship program. Others developed an interest in retraining their journeymen only when the Manpower Development and Training Act supplied money and momentum. Members of some large international unions were forced to drop into the ranks of the unemployed or to drift off into other occupations when local conditions brought about the closing-down or relocation of the companies for whom they had worked. Despite advance notice of these events, no steps were taken to help retool the workers. It is true that the pipefitters and electricians included in the study belonged to large unions that have acquired a national reputation for their forward-looking retraining policies. But the earnest efforts of the unions for marine cooks and stewards and for the radio operators underscore that size alone is not a decisive factor.

Membership in a union may provide an individual worker with some degree of safeguard against skill obsolescence and technological displacement only under limited conditions. Even if the local is one that has recognized the need for skill development and improvement sufficiently to have provided instruction, and if the worker has the perspicacity to want to take advantage of it, it was found that unions are likely to impose arbitrary criteria for entry. Selection of members who will be allowed access to the upgraded occupations is not entirely free of political considerations since it is in the hands of a committee that probably reflects the power structure of the local.

CONCLUSIONS

Regarded with unemployment as the frame of reference, retraining can be considered as (1) a means to keep workers maximally and optimally employed and (2) a way of making them employable. Up to this point in the résumé, focus has been closer on the first proposition. The remainder of this section, except for the portion dealing with the relatively small on-the-job activity under the Manpower Development and Training Act, is concerned largely with retraining as a vehicle to helping unemployed workers acquire the skills necessary to compete successfully for jobs. The findings of the research into the programs designed to aid vocationally handicapped persons are reported in the latter context.

Ethnic Minorities

That the employment prospects for members of minority groups are governed to some extent by the social climate was evident throughout the case studies. Civil rights pressures or fair employment considerations, and not conditions of the marketplace, suddenly opened career avenues in the San Francisco Bay area. While both Mexican-Americans and Negroes may stand to benefit from the dropping of discriminatory bars, no effort has been made here to assess the respective positions of these minority groups. Research emphasis has not been on those members of either who are equipped educationally and vocationally to take advantage of the change in employer attitudes, but rather on the persons who need jobs but are not prepared to compete for them nor to hold them when they are obtained. The process applied in such cases comes more appropriately under the heading of rehabilitation than of retraining, but, whatever its nomenclature, it cannot be ignored in a study of this kind.

In Chapter 5 there was presented a program which is unique because it is designed to meet an interrelated complex of deprivations that add up to unemployability. The men included in the project are from an almost totally segregated Negro community characterized by such cultural alienation as to be treated as an outcast group by other Negroes. More knowing in the ways of the police court than of the Employment Service, prone to regard work as a less likely and less respectable way of life than petty crime, they represent a hardcore amalgam inaccessible to traditional ameliorative approaches. The identification of a hierarchy of objectives has resulted in a developmental program made up of stages through which each individual is moved. In helping him build self-confidence, readjust attitudes, and acquire basic skills, the professional staff has brought to bear casework and vocational service methods with a flexibility rarely achieved in one organization. The trainee is guided through the steps of motivation, socialization, supervised work at assigned work-stations, and training and employment at a pace appropriate to his needs.

By recognizing and coping realistically with the educational, cultural, and social problems of the alienated and deprived, the workers associated with the Neighborhood House program address the combined tasks of building confidence, developing capabilities, and reformulating attitudes consistent with those of the larger society. The enrollees in the program exemplify a situation where long-time unemployment on the part of the adult members of a family has contributed directly to a state of virtual unemployability in the sons, almost irrespective of the availability of jobs. That there are many persons such as these in our society, who are incapable of taking advantage of a tight labor market and who could not hold a job if one were found for them, indicates the need for the kind of prevocational training reported in Chapter 5. That even the bottom rungs of the occupational ladder are out of reach of many persons who want and need employment underscores the importance of adapting and applying techniques such as were developed at Neighborhood House to other groups suffering disadvantage in competing for ways to earn an honest livelihood.

Just what will be the role played and the contribution made by the Job Corps cannot be predicted at this date. Whether the children of the poor will benefit from the cultural shock treatment intended to break old syndromes remains to be seen. The wisdom of combining the vocational training with the new way of life may be definitely demonstrated or refuted by the evidence still to come. Private industry's participation may be the Job Corps' great strength; it may be its Achilles' heel. Whatever the outcome of this particular endeavor, there is no question about the urgency of measures for young Americans, who at this time experience triple the national unemployment rate.

County Welfare Preemployment Training

It was in the analysis of case records of county welfare recipients enrolled in preemployment classes that the shortage of jobs, especially for Negro men with little or no skill, was most apparent. This poses a particularly serious problem for welfare agencies, where the official focus has shifted away from the mother and to the family with dependent children. Concomitant with this is an increased emphasis on willingness to accept training or a job as a condition for eligibility to receive aid. Even though the new rules include the father as a family member, he cannot assume a role of authority and respect in his household until he becomes the prime wage earner. Legislation can recognize him as a head of family and can even support him and his dependents, but it cannot provide him with a job. Thus, the matriarchal pattern among the lowest socioeconomic classes of the Negro population will probably continue; employment chances for Negro women are somewhat more promising than for men, and amendments to the Manpower Development and Training Act have designated mothers as head of families under certain conditions. Study of the individual records of the men and women for whom attendance in preemployment classes was a condition of eligibility to receive public assistance brought forth these basic facts. (1) The high school diploma covers a great variety of educational experience, regardless of its origin. (2) Absence of educational handicaps per se is not the sole index of employability. (3) While the state of the job market is a prime determinant of employability, certain fundamentals are indispensable in the successful quest for and holding of jobs. (4) Instruction in these basic matters and supervised work-experience, such as were predominant in the Neighborhood House program, are essential to the process of helping welfare recipients attain economic self-sufficiency. The preemployment classes did not lead to many jobs, perhaps because there just were not enough at the unskilled level to go around; but in a number of cases, the clients were successful in subsequent programs where they received training for specific occupations.

To supply meaningful work opportunity for persons "genuinely in the labor force," the National Commission on Technology, Automation, and Economic Progress endorsed a program of public service in which the government would be "an employer of last resort, providing work for the 'hard-core unemployed' in useful community enterprises." [3] Specifically recommended were:

(1) that public service employment opportunities be provided to those unsuccessful in the competition for existing jobs;

(2) that a five-year program be established, with the amount of public service employment increased each year, depending upon previous experience and labor market conditions;

(3) that an initial sum of perhaps two billion dollars be appropriated to provide about 500,000 additional full-time public service jobs; and

(4) that the program be coupled with a serious attempt to learn more about the nature and causes of "hard-core" unemployment by case and survey methods. [4]

The current social welfare emphasis on retraining and employment has considerable merit if administered with care. Because of the scarcity of employment opportunities for the unskilled, serious hardship could be imposed. Unless caution is exercised, some female clients will be forced into hunting for and accepting low-paying domestic work when it would be more sensible for them to stay at home and look after their young children, whose care would cost more than the mother could earn. Other recipients might be impelled to accept substandard jobs at wages so low that the agency, in supplementing for adequate living, would find itself in the anomalous position of subsidizing the cut-rate employer. Some of the lessons learned from study of the training efforts of welfare agencies may be usefully applied when planning national measures to combat poverty. If our society genuinely subscribes to the thesis that a paying job is a social good, we may have to alter our conception of the labor market as an arena where the fittest survive and others are relegated to the relief rolls, especially as labor-displacing mechanisms deprive more and more workers of their means of livelihood. If job-holding is to become a privilege, then it is quite apparent that we must be prepared to see large numbers remaining in or entering into the ranks of the underprivileged unless other alternative ways to earn an honest living are devised. One such alternative may be the public works program mentioned above.

---

[3] National Commission on Technology, Automation and Economic Progress, *Technology and the American Economy*, Vol. I (Feb., 1966), p. 110.

[4] *Ibid.*, p. 37.

Retraining Under the Manpower Development and Training Act

It is against the background of research into the kinds of retraining programs available to the American worker prior to mid-1963 that we can best appraise the problems, progress, and prospects of the MDTA. As was noted in earlier chapters, there are two distinct types of projects under this legislation; their only common feature is the source of funding. The on-the-job project was supposed to encourage employers to update and upgrade their work force through retraining for which federal compensation was to be made available; this prevention of skill obsolescence and enhancement of promotional opportunity was construed as a kind of escalator to move journeymen up into higher classifications to make room at the bottom for the young, the inexperienced, or the less talented. Implicit here were the assumptions that there were job openings going unfilled somewhere in the upper middle of the blue-collar occupational structure, and that correcting this hidden underemployment would help cure unemployment.

The long-time, hard-core unemployed were to be served under the MDTA through the establishment of institutional courses. These were to be programs set up by local school systems expressly for such persons and by agreement with the State Department of Employment, whose responsibility it was to survey the local job market to find occupations in which there was a continuing need for employees. Having satisfied certain criteria for eligibility, jobless heads of families were to be referred for training and were to receive monetary allowances.

Case materials on on-the-job training projects provide little evidence that the original objectives of the MDTA were being realized. Grants seem to have been made on the basis of some criteria other than merit or worker need. Perhaps government administrators, cognizant of organized labor's opposition to the Act, have been inordinately eager to curry favor with the unions by making funds available to them; or perhaps the Bureau of Apprenticeship and Training, through which requests for on-the-job grants are funneled, has not interpreted its own role with sufficient understanding. There seems little justification for supplying money to update journeymen who are employed full-time in an elite trade that has its own training fund and facilities, especially since this has not visibly affected the union's intake policies. Promotion may have come to some of the participants, but there is no evidence that new hirings at the threshold occurred as a result. No substantiation could be found for another union's claim that its

MDTA program had reduced underemployment among its members and thus opened a number of starting jobs. Comparison of the employment status of trainees at similar periods before and after the project showed no improvement in their earning capacity at the height of the season. More of them were unemployed in the summer of 1964 after having graduated than in the summer of 1963, before the training. That a claim of success was used as leverage to obtain an even larger appropriation indicates the need for reappraisal of the criteria by which such applications are judged. As operated at the time, the on-the-job portion of the MDTA demonstrated little raison d'être except that, to quote one official, "it made everyone look good."

More numerous, more publicized, and more vulnerable to criticism are the institutional programs under the MDTA. As was pointed out in Chapters 7 and 8, the regulation that the occupations for which training could be supplied had to be in demand in a particular labor market area led to an endless repetition of programs for entry into the high-turnover, low-paying fields. Some of the difficulties in establishing firm demand came into focus in the examination of classes in retail saleswork set up in response to certain local merchants' calls for trained Negro personnel. The course received much publicity, and the businessmen demonstrated their cooperative spirit in fervent graduation speeches. But even though the Easter season was at its height, the need for workers dwindled to almost nothing as civil rights demonstrations moved elsewhere. That a second class could have been justified on the basis of the job calls unfilled by the first group of graduates provides an interesting exercise in conjecture as to what really constitutes local demand.

The selection of trainees has posed a dilemma. Should the more needy but less qualified applicant be bypassed in favor of the person who is more likely to persevere and improve the record? With Congress and the taxpayers weighing the accomplishments of the MDTA and very conscious of dropouts and failures, the Employment Service interviewers have tended to enroll the best prospects, consistent with the letter if not the spirit of the Act. When courses were so long in getting started that the best prospects took flight, the vacant seats were then likely to be filled with little reference to the established norms. Thus, the chemical assistants' program included a man whose psychiatrist had specifically warned him against the close confinement of laboratory work because of a pathological tendency to claustrophobia. Girls who could not pass spelling tests were found in stenography classes. Tenth grade dropouts were enrolled in classes calling for high school graduates.

These are far from isolated instances of unsuitable referrals, and they have been interpreted by officials of the State Employment Service as evidence of the need to reconsider budgetary practices in that agency both for its regular operations and for its special and mounting responsibilities under the MDTA. Generally, its testing and guidance time must be "earned" by number of placements made. This has given rise to frenetic employment activity to the detriment of job development, occupational counseling, and judicious referral. In the screening, selecting, and assigning of persons to MDTA programs, hours are carefully rationed so as to make provision for the periodic checks on employment status of graduates required as follow-up for reports. As was shown in the case materials, this is often a frustrating and time-consuming task, which may result in wishful guesses based on ephemeral evidence. If the State Employment Office is to eradicate its public image as an unemployment bureau primarily concerned with disbursing insurance claims and assume instead the role of a dynamic manpower center, fundamental alterations in funding procedures are in order.

With all its mechanical weaknesses and functional shortcomings, the Manpower Development and Training Act has much to be said in its favor. Even when duplicating the form and some of the substance of ongoing classes, the institutional projects have incorporated didactic methods not to be found elsewhere. Counseling and remedial work in weak subjects have formed an intrinsic part of the programs. Indeed, experience with trainees during the first two years of operation pointed up so pressing a need for these aspects of the curriculum that the recommendation was made to Congress to amend the Act to allow for more remedial emphasis. The 1963 version of the legislation authorizes the development of basic knowledge of reading, writing, and arithmetic as a proper activity under the MDTA. Thus, courses are geared to the educational needs of the person with the more serious vocational handicap.

To evaluate the institutional projects completed to date simply in terms of their placements would be premature, for what can be achieved by the manpower policy still in its nascent stages cannot yet be objectively measured. We do know from our analysis of retraining activity in other sectors of our society that the disemployed or unemployed worker was virtually abandoned prior to the MDTA. After his unemployment benefits were exhausted, he was without professional help in his job hunt. Service of this kind was available to only certain select groups in the population—American Indians, the physically handicapped, the exconvict, and sometimes the welfare recipient. But even with these groups, the results were far from satisfactory. With no rehabilitative resources at his disposal, the unemployed worker was on the road to becoming unemployable, for no matter what his salable attributes were when he lost his job, the chances are that time would not add to or improve them.

Weaknesses in the Manpower Development and Training Act and in its implementation showed up in the first two years of operation, but they were acknowledged, and the 1963 Amendments to the Act were specifically designed to correct them. There is good reason to believe that the new provisions will address more directly the vocational needs of the deprived and the alienated while at the same time offering preventive maintenance and even skill development services to other sectors of the unemployed. As we found throughout our research, unemployment is both the cause and the effect of many problems amenable to no single, simple solution. The unemployed are not a homogeneous body, but a vastly varied aggregate under one statistical heading; their individual characteristics may be fully as important as the condition of the labor market in determining their chances of obtaining work.

On the credit side of the balance sheet, even before the amendments have taken significant effect, the Manpower Development and Training Act has made notable progress on several fronts. (1) It has vitalized the functions of the Department of Employment, a considerable accomplishment in small communities where that agency had previously operated in low gear as a farm labor exchange. (2) By forcing cooperative activity between the school system and the Department of Employment, the MDTA has been instrumental in bringing educators closer to the realities of the work world; perhaps this will lead to some basic readjustments in the archaic approach to vocational education. (3) Operating under the Act's mandate that data pertaining to all facets of labor force participation be gathered, compiled, and disseminated, the Office of Manpower, Automation, and Training has been the source of important information regarding unemployment and the unemployed. The special studies and analytical reports provide valuable insights into the dynamics of retraining. (4) Thanks to this legislation and its implementation, the American public has been made aware of the fact that unemployment is a complicated phenomenon and not exclusively a manifestation of a sluggish economy; as never before, we have come to recognize the existence of want in the midst of affluence. (5) The focus on unemployment and its characteristics and consequences, brought about by the MDTA, has contributed to widespread acceptance of the idea that nothing less than national manpower policy can cope with problems of the magnitude faced by America in the mid-1960's. While not a panacea for the combination of economic, social, educational, technological, and psychological ailments that comprise the unemployment problems of our time, the Manpower Development and Training Act is a necessary step in the right direction.

Policy Implications of the Research Findings

The empirical research into retraining opportunities under conventional types of sponsorship—such as adult vocational education, industry, and labor unions—has provided a substantive base on which to develop long-range and broad-gauged policy. While it is apparent that certain employed sectors of the labor force may reasonably expect to receive the retraining necessary for a measure of job security in a rapidly changing technological work world, no such expectation appears warranted for increasingly large categories of Americans. Unemployed, underemployed, or only marginally employed in a period of economic prosperity, these persons pose serious social problems, which are compounded as they become the bitter heritage of the permanently underprivileged.

Articulation of a realistic educational philosophy and establishment of suitable curricula at all age and skill levels represent only the starting point. The government as an employer, private industry, and labor unions must accept a responsible role, defined by a regard for the common good as well as their own immediate interests. With the advance of automation, the quantity and structure of jobs will continue to undergo change. Skill obsolescence could become a greater threat as new processes and procedures permeate field, factory, and office. The number of victims of "silent firing,"—those who never are hired—could increase as machines replace people at the workbench.

Established institutions have failed to provide the necessary services of occupational guidance and retraining; even a boom economy lacks the capacity to absorb the workers. Along with greater concentration on retraining there is an urgent need for a program of public works to provide the socially acceptable means for all persons to earn a livelihood.

The concept of manpower as a resource is nothing but an empty verbalism unless we adopt realistic measures leading to a comprehensive employment and manpower policy. A labor force with skills consonant with the highly developed technology of our time can be considered a resource. Once we subscribe to the thesis that manpower is not a commodity, to be declared surplus like a heap of old tires, we are forced into searching for meaningful uses of the talents and capabilities of human beings. Here is the point at which we must recognize that unemployment as a social problem demands solution at the very time that it may have only minor importance as an economic matter.

Index

273